T0289939

The Essence of
International Trade Theory

The Essence of
International
Trade Theory

Noritsugu Nakanishi

Kobe University, Japan

World Scientific

NEW JERSEY · LONDON · SINGAPORE · BEIJING · SHANGHAI · HONG KONG · TAIPEI · CHENNAI · TOKYO

Published by

World Scientific Publishing Co. Pte. Ltd.

5 Toh Tuck Link, Singapore 596224

USA office: 27 Warren Street, Suite 401-402, Hackensack, NJ 07601

UK office: 57 Shelton Street, Covent Garden, London WC2H 9HE

Library of Congress Cataloging-in-Publication Data
Names: Nakanishi, Noritsugu, 1963–   author.
Title: The essence of international trade theory / Noritsugu Nakanishi (Kobe University, Japan).
Description: New Jersey : World Scientific, [2018] | Includes bibliographical references.
Identifiers: LCCN 2018039246 | ISBN 9789813273818 (hc : alk. paper)
Subjects: LCSH: International trade. | International trade--Mathematical models.
Classification: LCC HF1379 .N335 2018 | DDC 382.01--dc23
LC record available at https://lccn.loc.gov/2018039246

British Library Cataloguing-in-Publication Data
A catalogue record for this book is available from the British Library.

For any available supplementary material, please visit
https://www.worldscientific.com/worldscibooks/10.1142/11085#t=suppl

Desk Editors: Herbert Moses/Lum Pui Yee

Typeset by Stallion Press
Email: enquiries@stallionpress.com

Printed in Singapore by Mainland Press Pte Ltd.

To

Kaori, Hikaru, and Shunsuke

Preface

International trade theory, as one of the applied fields of economics, encompasses not only import/export of tangible goods but also other issues such as trade in services, foreign direct investments, temporal/permanent migration of labor, various transactions conducted by multinational enterprises, trade policies and negotiations among countries, the roles of rules in international organizations, and so forth. There is a great number of issues to be examined in the real world, but, basically, the international trade theory pursues only two principal themes: one is to identify the determinants of trade patterns and the other is to clarify the welfare gains or losses from trade. (The term "trade" here should be taken in the broader sense so that it includes various cross-border economic activities.)

Trying to deal with all sorts of important issues in the real world as many as possible and to incorporate both the theoretical explanations and empirical evidence of those issues in a single volume, textbooks on international trade often get quite voluminous. Actually, some of the popular textbooks even come up to around 700 pages long. In my experience of teaching international trade at some universities, I have seen many times a lot of students being overwhelmed by the volume of the assigned textbook, not by the contents of it. I think, however, as far as we are focusing on the basic ideas and principles, the textbook can be made reasonably short and approachable with keeping the rigor of the contents. This is my primal motivation to prepare this book.

This book is intended to provide the readers with a "minimum toolkit" for the pursuit of the principal themes in international trade. This book contains seven chapters and they are devoted solely to theoretical issues, that is, to the construction and operation of models and the fundamental theorems derived from them. Chapter 1 introduces some basic concepts, technical terms, and analytical tools used in the later chapters. The subsequent three chapters explore the structure of comparative advantages and the gains from trade in the perfectly competitive circumstance. Chapter 2 deals with the Ricardian model and its variations, which focus on the roles of technologies. Some new intriguing issues such as the gravity equation derived from the Eaton–Kortum model, the technological leapfrogging, and the roles of time-zone differences are also discussed. Chapter 3 takes up the Heckscher–Ohlin–Samuelson model and the Specific-Factors model, which highlight the roles of the differences in factor endowments. Chapter 4 delves into the welfare economics of international trade. I first introduce various welfare criteria such as the Pareto-criterion, the compensation principle, and the revealed preference in the aggregate and examine their properties with paying attention to the relation to "social utility function". Then, I prove the gains-from-trade proposition and the Pareto-efficiency of free trade equilibrium in the perfectly competitive circumstance. I also review the argument of Pareto-inferior trade raised by Newbery and Stiglitz — the possibility of welfare losses from trade when the markets are incomplete. Chapters 5 and 6 are concerned with imperfectly competitive circumstances. By using a unified model, I examine both cases of a quantity-setting duopoly and a price-setting duopoly in Chapter 5. In addition, recent attempt of the general oligopolistic equilibrium approach proposed by Neary is discussed. Chapter 6 deals with the monopolistically competitive models, which emphasize the roles of product differentiation and increasing-returns-to-scale in production. I first introduce the monopolistically competitive model à la Krugman, which relies on the assumption of symmetric firms. Then, I move on to the model developed by Melitz that incorporates the heterogeneity of firms. Further, I review some elements of New Economic Geography (or Spatial Economics), which examines the locational distribution of agents and other geographic characteristics of an economy by using the monopolistically competitive model. Chapter 7 deals with trade policy issues. I examine the effects of tariffs and the relations to other policy measures in the perfectly competitive circumstance. The argument of strategic trade policy in an oligopolistic circumstance is also discussed.

Noritsugu Nakanishi
August 2, 2018

About the Author

 **Noritsugu Nakanishi** is a professor of economics at the Graduate School of Economics, Kobe University, Japan. He began studying economics at Hiroshima University, Japan. After he obtained the doctoral degree in economics from Kobe University in 1991, he joined the faculty of Kobe University and was promoted to full professor in 2004. His research interests are in both the general equilibrium aspects of international trade theory and the application of game theory to trade policy issues. He edited and authored two textbooks on international economics and also wrote two monographs on trade policy issues (all in Japanese). His research articles can be found in some academic journals such as *Journal of International Economics, Review of International Economics, International Economic Review, Games and Economic Behavior*, and *International Journal of Game Theory*. As an expert in international economics, he has long been an executive member of the Japan Society of International Economics (JSIE). He was awarded the *Kojima Kiyoshi Prize* of the JSIE in 2014 and served the Presidency of the JSIE from 2016 to 2018.

Acknowledgment

Since I started studying economics in earnest in my 20s, I have been benefited from discussions with my teachers, friends, colleagues, and students. They have helped to build my own view of economics and to deepen my understanding of the theory of international trade. I would like to thank Kenzo Abe, Koji Aoki, Fumio Dei, Junko Doi, Kenji Fujiwara, Taro Fukui, Taiji Furusawa, Hiroshi Goto, Masayuki Hara, Ken-ichi Hashimoto, Masayuki Hayashibara, Keisaku Higashida, Kenzo Hirose, Yunfang Hu, Yasukazu Ichino, Kazuhiro Igawa, Kiyoshi Ikemoto, Chihiro Inaba, Kaoru Ishiguro, Yasuko Ishiguro, Jota Ishikawa, Takekazu Iwamoto, Kazumichi Iwasa, Naoto Jinji, Isao Kamata, Takashi Kamihigashi, Toru Kikuchi, Tetsuya Kishimoto, Shin-ichi Kitasaka, Kazuharu Kiyono, Kenji Kondo, Ngo Van Long, Biswajit Mandal, Sugata Marjit, Yoichi Matsubayashi, Yuji Matsuoka, Sawako Maruyama, Shigeo Minabe, Eiichi Miyagawa, Hiroshi Mukunoki, Atsushi Murakami, Shigeo Muto, Takumi Naito, Shoji Nishijima, Hiroyuki Nishiyama, Masao Oda, Masayuki Ohkawa, Takao Ohkawa, Yoshifumi Ohkawa, Hiroshi Ohta, Michihiro Ohyama, Hisayuki Okamoto, Makoto Okamura, Shinsaku Sano, Hiroaki Sasaki, Masao Satake, Takashi Shibata, Koji Shimomura, Katsuhiko Suzuki, Yasuhiro Takarada, Sadayoshi Takaya, Shunpei Takemori, Makoto Tawada, Nobuo Teramachi, Ryuhei Wakasugi, Nobuyoshi Yamori, Akihiko Yanase, Koichi Yasutake, Masayuki Yoneyama, Chisato Yoshida, and Laixun Zhao.

My special thanks go to Shigeyuki Hamori, who suggested this textbook project several years ago, and also to Lum Pui Yee, the editor of this book. Without their advice and patience, this book would not have come into existence. In this textbook, I have included some materials from my research project supported by the Japan Society for the Promotion of Science (JSPS). I cordially acknowledge the JSPS Grant-in-Aid for Scientific Research (A), No. 16H02016. Lastly, I am particularly grateful to my wife Kaori for keeping our daily life cheerful and healthy. I am also grateful to my kids, Hikaru and Shunsuke, who always make me smile and provide me with good prospects for the future.

Noritsugu Nakanishi

August 2, 2018

Contents

Chapter 1

Preliminaries

In order to derive clear-cut results, international trade theory often makes use of simple small-scale models, which consist of only small numbers of goods, production factors, and/or countries. Those results obtained from small-scale models, however, can be extended to more general settings (with appropriate modifications and reinterpretations) as far as we fully recognize which properties are generic to an economy and which are specific to the model under consideration. In this preliminary chapter, we introduce some basic concepts, technical terms, and analytical tools in a general setting, which will be used in some specific contexts later in the book.

We consider an economy of a single country in which a number of different agents participate in various economic activities. Typical economic activities include production, consumption, and exchange of goods and services in the marketplace.[1] The agents that play central roles are *firms*, who produce and sell goods, and *households*, who buy and consume goods. All markets are assumed to be *perfectly competitive*.[2] That is, each individual agent cannot control the prices of goods and services; instead, the market mechanism determines the prices so as to establish the *market equilibrium* — a situation where the demand and supply for goods and services are equalized in all markets.

---

[1]We frequently use a simpler term "goods" to refer to the objects of economic transactions, unless it is necessary to draw an explicit distinction between goods and services.

[2]In Chapters 5, 6, and a part of Chapter 7, we deal with imperfectly competitive circumstances.

1.1 Production

Production is a firm's activity of converting a set of some objects (i.e., *inputs*) into different kinds of objects (i.e., *outputs*). In general, inputs are classified into two categories: *intermediate goods* and *primary factors of production* (production factors or, simply, factors). Intermediate goods are inputs to a production activity that themselves are the outputs of other production activities. On the other hand, primary factors are productive services provided by such things as *labor*, *capital*, and *land* that are not (considered to be) the outputs of other production activities (at least) within a certain period of time. We have to distinguish the productive services provided by a primary factor from the factor itself as a physical object that generates productive services. For example, when we refer to "capital" as a physical object, it means a *stock* variable such as machine tools, equipments, and factories, which are indeed the outputs of some production activities completed before the period of time we are concerned. On the other hand, when we refer to "capital" as a production factor, it means the workings or services generated by the physical capital and is considered as a *flow* variable defined for a certain period of time.[3]

1.1.1 *Description of Technology*

Production function: Technology of producing a good is the entirety of firm's knowledge of how to use and process inputs and how to organize and manage an appropriate system of production in order to obtain outputs efficiently. We can think of production technology as a certain relationship between possible combinations of inputs and the corresponding maximum outputs of the good. For simplicity, we often assume that inputs consist only of primary factors.

Suppose that there are m primary factors indexed by $i = 1, 2, \ldots, m$. Let $v_i \in \mathbb{R}_+$ be the quantity of the ith primary factor (i.e., factor i). A combination of factor inputs, $v = (v_1, v_2, \ldots, v_m) \in \mathbb{R}_+^m$, is called an *input vector*. Production technology of producing a certain good can be represented

---

[3] We usually assume that one unit of the stock of a physical production factor generates one unit flow of its services during one period of time.

by a non-negative, real-valued function $F : \mathbb{R}_+^m \to \mathbb{R}_+$, which we call a *production function*:

$$F(v) \equiv F(v_1, v_2, \ldots, v_m),$$

which represents the *maximum* amount of the good obtained from putting an input vector v into the production process under the current technology. We say that factor i is *indispensable in production* if the good cannot be produced without factor i, that is, if $v_i = 0$ implies $F(v_1, \ldots, v_i, \ldots, v_m) = 0$.

Production function is usually assumed to be continuous or differentiable in its domain; continuity and/or differentiability are rather mathematical regularity conditions. F is *monotonically increasing* if $0 \ll v < v'$ implies $F(v) < F(v')$.[4] The monotonicity of F means that an increase in the input of one production factor brings about an increase in the output (as far as the other factor inputs are strictly positive and remain constant). F is *concave* if for any $v, v' \in \mathbb{R}_+^m$ and any real number λ with $0 \le \lambda \le 1$,

$$\lambda F(v) + (1 - \lambda)F(v') \le F(\lambda v + [1 - \lambda]v').$$

If the above condition is satisfied with strict inequality for any distinct $v, v' \in \mathbb{R}_+^m$ and any λ with $0 < \lambda < 1$, F is said to be *strictly concave*. Further, F is said to be positively homogeneous of degree r if for any $v \in \mathbb{R}_+^m$ and any positive real number $\lambda > 0$,

$$F(\lambda v) = \lambda^r F(v).$$

The homogeneity of F is related to the economic concept of "returns to scale". According to cases where (i) $r = 1$, (ii) $r > 1$, and (iii) $0 < r < 1$, we say that F exhibits (i) *constant-returns-to-scale* (CRS), (ii) *increasing-returns-to-scale* (IRS), and (iii) *decreasing-returns-to-scale* (DRS), respectively. If F exhibits CRS (IRS, DRS), the output increases proportionally (more-than-proportionally, less-than-proportionally, respectively) as *all* the inputs increase simultaneously at a common rate. CRS and DRS

---

[4]The symbol "0" denotes both the real number "zero" and a "zero-vector" of a certain dimension. For two m-vectors $v = (v_1, v_2, \ldots, v_m)$ and $v' = (v'_1, v'_2, \ldots, v'_m)$, we write (i) $v = v'$ if $v_i = v'_i$ for all $i = 1, 2, \ldots, m$; (ii) $v \le v'$ if $v_i \le v'_i$ for all $i = 1, 2, \ldots, m$; (iii) $v < v'$ if $v \le v'$ and $v \ne v'$; (iv) $v \ll v'$ if $v_i < v'_i$ for all $i = 1, 2, \ldots, m$.

are compatible with the concavity of F, while IRS is not; DRS is also compatible with the strict concavity of F, while CRS and IRS are not. A production function that is (twice) differentiable, monotonically increasing, concave, and homogeneous of degree one (i.e., *linearly homogeneous*) is frequently called a *neoclassical production function*.

Marginal productivity: The partial derivative of F with respect to v_i represents the *marginal product of factor i*, which indicates how much output will be increased by one-unit increase in the input of factor i with keeping the other inputs unchanged. We say that factor i is *productive* at v if the marginal product of factor i is positive:

$$\frac{\partial F(v)}{\partial v_i} > 0. \tag{1.1}$$

F is monotonically increasing if Eq. (1.1) holds for all $i = 1, 2, \ldots, m$ and for all $v \gg 0$. If F is homogeneous of degree r, the marginal products of factors satisfy the following equation:

$$rF(v) = \sum_{i=1}^{m} \frac{\partial F(v)}{\partial v_i} \cdot v_i,$$

which is known as *Euler's theorem for homogeneous functions*.

If F is concave, the $m \times m$ matrix

$$[F_{ij}] \equiv \left[\frac{\partial^2 F}{\partial v_i \partial v_j}\right]_{i,j=1,\ldots,m} \equiv \begin{pmatrix} \dfrac{\partial^2 F}{\partial v_1^2} & \dfrac{\partial^2 F}{\partial v_1 \partial v_2} & \cdots & \dfrac{\partial^2 F}{\partial v_1 \partial v_m} \\ \dfrac{\partial^2 F}{\partial v_2 \partial v_1} & \dfrac{\partial^2 F}{\partial v_2^2} & \cdots & \dfrac{\partial^2 F}{\partial v_2 \partial v_m} \\ \vdots & \vdots & \ddots & \vdots \\ \dfrac{\partial^2 F}{\partial v_m \partial v_1} & \dfrac{\partial^2 F}{\partial v_m \partial v_2} & \cdots & \dfrac{\partial^2 F}{\partial v_m^2} \end{pmatrix} \tag{1.2}$$

consisting of the second-order partial derivatives of F is *negative semi-definite*.[5] In particular, every diagonal element of $[F_{ij}]$ is non-positive:

---

[5]By Young's theorem, (i, j)-element of the matrix $[F_{ij}]$ is equal to (j, i)-element; therefore, $[F_{ij}]$ is a symmetric matrix. In general, a real $k \times k$ symmetric matrix A is said to be *negative semi-definite* if $\xi A \xi^t \leq 0$ for any real k-vector ξ; it is said to be *negative definite* if $\xi A \xi^t < 0$ for any *non-zero* k-vector ξ (here, ξ is a row vector and ξ^t denotes the transposition of ξ).

for $i = 1, 2, \ldots, m$,

$$\frac{\partial^2 F(v)}{\partial v_i^2} \le 0.$$

This is sometimes referred to as the *law of diminishing marginal product* of factor i.

1.1.2 *Behavior of a Firm*

Let us consider the behavior of a firm that knows the technology (production function F) of producing a certain good. Let p and y be the price and quantity of the good, respectively, and let w_i be the reward rate (i.e., *factor price*) for factor i. An array of reward rates, $w = (w_1, w_2, \ldots, w_m) \in \mathbb{R}_+^m$, is called a *factor price vector*. Then, the firm's profit can be written as $\pi \equiv py - wv$. Given F, p, and w, the firm chooses the output y and the input vector v so as to maximize π.

Cost minimization: To produce a certain amount of a good, the firm has to find an appropriate combination of inputs to minimize the cost of producing the specified amount of the output. That is, the firm has to solve the following cost minimization problem: for a given y and w,

$$\min_v \; wv \equiv \sum_{i=1}^{m} w_i v_i \quad \text{subject to } F(v) \ge y. \tag{1.3}$$

Let us define the Lagrangian function $\mathscr{L} \equiv \sum_{i=1}^{m} w_i v_i + \mu \{F(v) - y\}$ for the above cost minimization problem, where μ is the Lagrangian multiplier. The first-order necessary conditions for the cost minimization are[6]

$$\frac{\partial \mathscr{L}}{\partial \mu} \equiv F(v_1, v_2, \ldots, v_m) - y = 0,$$

$$\frac{\partial \mathscr{L}}{\partial v_i} \equiv w_i - \mu \frac{\partial F(v)}{\partial v_i} = 0, \quad i = 1, 2, \ldots, m.$$

The first line simply means that the cost minimizing input vector just realizes the specified output y. Eliminating the Lagrange multiplier from the

---

[6]We are assuming here that there exits a unique interior solution to the cost minimization problem. There can be cases where no solution exists for some (w, y).

second line, we obtain

$$\left[\frac{\partial F(v)}{\partial v_i}\right]\Bigg/\left[\frac{\partial F(v)}{\partial v_m}\right] = \frac{w_i}{w_m}, \quad i = 1, 2, \ldots, m - 1. \tag{1.4}$$

The left-hand side of the above equation is the *marginal rate of technical substitution* of factor m for factor i (hereafter, we write MRTS_{im}), which indicates the minimum amount of factor m necessary to increase in order to keep the quantity of the good unchanged when factor i is decreased by one unit. Then, the cost minimization requires that MRTS_{im} coincides with the *relative factor price* of factor i in terms of factor m for all $i = 1, 2, \ldots, m-1$.

The solution to the cost minimization problem (1.3) can be written as a function of (w, y), which is called the *conditional factor demand function*: $\tilde{v}(w, y) \equiv (\tilde{v}_1(w, y), \ldots, \tilde{v}_m(w, y))$. If we replace w in (1.3) with λw where $\lambda > 0$, we obtain another cost minimization problem. As is obvious from the definitions of these problems, the solutions to them, $\tilde{v}(w, y)$ and $\tilde{v}(\lambda w, y)$, must be the same. That is, the conditional factor demand function $\tilde{v}$ is homogeneous of degree zero in w. For a given y and for any w and w', we have $w\tilde{v}(w, y) \leq w\tilde{v}(w', y)$ and $w'\tilde{v}(w', y) \leq w'\tilde{v}(w, y)$ by the definition of $\tilde{v}$. Combining these inequalities, we obtain $(w' - w)\{\tilde{v}(w', y) - \tilde{v}(w, y)\} \leq 0$. If w and w' are such that $w_i < w'_i$ and $w_j = w'_j$ for all $j \neq i$, we have $(w'_i - w_i)\{\tilde{v}_i(w', y) - \tilde{v}_i(w, y)\} \leq 0$. This means that the conditional factor demand for factor i, $\tilde{v}_i$, is non-increasing in its own factor price w_i.

By substituting $v = \tilde{v}(w, y)$ into the objective function of (1.3), we obtain the *minimum cost function*:

$$C(w, y) \equiv w\tilde{v}(w, y).$$

It is easy to verify that C is non-decreasing in (w, y); concave and linearly homogeneous in w. If C is differentiable with respect to w, we have

$$\frac{\partial C(w, y)}{\partial w_i} = \tilde{v}_i(w, y), \quad i = 1, 2, \ldots, m.$$

This is known as *Shephard's lemma* (Shephard, 1953). Young's theorem implies $\partial \tilde{v}_i(w, y)/\partial w_j = \partial \tilde{v}_j(w, y)/\partial w_i$ for all $i, j = 1, 2, \ldots, m$. That is, the effect of an increase in w_j on $\tilde{v}_i$ is equivalent to that of an increase in w_i on $\tilde{v}_j$. The concavity of C implies that the $m \times m$ matrix $[C_{ij}] \equiv [\partial^2 C / \partial w_i \partial w_j]_{i,j=1,\ldots,m}$ consisting of the second-order derivatives is *negative semi-definite*.[7] Every diagonal element of $[C_{ij}]$ is non-positive.

Factor substitution: When w_j increases, the input of factor j decreases and, to keep the output at a specified level, inputs of some factors have to increase (of course, it is possible that inputs of some other factors decrease). If the conditional demand for factor i increases (decreases) against an increase in w_j ($j \neq i$), we say that factor i is a *substitute* (*complement*, respectively) for factor j in production. The *elasticity of substitution* between factors i and j, denoted by σ_{ij}, measures the degree of substitutability/complementarity[8]: for $i, j = 1, 2, \ldots, m$ with $i \neq j$,

$$\sigma_{ij} \equiv \frac{\partial \tilde{v}_i(w, y)}{\partial w_j} \cdot \frac{C(w, y)}{\tilde{v}_i(w, y)\tilde{v}_j(w, y)}. \tag{1.5}$$

Factor i is a substitute for factor j if $\sigma_{ij} > 0$; a complement if $\sigma_{ij} < 0$. Further, because $\sigma_{ij} = \sigma_{ji}$ ($i \neq j$), we can say that factors i and j are substitutes or complements with each other.

Supply and factor-demand functions: Given the minimum cost function C, the profit π of a firm can be written as a function of the output level y as well as the prices (p, w) of the good and factors: $\pi = py - C(w, y)$. The *supply function* associates the profit maximizing output level with a given combination of prices:

$$S(p, w) \equiv \arg \max_y \{ py - C(w, y) \mid y \in \mathbb{R}_+ \}.$$

It is easy to verify that S is increasing in p, decreasing in w, and homogeneous of degree zero in (p, w). Substituting $y = S(p, w)$ into the conditional factor demand function, we obtain the *factor demand function*: $v^*(p, w) \equiv \tilde{v}(w, S(p, w))$.

The supply function S and the factor demand function v^* have been derived in two steps: first, given y and w, the firm chooses an appropriate input vector to minimize the cost of producing y; second, given p and w, the firm chooses the output that maximizes the profit. We can consider

---

[7]The matrix $[C_{ij}]$ is defined in a similar way as $[F_{ij}]$ in Eq. (1.2).

[8]For the definition of the elasticity of substitution, see, for example, Takayama (1985).

the firm's profit maximization problem in a more direct manner: given p and w, find an appropriate input vector v that maximizes $\pi = pF(v) - wv$. The solution to this problem (if it exists) is nothing but the factor demand function $v^*(p, w)$ obtained above. Similar to the conditional factor demand function, the factor demand function of factor i, v_i^*, is decreasing in w_i. By substituting $v = v^*(p, w)$ into the production function F, we obtain the supply function: $S(p, w) \equiv F(v^*(p, w))$.

Remark on the CRS technology:　If the production function F is linearly homogeneous (i.e., the technology exhibits CRS), the corresponding minimum cost function becomes multiplicatively separable such that $C(w, y) \equiv c(w)y$, where $c(w)$ denotes the *unit cost function*: for $y > 0$,

$$C(w, y) \equiv \max_{v} \{wv \mid F(v) \geq y\} = \max_{y[v/y]} \left\{ y\,[w(v/y)] \;\middle|\; y\,[F(v/y) \geq 1] \right\}$$

$$= \left[\max_{a} \{wa \mid F(a) \geq 1\} \right] y = c(w)y,$$

where $v/y \equiv (v_1/y, v_2/y, \ldots, v_m/y)$ and $a \equiv (a_1, a_2, \ldots, a_m)$. Due to Shephard's lemma, $a_i(w) \equiv \partial c(w)/\partial w_i$ represents the *input coefficient* of factor i, that is, the cost minimizing input of factor i to produce one unit of the good when the factor prices are given by w. Of course, we have $\sum_{i=1}^{m} w_i a_i(w) \equiv c(w)$.

Under the CRS technology, the firm's profit becomes a linear function of the output: $\pi = [p - c(w)]y$. Therefore, it may be the case that the supply function S and the factor demand function v^* are not defined well for some pairs of (p, w).

1.2　Consumption

Consumption is, in a sense, the ultimate goal for households. Household is an economic agent who owns production factors, earns monetary income in exchange for supplying factor services to the factor markets, and spends the income to buy goods and services for consumption. A household may consist of a single individual or of several individuals (e.g., a married couple with some children). Even if the household under consideration is actually a group of individuals, it will be identified with a single individual as far as it can make *consistent decisions* on the group's activities. In international trade theory, even the household sector of a country as a whole, which actually consists of many households and individuals, is frequently treated as if it were a single individual.

1.2.1 *Preference and Utility*

Let us consider the behavior of a single household. There are n consumption goods indexed by $j = 1, 2, \ldots, n$. Let $x_j \in \mathbb{R}_+$ be the quantity of consumption of good j. An array of quantities of the goods, $x = (x_1, x_2, \ldots, x_n) \in \mathbb{R}_+^n$, is called a *consumption vector* or a consumption bundle. The *consumption set* is the set of all physically possible consumption vectors; we assume it coincides with $\mathbb{R}_+^n$.

Preference relation: Take two consumption vectors arbitrarily: x and x'. When a household thinks "x is at least as good as x'", we write $x \succcurlyeq x'$. The relation $\succcurlyeq$ represents the household's valuation on consumption bundles and it is called the *preference relation*. When both $x \succcurlyeq x'$ and $x' \succcurlyeq x$ hold, we write $x \sim x'$ and say that the household is *indifferent* between x and x' — the household evaluates x exactly the same as x'. On the other hand, if $x \succcurlyeq x'$ but not $x' \succcurlyeq x$, we write $x \succ x'$ and say that the household *prefers* x to x' — the household thinks that x is strictly better than x'. A preference relation is said to be *complete* if we have $x \succcurlyeq x'$ or $x' \succcurlyeq x$ for any x and x'; to be *transitive* if both $x \succcurlyeq x'$ and $x' \succcurlyeq x''$ together imply $x \succcurlyeq x''$ for any x, x', and x''.

Utility function: It is well known that under certain regularity conditions there exists a continuous real-valued function $U \colon \mathbb{R}_+^n \to \mathbb{R}$, called a *utility function*, that represents a complete transitive preference relation $\succcurlyeq$ in such a way that for any $x, x' \in \mathbb{R}_+^n$, $U(x) \geq U(x')$ if and only if $x \succcurlyeq x'$.[9] If a utility function U represents a certain preference relation $\succcurlyeq$, any monotonic transformation of U also represents $\succcurlyeq$ equally as well.[10]

---

[9]See Debreu (1959). It is also well known that not all complete transitive preferences can be represented by real-valued functions.

[10]Let $g \colon \mathbb{R} \to \mathbb{R}$ be a strictly increasing function. A monotonic transformation of U is a function that can be represented by the composite function $g \circ U \colon \mathbb{R}_+^n \to \mathbb{R}$ where $[g \circ U](x) \equiv g(U(x))$ for all $x \in \mathbb{R}_+^n$.

If a utility function U is monotonically increasing, that is, if $0 \ll x < x'$ implies $U(x) < U(x')$, then the preference represented by U is said to be *monotonic*. The monotonic preference means that the household prefers more consumption of goods and services to less. A utility function U is *quasi-concave* if for any $x, x' \in \mathbb{R}_+^n$ and for any real number λ with $0 \le \lambda \le 1$,

$$\min\{U(x), U(x')\} \le U(\lambda x + [1 - \lambda]x'). \qquad (1.6)$$

A utility function is *strictly quasi-concave* if (1.6) holds with strict inequality for any distinct $x, x' \in \mathbb{R}_+^n$ and for any λ with $0 < \lambda < 1$. The preference represented by a quasi-concave (strictly quasi-concave) utility function is said to be *convex* (*strictly convex*, respectively). The convex preference implies that the household prefers a more diversified consumption vector to more biased consumption vectors. Unless otherwise stated explicitly, we assume both the monotonicity and the (strict) convexity of preferences throughout the book.

For a given $x \in \mathbb{R}_+^n$, the *indifference set* for x is the set of all consumption vectors indifferent to x, i.e., $\{x' \in \mathbb{R}_+^n | U(x') = U(x)\}$. The graph of an indifference set is called an *indifference surface (curve)*. Given a utility function or a preference relation, the consumption set is partitioned into a collection of indifference sets.[11]

1.2.2 *Demand for Goods*

For simplicity, we assume in this subsection that the income of a household, denoted by I, is given exogenously.

Budget constraint: Let $p_j \in \mathbb{R}_+$ be the price of good j. An array of prices, $p = (p_1, p_2, \ldots, p_n) \in \mathbb{R}_+^n$, is called a *price vector*. A household cannot buy any consumption vector of which the total expenditure exceeds its income — the *budget constraint*. The *budget set* of a household is a subset of consumption vectors that satisfy the budget

---

[11] A collection of non-empty subsets of $\mathbb{R}_+^n$, i.e., $\{A_\lambda\}_{\lambda \in \Lambda}$, is said to be a *partition* of $\mathbb{R}_+^n$ if $A_\lambda \cap A_{\lambda'} = \emptyset$ for any distinct $\lambda, \lambda' \in \Lambda$ and $\mathbb{R}_+^n = \cup_{\lambda \in \Lambda} A_\lambda$, where Λ is a certain index set.

constraint: for p and I,

$$\mathscr{B}(p, I) \equiv \left\{ x \in \mathbb{R}^n_+ \middle|\ px \leq I \right\}.$$

If $p_j > 0$ for all $j = 1, 2, \ldots, n$ and $I > 0$, then the budget set $\mathscr{B}(p, I)$ becomes a non-empty, compact (bounded and closed) subset of $\mathbb{R}^n_+$. It is obvious that for any positive real number $\lambda > 0$, we have $\mathscr{B}(\lambda p, \lambda I) = \mathscr{B}(p, I)$. The graph of consumption vectors satisfying the budget constraint with equality (i.e., $px = I$) is called the *budget plane (line)*.

Utility maximization: A household chooses a consumption vector from those contained in the budget set so as to maximize its utility. In other words, the household solves the following problem: given p and I,

$$\max_x\ U(x) \quad \text{subject to } x \in \mathscr{B}(p, I).$$

Let us define the Lagrangian function $\mathscr{L} \equiv U(x) + \mu\{I - px\}$ for the utility maximization problem, where μ is the Lagrange multiplier. The first-order necessary conditions are

$$\frac{\partial \mathscr{L}}{\partial \mu} \equiv I - \sum_{k=1} p_k x_k = 0,$$

$$\frac{\partial \mathscr{L}}{\partial x_j} \equiv \frac{\partial U(x)}{\partial x_j} - \mu p_j = 0, \quad j = 1, 2, \ldots, n.$$

The first line is simply the budget constraint (with equality). Eliminating μ from the second line, we obtain

$$\left[\frac{\partial U(x)}{\partial x_j}\right] \middle/ \left[\frac{\partial U(x)}{\partial x_n}\right] = \frac{p_j}{p_n}, \quad j = 1, 2, \ldots, n - 1, \tag{1.7}$$

The left-hand side of the above equation is the *marginal rate of substitution* of good n for good j (hereafter, we write MRS_{jn}), which indicates the minimum amount of good n that is necessary to increase in order to keep the utility level unchanged when good j is decreased by one unit. Graphically, MRS_{jn} represents (the absolute value of) the slope of an indifference surface (curve) along the directions of good j and good n. Equation (1.7) means that MRS_{jn} coincides with the *relative price* of good j in terms of good n, which in turn means that an indifference surface is tangent to the budget plane at the optimal point. The budget constraint with equality means that the household spends all available income to buy consumption goods. The solution to the utility maximization problem can be written as a function of (p, I), which is called the *demand function*: $D(p, I) \equiv (D_1(p, I), \ldots, D_n(p, I))$.[12] As is obvious from the definition and the property of the budget set, the demand function $D(p, I)$ is homogeneous of degree zero in (p, I), that is, $D(\lambda p, \lambda I) = D(p, I)$ for any $\lambda > 0$.

Good j is called a *normal good* if $D_j(p, I)$ is increasing in income I; an *inferior good* if $D_j(p, I)$ is decreasing in I. The *law of demand* says that the demand for good j decreases as its own price p_j increases. However natural it may seem, the law of demand does not always hold true. If good j is a normal good, then the law of demand holds. If, on the other hand, good j is an inferior good, it may be the case that the demand for good j increases despite that p_j increases; this somewhat unusual case is known as *Giffen's paradox*.

By substituting $x = D(p, I)$ into the utility function, we obtain the *indirect utility function*, which represents the maximized utility level as a function of (p, I):

$$V(p, I) \equiv U(D(p, I)).$$

The indirect utility function V is decreasing in p; increasing in I; homogeneous of degree zero in (p, I); *quasi-convex* in (p, I), that is, for any (p, I) and (p', I') and for any real number λ with $0 \leq \lambda \leq 1$, we have

$$\max\{V(p, I), V(p', I')\} \geq V(\lambda p + [1 - \lambda]p', \lambda I + [1 - \lambda]I').$$

Further, V satisfies *Roy's identity* (Roy, 1947): for $j = 1, 2, \ldots, n$,

$$-\left[\frac{\partial V(p, I)}{\partial p_j}\right] \bigg/ \left[\frac{\partial V(p, I)}{\partial I}\right] = D_j(p, I).$$

The indirect utility function intensively describes the behavior of a household.

Expenditure minimization: Looking at the behavior of a household from a different angle, let us consider the following problem in which the

---

[12]The demand function is also called the *ordinary demand function* or the *Marshallian demand function*.

household minimizes the expenditure on the purchase of a consumption vector that guarantees a specified utility level: given p and u,

$$\min_x px \quad \text{subject to } U(x) \geq u. \tag{1.8}$$

The solution to the above problem depends on the pair of (p, u) and is called the *compensated demand function*: $\widetilde{D}(p, u) \equiv (\widetilde{D}_1(p, u), \ldots, \widetilde{D}_n(p, u))$.[13] By substituting $x = \widetilde{D}(p, u)$ into the objective function in (1.8), we obtain the *expenditure function*:

$$E(p, u) \equiv p\widetilde{D}(p, u).$$

The formal definitions of the compensated demand function and the expenditure function are parallel to those of the conditional factor demand function $\tilde{v}$ and the minimum cost function C. Therefore, similar to $\tilde{v}$ and C, we can show that the compensated demand function $\widetilde{D}(p, u)$ is homogeneous of degree zero in p; $(p' - p)\{\widetilde{D}(p', u) - \widetilde{D}(p, u)\} \leq 0$ for any p and p'; and $E(p, u)$ is monotonically increasing in u, concave and linearly homogeneous in p, and it satisfies Shephard's lemma: $\partial E(p, u)/\partial p_i = \widetilde{D}_i(p, u)$ for $i = 1, 2, \ldots, n$. The $n \times n$ matrix $[E_{ij}] \equiv [\partial^2 E/\partial p_i \partial p_j]_{i,j=1,\ldots,n}$ consisting of the second-order derivatives of E with respect to p is negative semi-definite. Further, similar to Eq. (1.5), we can define the elasticity of substitution between good i and good j in consumption; with a slight abuse of notation, we shall denote it by σ_{ij}. If $\sigma_{ij} > 0$ ($\sigma_{ij} < 0$), then good i and good j are mutually substitutes (complements, respectively) in consumption.

Slutsky equation: As is obvious from the definitions of D and $\widetilde{D}$, we have $D_i(p, E(p, u)) \equiv \widetilde{D}_i(p, u)$ for any pair of (p, u). By differentiating this identity with respect to p_j, we can show that the effect of a price change on the (ordinary) demand for good i is decomposed into two effects. The decomposition is known as the *Slutsky equation*: for $i, j = 1, 2, \ldots, n$,

$$\frac{\partial D_i(p, I)}{\partial p_j} = \frac{\partial \widetilde{D}_i(p, u)}{\partial p_j} - x_j \frac{\partial D_i(p, I)}{\partial I}, \tag{1.9}$$

where $x_j = D_j(p, I) = \widetilde{D}_j(p, u)$ is the quantity of demand for good j. The first term of the right-hand side of (1.9), $\partial \widetilde{D}_i(p, u)/\partial p_j$, is the *substitution*

---

[13]The compensated demand function is also called the *Hicksian demand function*.

effect and the second term, $-x_j \partial D_i(p, I)/\partial I$, is the *income effect*. The substitution effect is positive (negative) if good i and good j are substitutes (complements, respectively). The substitution effect of its own price, $\partial \widetilde{D}_i(p, u)/\partial p_i$, is always negative. We say that good i is a *normal good* (an *inferior good*) if $\partial D_i(p, I)/\partial I$ is positive (negative, respectively). Accordingly, the income effect in the Slutsky equation is negative (positive) if good i is a normal good (inferior good, respectively). Therefore, the *law of demand*, which is equivalent to $\partial D_i(p, I)/\partial p_i < 0$, holds true if good i is a normal good.

1.2.3 *Restrictions on Preferences*

It is sometimes convenient to place some restrictions on the preference structure or on the utility function.

Homotheticity: If a utility function U is represented by a monotonic transformation of a real-valued, linearly homogeneous function $f: \mathbb{R}^n_+ \to \mathbb{R}$, that is, if there exists a strictly increasing function $g: \mathbb{R} \to \mathbb{R}$ such that $U(x) \equiv g(f(x))$ for all $x \in \mathbb{R}^n_+$, then the preference represented by U is said to be *homothetic*. The demand function derived from a homothetic preference becomes linear in income: there exists a vector function $\phi: \mathbb{R}^n_+ \to \mathbb{R}^n_+$ such that

$$D(p, I) \equiv \phi(p)I = (\phi_1(p)I, \phi_2(p)I, \dots, \phi_n(p)I).$$

This implies that all goods are normal and that the ratio of the demands for goods i and j becomes independent of the income level: $x_i/x_j = \phi_i(p)/\phi_j(p)$ for all $i, j = 1, 2, \dots, n$ with $i \neq j$.

Quasi-linearity: If, for a utility function $U: \mathbb{R}^n_+ \to \mathbb{R}$, there exists a sub-utility function $U^\circ: \mathbb{R}^{n-1}_+ \to \mathbb{R}$ such that

$$U(x_1, x_2, \dots, x_{n-1}, x_n) \equiv U^\circ(x_1, x_2, \dots, x_{n-1}) + x_n,$$

then U is said to be *quasi-linear*.[14] In this case, utility is measured in the units of good n and, therefore, the marginal utility of good n is equal

---

[14]The sub-utility function U° is often assumed to be *strictly concave*.

to unity for all $x \in \mathbb{R}_+^n$. Then, it is convenient to consider good n as a *numéraire*.

It can be shown that the demand function for a non-numéraire good derived from a quasi-linear function depends only on the price vector, but not on the income level: $D_j(p, I) \equiv D_j^\circ(p)$ for $j = 1, 2, \ldots, n - 1$. The income effect concentrates in the demand for the numéraire: $D_n(p, I) \equiv I/p_n - \sum_{k=1}^{n-1} p_k D_k^\circ(p)/p_n$. The assumption of a quasi-linear utility function is particularly convenient when we consider some oligopolistic situations in a general equilibrium setting, because we can safely ignore the income effects of the non-numéraire goods.

1.3 Autarky

We consider the autarkic situation of a country, where the demand and supply for all goods and factors have to be met in its own domestic markets. There are n goods and m factors. For simplicity, intermediate goods are assumed away. All the factors are owned by the households in the country and supplied inelastically to the domestic factor markets, but they are not consumed by the households. With these assumptions, we can examine the factor markets and the goods markets separately.

1.3.1 *Production Sector*

To distinguish the production activities of various goods, we need to modify notation slightly. Let y_j and F_j be the quantity and production function of good j, and let v_{ij} and $v_{\bullet j} = (v_{1j}, v_{2j}, \ldots, v_{mj})$ be the amount of factor i used to produce good j and an input vector for good j production, respectively ($i = 1, 2, \ldots, m$ and $j = 1, 2, \ldots, n$). The marginal rate of technical substitution of factor m for factor i in good j production is denoted by $\mathrm{MRTS}_{im}^{(j)}$. As we assume the CRS technology, the number of firms who produce a particular good becomes indeterminate in equilibrium. We call a firm that produces good j as "firm j".

Production possibility set: Let $\bar{v}_i$ be the existing amount (i.e., *endowment*) of factor i in this country. An array of factor input vectors $\{v_{\bullet 1}, v_{\bullet 2}, \ldots, v_{\bullet n}\}$ is called a *factor allocation*. Not all factor allocations are physically possible; they are subject to the *resource constraint*, which means that the total amounts of factors used in production cannot exceed the endowments: for $i = 1, 2, \ldots, m$,

$$\bar{v}_i \geq \sum_{j=1}^{n} v_{ij}, \tag{1.10}$$

A factor allocation that satisfies the resource constraint is said to be *feasible*.

An array of outputs, $y = (y_1, y_2, \ldots, y_n) \in \mathbb{R}_+^n$, is called a *production vector* or a *production structure* and it is said to be feasible if there exists a feasible factor allocation $\{v_{\bullet 1}, v_{\bullet 2}, \ldots, v_{\bullet n}\}$ such that $y_j \leq F_j(v_{\bullet j})$ for all $j = 1, 2, \ldots, n$. The *production possibility set* is the set of all feasible production vectors:

$$\mathcal{Y} \equiv \left\{ y \in \mathbb{R}_+^n \,\middle|\, \begin{array}{l} y_j \leq F_j(v_{\bullet j}),\ v_{ij} \geq 0,\ \bar{v}_i \geq \sum_{j=1}^{n} v_{ij}, \\ j = 1, 2, \ldots, n;\ i = 1, 2, \ldots, m \end{array} \right\}.$$

When we emphasize the fact that $\mathcal{Y}$ depends on a given *endowment vector* $\bar{v} \equiv (\bar{v}_1, \bar{v}_2, \ldots, \bar{v}_m)$, we write $\mathcal{Y}(\bar{v})$.[15] As we assume neoclassical production functions, the production possibility set becomes a compact convex subset of $\mathbb{R}_+^n$. Further, it is *comprehensive* in the sense that $y \in \mathcal{Y}$, $y' \in \mathbb{R}_+^n$, and $y' \leq y$ together imply $y' \in \mathcal{Y}$. Furthermore, for any $\bar{v}, \bar{v}' \gg 0$ and any positive real number $\lambda > 0$, we have both $\mathcal{Y}(\bar{v}) + \mathcal{Y}(\bar{v}') \subset \mathcal{Y}(\bar{v} + \bar{v}')$ and $\lambda \mathcal{Y}(\bar{v}) = \mathcal{Y}(\lambda \bar{v})$.[16]

Production efficiency: A feasible production vector $y \in \mathcal{Y}$ is said to be *efficient* if there is *no* other feasible production vector $y' \in \mathcal{Y}$ such that $y < y'$. Thus, if we want to increase an output of a particular good from an efficient production vector, we have to decrease the production of at least one of the other goods. The set of all efficient production vectors is called the *production possibility frontier* or the *transformation surface (curve)*. A feasible factor allocation $\{v_{\bullet 1}, v_{\bullet 2}, \ldots, v_{\bullet n}\}$ that realizes an efficient production vector y is also said to be *efficient*.

---

[15]Throughout the analysis, we assume the endowment vector $\bar{v}$ is strictly positive, i.e., $\bar{v}_i > 0$ for all $i = 1, 2, \ldots, m$.
[16]$\mathcal{Y}(\bar{v}) + \mathcal{Y}(\bar{v}') \equiv \{y'' \in \mathbb{R}_+^n \mid y'' = y + y' \text{ for some } y \in \mathcal{Y}(\bar{v}) \text{ and } y' \in \mathcal{Y}(\bar{v}')\}$ and $\lambda \mathcal{Y}(\bar{v}) \equiv \{y' \in \mathbb{R}_+^n \mid y' = \lambda y \text{ for some } y \in \mathcal{Y}(\bar{v})\}$.

An efficient factor allocation can be characterized as the solution to the following maximization problem:

$$\max y_n \quad \text{subject to} \quad y = (y_1, y_2, \ldots, y_n) \in \mathcal{Y} \text{ and}$$
$$y_j : \text{given}, \quad j = 1, 2, \ldots, n-1.$$

One of the first-order necessary conditions for the above problem is Eq. (1.10) with equality, which means the full employment of all factors. The others are the following equations: for $i = 1, 2, \ldots, m-1$ and for $j, k = 1, 2, \ldots, n$ with $j \neq k$,

$$\text{MRTS}_{im}^{(j)} = \text{MRTS}_{im}^{(k)}. \tag{1.11}$$

Let y be an efficient production vector and let us choose two goods j and k arbitrarily. If we decrease good j from y, some factors of production are released from the production of good j and we can use those resources to increase good k. The *marginal rate of transformation* of good k for good j (MRT_{jk}) is the maximum amount of good k that can be increased when good j is decreased by one unit from an efficient production vector with keeping the production of the other goods unchanged. MRT_{jk} at an efficient production vector y can be represented by the ratio of the marginal product of any factor in the good j production and that in the good k production evaluated at the efficient factor allocation corresponding to y:

$$\text{MRT}_{jk} \equiv -\frac{dy_k}{dy_j}\bigg|_{y:\text{efficient}} = \left[\frac{\partial F_k(v_{\bullet k})}{\partial v_{ik}}\right] \bigg/ \left[\frac{\partial F_j(v_{\bullet j})}{\partial v_{ij}}\right]. \tag{1.12}$$

Note that the right-hand side of the above expression is independent of the choice of factor i, because Eq. (1.11) holds true at the point of evaluation.

1.3.2 *Factor Markets*

Let us examine how the production structure for a given price vector p is determined through the factor market equilibrium.

Production equilibrium: As described in Section 1.1.2, the factor demand of firm j can be written as a function of the prices of goods and factors, that is, $v_{\bullet j}^*(p, w) \equiv (v_{1j}^*(p, w), \ldots, v_{mj}^*(p, w))$. Given a price vector p and the factor endowment vector $\bar{v}$, the factor market equilibrium is attained if

$$\bar{v}_i = \sum_{j=1}^{n} v_{ij}^*(p, w), \quad i = 1, 2, \ldots, m. \tag{1.13}$$

The above system of equations determines the factor prices as a function of p and $\bar{v}$: $\tilde{w}(p, \bar{v}) = (\tilde{w}_1(p, \bar{v}), \ldots, \tilde{w}_m(p, \bar{v}))$. Substituting the results into the factor demand function and the production function of firm j in turn, we obtain $\tilde{v}_{ij}(p, \bar{v}) = v_{ij}^*(p, \tilde{w}(p, \bar{v}))$ and $\tilde{y}_j(p, \bar{v}) \equiv F_j(\tilde{v}_{\bullet j}(p, \bar{v}))$.[17] In vector form, $\tilde{v}_{\bullet j}(p, \bar{v}) = (\tilde{v}_{1j}(p, \bar{v}), \ldots, \tilde{v}_{mj}(p, \bar{v}))$ and $\tilde{y}(p, \bar{v}) = (\tilde{y}_1(p, \bar{v}), \ldots, \tilde{y}_n(p, \bar{v}))$. The latter is called the *production point* for p. For a given p, the triple of production point, factor allocation, and factor price vector, that is, $\{\tilde{y}(p, \bar{v}), \{\tilde{v}_{ij}(p, \bar{v})\}, \tilde{w}(p, \bar{v})\}$ is called the *production equilibrium* for p.

Now let us examine the characteristics of the production equilibrium for p. First, we show that the production vector and the factor allocation that correspond to the production equilibrium for p are efficient. Firm j equates $\text{MRTS}_{im}^{(j)}$ to the relative factor price w_i/w_m for all $i = 1, 2, \ldots, m-1$ in order to minimize the production cost of good j. Because the relative factor prices are common to all firms, $\text{MRTS}_{im}^{(j)}$ $(j = 1, 2, \ldots, n)$ are equalized among all firms. This implies Eq. (1.11). In addition, because of Eq. (1.13), the resource constraint (1.10) is satisfied with equality. Thus, all of the conditions for the production efficiency are satisfied.

Next, we show that MRT_{jk} at the production equilibrium for p is equal to the relative price of good j in terms of good k: for $j, k = 1, 2, \ldots, n$ with $j \neq k$,

$$\text{MRT}_{jk} = \frac{p_j}{p_k}. \tag{1.14}$$

Totally differentiating $y_\ell = F_\ell(v_{\bullet \ell})$ and the resource constraint with keeping $\bar{v}_i$ unchanged, we obtain the following results: for $i = 1, 2, \ldots, m$

---

[17]The function $\tilde{y}_j(p, \bar{v})$ can be seen as a kind of supply function of firm j. However, because $\tilde{y}_j(p, \bar{v})$ embodies the factor market equilibrium conditions and depends on the endowment vector $\bar{v}$, it should be distinguished from the usual supply function of an individual firm that depends on p and w but not on $\bar{v}$.

and $\ell = 1, 2, \ldots, m$,

$$d\bar{v}_i = 0 = \sum_{\ell=1}^{n} dv_{i\ell},$$

$$p_\ell \cdot dy_\ell = \sum_{i=1}^{m} p_\ell \frac{\partial F_\ell(v_{\bullet\ell})}{\partial v_{i\ell}} \cdot dv_{i\ell} = \sum_{i=1}^{m} w_i \cdot dv_{i\ell}.$$

Combining these results, we get

$$\sum_{\ell=1}^{n} p_\ell \cdot dy_\ell = \sum_{\ell=1}^{n}\sum_{i=1}^{m} w_i \cdot dv_{i\ell} = \sum_{i=1}^{m} w_i \left\{ \sum_{\ell=1}^{n} dv_{i\ell} \right\} = 0.$$

Hence, setting $dy_\ell = 0$ for all ℓ other than j and k yields Eq. (1.14).

GDP maximization: Given a price vector p and a production vector y, we can calculate the value of the total production $py \equiv \sum_{j=1}^{n} p_j y_j$, which is nothing but the Gross Domestic Product (GDP) of the country. Let us consider the GDP maximization problem under the resource constraint:

$$\max_{y} py \quad \text{subject to} \quad y \in \mathscr{Y}(\bar{v}). \tag{1.15}$$

We can show that the production point $\tilde{y}(p, \bar{v})$ of the production equilibrium for p coincides with the solution to the GDP maximization problem. It suffices to show that the production equilibrium satisfies the conditions for the GDP maximization.

Taking account of the definition of $\mathscr{Y}(\bar{v})$, let us define the Lagrangian function for (1.15):

$$\mathscr{L} \equiv \sum_{j=1}^{n} p_j y_j + \sum_{j=1}^{n} \mu_j \left\{ F_j(v_{\bullet j}) - y_j \right\} + \sum_{i=1}^{m} \xi_i \left\{ \bar{v}_i - \sum_{j=1}^{n} v_{ij} \right\},$$

where μ_j $(j = 1, 2, \ldots, n)$ and ξ_i $(i = 1, 2, \ldots, m)$ are the Lagrange multipliers. The first-order necessary conditions for the GDP maximization become as follows: for $i = 1, 2, \ldots, m$ and $j = 1, 2, \ldots, n$,

$$\frac{\partial \mathcal{L}}{\partial y_j} = p_j - \mu_j = 0,$$

$$\frac{\partial \mathcal{L}}{\partial \mu_j} = F_j(v_{\bullet j}) - y_j = 0,$$

$$\frac{\partial \mathcal{L}}{\partial v_{ij}} = \mu_j \frac{\partial F_j(v_{\bullet j})}{\partial v_{ij}} - \xi_i = 0,$$

$$\frac{\partial \mathcal{L}}{\partial \xi_i} = \bar{v}_i - \sum_{k=1}^{n} v_{ik} = 0.$$

The first line means the Lagrange multiplier μ_j is equal to the price of good j. The second line is simply the production function (i.e., $v_{\bullet j}$ realizes y_j through F_j). If we set $\xi_i = w_i$, the third line implies Eq. (1.4). The fourth line is the resource constraint. Clearly, the production equilibrium for p satisfies all of the above conditions. Therefore, $\tilde{y}(p, \bar{v})$ coincides with the solution to the GDP maximization problem (1.15).

Some properties of $\tilde{y}(p, \bar{v})$ can be derived easily from the fact that it is the solution to the GDP maximization problem. Because $(\lambda p)y = \lambda(py)$ for any $\lambda > 0$, the maximization of $(\lambda p)y$ with respect to $y \in \mathcal{Y}(\bar{v})$ is equivalent to that of py with respect to $y \in \mathcal{Y}(\bar{v})$. Hence, the solutions to these problems have to coincide with each other: $\tilde{y}(\lambda p, \bar{v}) = \tilde{y}(p, \bar{v})$, which implies that $\tilde{y}(p, \bar{v})$ is homogeneous of degree zero in p. Further, for any price vectors p and p', we have $p\tilde{y}(p, \bar{v}) \geq p'\tilde{y}(p, \bar{v})$ and $p'\tilde{y}(p', \bar{v}) \geq p\tilde{y}(p', \bar{v})$ by definition. These inequalities together imply $(p' - p)\{\tilde{y}(p', \bar{v}) - \tilde{y}(p, \bar{v})\} \geq 0$. If p and p' are such that $p_j < p'_j$ and $p_\ell = p'_\ell$ for all $\ell \neq j$, then $(p'_j - p_j)\{\tilde{y}_j(p', \bar{v}) - \tilde{y}_j(p, \bar{v})\} \geq 0$, which implies that $\tilde{y}_j(p, \bar{v})$ is nondecreasing in its own price p_j.

Furthermore, we can show that $\tilde{y}(p, \bar{v})$ is linearly homogeneous in $\bar{v}$. Let us consider $\tilde{y}(p, \lambda \bar{v})$ for $\lambda > 0$. Because $\tilde{y}(p, \lambda \bar{v}) \in \mathcal{Y}(\lambda \bar{v}) = \lambda \mathcal{Y}(\bar{v})$, there exists $y' \in \mathcal{Y}(\bar{v})$ such that $\lambda y' = \tilde{y}(p, \lambda \bar{v})$. We have to show $y' = \tilde{y}(p, \bar{v})$. Suppose, in negation, that $y' \neq \tilde{y}(p, \bar{v})$. Then, we have $p\tilde{y}(p, \bar{v}) > py'$ by definition. It follows that $p[\lambda \tilde{y}(p, \bar{v})] = \lambda p\tilde{y}(p, \bar{v}) > \lambda py' = p[\lambda y'] = p\tilde{y}(p, \lambda \bar{v})$. On the other hand, $\lambda \tilde{y}(p, \bar{v}) \in \lambda \mathcal{Y}(\bar{v}) = \mathcal{Y}(\lambda \bar{v})$ implies $p[\lambda \tilde{y}(p, \bar{v})] \leq p\tilde{y}(p, \lambda \bar{v})$ by definition — a contradiction. Hence, $\lambda \tilde{y}(p, \bar{v}) = \tilde{y}(p, \lambda \bar{v})$ for any $\lambda > 0$.

GDP function: The maximized GDP is written as a function of p and $\bar{v}$:

$$Y(p, \bar{v}) \equiv p\tilde{y}(p, \bar{v}) \equiv \max \{ py \mid y \in \mathscr{Y}(\bar{v}) \}.$$

We call it the *GDP function*.[18] The GDP function is a convenient analytical tool that describes intensively the behavior of the production sector of a country as a whole. We show some of the properties of the GDP function below.

The GDP function is linearly homogeneous, non-decreasing, and convex in p. The linear homogeneity of Y in p directly follows from the definition. To show Y is non-decreasing in p, let us take two price vectors p and p' such that $p_j < p'_j$ and $p_\ell = p'_\ell$ for all $\ell \neq j$. Then, we have $Y(p', \bar{v}) - Y(p, \bar{v}) = Y(p', \bar{v}) - p'\tilde{y}(p, \bar{v}) + p'\tilde{y}(p, \bar{v}) - p\tilde{y}(p, \bar{v}) = [Y(p', \bar{v}) - p'\tilde{y}(p, \bar{v})] + (p'_j - p_j)\tilde{y}_j(p, \bar{v})$. The first bracketed term is non-negative by the definition of Y and, because $p'_j - p_j > 0$ and $\tilde{y}_j(p, \bar{v}) \geq 0$, the second term is also non-negative, implying Y is non-decreasing in p. Let us turn to the convexity in p. For arbitrary price vectors p and p' and a real number λ such that $0 < \lambda < 1$, define $p^\lambda \equiv \lambda p + [1 - \lambda]p'$. Then, by definition, we have $Y(p, \bar{v}) \geq p\tilde{y}(p^\lambda, \bar{v})$ and $Y(p', \bar{v}) \geq p'\tilde{y}(p^\lambda, \bar{v})$. Multiplying the former by λ and the latter by $[1 - \lambda]$ and adding both sides, we obtain $\lambda Y(p, \bar{v}) + [1 - \lambda]Y(p', \bar{v}) \geq (\lambda p + [1 - \lambda]p')\tilde{y}(p^\lambda, \bar{v}) = Y(p^\lambda, \bar{v})$.

In addition, the GDP function is linearly homogeneous, non-decreasing, and concave in $\bar{v}$. As shown before, $\tilde{y}(p, \lambda \bar{v}) = \lambda \tilde{y}(p, \bar{v})$ for any $\lambda > 0$. Multiplying both sides by p, we have $Y(p, \lambda \bar{v}) = p\tilde{y}(p, \lambda \bar{v}) = p[\lambda \tilde{y}(p, \bar{v})] = \lambda p\tilde{y}(p, \bar{v}) = \lambda Y(p, \bar{v})$. To show that Y is non-decreasing in $\bar{v}$, let us consider two endowment vectors $\bar{v}$ and $\bar{v}'$ such that $\bar{v} < \bar{v}'$. From the definition of the production possibility set, we have $\mathscr{Y}(\bar{v}) \subset \mathscr{Y}(\bar{v}')$, which implies $Y(p, \bar{v}) \leq Y(p, \bar{v}')$. Let us turn to the concavity. For arbitrary factor endowment vectors $\bar{v}$ and $\bar{v}'$ and a real number λ such that $0 < \lambda < 1$, define $\bar{v}^\lambda \equiv \lambda \bar{v} + [1 - \lambda]\bar{v}'$. Then, we have $\lambda Y(p, \bar{v}) + [1 - \lambda]Y(p, \bar{v}') = \lambda p\tilde{y}(p, \bar{v}) + [1 - \lambda]p\tilde{y}(p, \bar{v}') = p\{\lambda \tilde{y}(p, \bar{v}) + [1 - \lambda]\tilde{y}(p, \bar{v})\} = p\{\tilde{y}(p, \lambda \bar{v}) + \tilde{y}(p, [1 - \lambda]\bar{v}')\} \leq Y(p, \bar{v}^\lambda)$. The last inequality follows from the fact that $\tilde{y}(p, \lambda \bar{v}) + \tilde{y}(p, [1 - \lambda]\bar{v}') \in \mathscr{Y}(\lambda \bar{v}) + \mathscr{Y}([1 - \lambda]\bar{v}') \subset \mathscr{Y}(\bar{v}^\lambda)$.

---

[18] Woodland (1982) has introduced the concept of GDP function and investigated its properties thoroughly. Dixit and Norman (1980) have introduced intrinsically the same concept as the GDP function and called it the *revenue function*.

If the GDP function is (twice) differentiable in p and $\bar{v}$,[19] we can prove some additional properties:

$$\frac{\partial Y(p, \bar{v})}{\partial p_j} = \tilde{y}_j(p, \bar{v}), \quad j = 1, 2, \ldots, n,$$

$$\frac{\partial Y(p, \bar{v})}{\partial \bar{v}_i} = \tilde{w}_i(p, \bar{v}), \quad i = 1, 2, \ldots, m.$$

Because Y is linearly homogeneous in p and in $\bar{v}$, respectively, the above results and Euler's theorem for homogeneous functions together imply

$$Y(p, \bar{v}) = \sum_{j=1}^{n} \frac{\partial Y(p, \bar{v})}{\partial p_j} \cdot p_j = \sum_{i=1}^{m} \frac{\partial Y(p, \bar{v})}{\partial \bar{v}_i} \cdot \bar{v}_i = w(p, \bar{v})\bar{v}.$$

This means that the total value of production (GDP) is equal to the total factor income. Furthermore, Young's theorem implies

$$\frac{\partial \tilde{y}_j(p, \bar{v})}{\partial \bar{v}_i} = \frac{\partial}{\partial \bar{v}_i}\left[\frac{\partial Y(p, \bar{v})}{\partial p_j}\right] = \frac{\partial}{\partial p_j}\left[\frac{\partial Y(p, \bar{v})}{\partial \bar{v}_i}\right] = \frac{\partial \tilde{w}_i(p, \bar{v})}{\partial p_j}.$$

That is, the effect of an increase in the endowment of factor i on the equilibrium supply of good j is equivalent to the effect of an increase in the price of good j on the equilibrium factor price i — this is known as the *reciprocity relation*.[20] The $n \times n$ matrix $[Y_{ij}] \equiv [\partial^2 Y/\partial p_i \partial p_j]_{i,j=1,\ldots,n}$ consisting of the second-order partial derivatives of Y with respect to p is symmetric and *positive semi-definite*.[21]

1.3.3 *Goods Markets*

Household sector: For simplicity, we assume that the household sector of this country consists only of a single household, who possesses all the

---

[19]The differentiability of Y in p is related to the uniqueness of the solution to the GDP maximization problem (1.15). If the number of goods is greater than the number of factors, the production possibility frontier contains a "flat" portion and this flat portion itself can be the solution to (1.15) for a certain price vector; in this case, Y fails to be differentiable at that price vector.

[20]Samuelson (1953–1954). It should be noted that we have not mentioned the signs of $\partial y_j/\partial \bar{v}_i$ and $\partial w_i/\partial p_j$; they may be either positive or negative or zero, depending on the structure of each specific model.

[21]In general, a real symmetric $k \times k$ matrix A is positive semi-definite if $\xi A \xi^t \geq 0$ for any real k-vector ξ. By definition, A is positive semi-definite if and only if $-A$ is negative semi-definite.

factors of production and all the claims to the profits of firms. The preference of the household is represented by a monotonic, strictly quasi-concave utility function U.[22] The total income of the household, denoted by I, consists of both the factor incomes $\sum_{i=1}^{m} w_i \bar{v}_i$ and the profits $\sum_{j=1}^{n} \pi_j$. Then, taking account of the definition of profit, $\pi_j \equiv p_j y_j - \sum_{i=1}^{m} w_i v_{ij}$, the household's income I becomes as follows:

$$I \equiv \sum_{i=1}^{m} w_i \bar{v}_i + \sum_{j=1}^{n} \pi_j = \sum_{i=1}^{m} w_i \left\{ \bar{v}_i - \sum_{j=1}^{n} v_{ij} \right\} + \sum_{j=1}^{n} p_j y_j. \qquad (1.16)$$

Because of the factor market equilibrium conditions, the braced term in the right-hand side of Eq. (1.16) becomes zero. In addition, we have $Y(p, \bar{v}) = \sum_{j=1} p_j y_j$ in the production equilibrium. Therefore, $I = Y(p, \bar{v})$. Accordingly, we can write the household's demand for good j as a function of p and $\bar{v}$: for $j = 1, 2, \ldots, n$,

$$\tilde{x}_j(p, \bar{v}) \equiv D_j(p, Y(p, \bar{v})).$$

Because Y is linearly homogeneous in p and D_j is homogeneous of degree zero in (p, I), the function $\tilde{x}_j(p, \bar{v})$ becomes homogeneous of degree zero in p.

Walras law and the relative prices: The autarkic general equilibrium of the country is attained if $\tilde{x}_j(p, \bar{v}) = \tilde{y}_j(p, \bar{v})$ for all $j = 1, 2, \ldots, n$. However, these n equations are not independent. Rearranging the budget constraint of the household, Eq. (1.16), we obtain

$$\sum_{j=1}^{n} p_j \left\{ x_j - y_j \right\} = 0.$$

Therefore, if the markets for arbitrary $n - 1$ goods are in equilibrium, the only remaining market will also be in equilibrium (e.g., if $x_j = y_j$ for $j = 1, 2, \ldots, n - 1$, then $x_n = y_n$). This is known as the *Walras law*.

Taking account of the homogeneity of $\tilde{x}(p, \bar{v})$ and $\tilde{y}(p, \bar{v})$ in p and the Walras law, we can rewrite the equilibrium conditions as follows:[23]

---

[22]Strict quasi-concavity of the utility function guarantees the uniqueness of the solution to the constrained utility maximization problem of the household.

[23]We assume $p_n > 0$, i.e., good n is not a *free good* in equilibrium.

for $1, 2, \ldots, n - 1$,

$$\tilde{x}_j \left(\frac{p_1}{p_n}, \frac{p_2}{p_n}, \ldots, \frac{p_{n-1}}{p_n}, 1, \tilde{v} \right) = \tilde{y}_j \left(\frac{p_1}{p_n}, \frac{p_2}{p_n}, \ldots, \frac{p_{n-1}}{p_n}, 1, \tilde{v} \right). \qquad (1.17)$$

The above system of $n - 1$ equations determines $n - 1$ relative prices p_j / p_n for $j = 1, 2, \ldots, n - 1$. To avoid notational complexity, we set $p_n = 1$ and regard p_j ($j \neq n$) itself as the relative price of good j in terms of good n. Let $\bar{p}_j$ be the autarkic equilibrium price (or, autarkic price) of good j; $\bar{p}$ denotes the corresponding price vector. In general, $\bar{p}$ depends on the factor endowment vector.

Characterization of the autarkic equilibrium: For a given factor endowment vector $\bar{v}$, the array of the autarkic price vector $\bar{p}$, the consumption vector $\bar{x} \equiv \tilde{x}(\bar{p}, \bar{v})$, the production vector $\bar{y} \equiv \tilde{y}(\bar{p}, \bar{v})$, the factor allocation $\{\bar{v}_{ij}\} \equiv \{\tilde{v}_{ij}(\bar{p}, \bar{v})\}$, and the factor price vector $\bar{w} \equiv \tilde{w}(\bar{p}, \bar{v})$, that is, $\{\bar{p}, \bar{x}, \bar{y}, \{\bar{v}_{ij}\}, \bar{w}\}$ is called the *autarkic equilibrium* of the country.

The autarkic equilibrium can be characterized as the point at which the household's utility is maximized under the constraint of the production possibility set (PPS). To see this, let us consider the following problem:

$$\max_x \ U(x) \quad \text{subject to } x = y \quad \text{and} \quad y \in \mathscr{Y}(\bar{v}).$$

The first-order necessary conditions consist of all the conditions for the production equilibrium and the following equations: for $j = 1, 2, \ldots, n - 1$,

$$\text{MRT}_{jn} = \text{MRS}_{jn}.$$

The coincidence of the marginal rate of transformation and the marginal rate of substitution in consumption means that an indifference surface is tangent to the production possibility frontier at the optimal point. Clearly, the autarkic equilibrium satisfies all of these conditions.[24]

Alternative characterization of the autarkic equilibrium: By substituting the GDP function $Y(p, \bar{v})$ into the indirect utility function $V(p, I)$, we

---

[24] We omit to list all the conditions for the constrained utility maximization subject to the production possibility set; they can be derived by making use of the usual Lagrangian method as in the case of the production equilibrium.

can represent the utility level u of the country by a function V^* of p and $\bar{v}$:

$$u = V^*(p, \bar{v}) \equiv V(p, Y(p, \bar{v})),$$

which we call the *integrated indirect utility function*.[25] For an arbitrary price vector p and a positive real number λ, we have $V^*(\lambda p, \bar{v}) = V(\lambda p, Y(\lambda p, \bar{v})) = V(\lambda p, \lambda Y(p, \bar{v})) = V(p, Y(p, \bar{v})) = V^*(p, \bar{v})$. The second equality follows from the linear homogeneity of Y in p; the third from the zero-degree homogeneity of V in (p, I). That is, V^* is homogeneous of degree zero in p. On the other hand, for arbitrary price vectors p and p' and a real number λ with $0 < \lambda < 1$, we have

$$\max\{V^*(p, \bar{v}), V^*(p', \bar{v})\} = \max\{V(p, Y(p, \bar{v})), V(p', Y(p', \bar{v}))\}$$

$$\geq V(\lambda p + [1 - \lambda]p', \lambda Y(p, \bar{v}) + [1 - \lambda]Y(p', \bar{v}))$$

$$\geq V(\lambda p + [1 - \lambda]p', Y(\lambda p + [1 - \lambda]p', \bar{v}))$$

$$= V^*(\lambda p + [1 - \lambda]p', \bar{v}).$$

The first inequality follows from the quasi-convexity of V in (p, I); the second from the convexity of Y in p and the monotonicity of V in I. This proves that V^* is quasi-convex in p.

We now show that the autarkic equilibrium price vector $\bar{p}$ is the *minimizer* of the integrated indirect utility function V^*.[26] Assuming the differentiability of relevant functions and taking account of Roy's identity and the properties of the GDP function, the first-order necessary conditions for the minimization of V^* with respect to p become as follows: for $j = 1, 2, \ldots, n - 1$,

$$\frac{\partial V^*(p, \bar{v})}{\partial p_j} = \frac{\partial V(p, I)}{\partial p_j} + \frac{\partial V(p, I)}{\partial I} \cdot \frac{\partial Y(p, \bar{v})}{\partial p_j}$$

$$= \frac{\partial V(p, I)}{\partial I} \cdot \left\{ \tilde{y}_j(p, \bar{v}) - \tilde{x}_j(p, \bar{v}) \right\} = 0,$$

---

[25] Woodland (1982) called this function as the *trade indirect utility function*.

[26] Although we give here the sketch of the proof of this fact based on the differentiability of relevant functions, it can be proved without the differentiability assumptions. See Woodland (1982).

where $I = Y(p, \bar{v})$. Because the marginal utility of income $[\partial V/\partial I]$ is positive, the above conditions are equivalent to the autarkic equilibrium conditions (1.17). Clearly, the autarkic equilibrium price vector satisfies these conditions.

Further, the second-order necessary condition for the minimization of V^* is that the $n \times n$ matrix $[V_{ij}^*] \equiv [\partial^2 V^*/\partial p_i \partial p_j]_{i,j=1,\ldots,n}$ evaluated at $\bar{p}$ is positive semi-definite. The second-order derivatives become as follows: for $i, j = 1, 2, \ldots, n$,

$$\frac{\partial^2 V^*}{\partial p_i \partial p_j} = \frac{\partial^2 V^*}{\partial p_i \partial I} \cdot \underbrace{\left[\tilde{y}_j(p, \bar{v}) - \tilde{x}_j(p, \bar{v}) \right]}_{=0} + \frac{\partial V}{\partial I} \cdot \frac{\partial}{\partial p_i} \left[\tilde{y}_j(p, \bar{v}) - \tilde{x}_j(p, \bar{v}) \right]$$

$$= \frac{\partial V}{\partial I} \cdot \left\{ \frac{\partial y_j(p, \bar{v})}{\partial p_i} - \frac{\partial \widetilde{D}_j(p, u)}{\partial p_i} - \underbrace{\left[\tilde{y}_j(p, \bar{v}) - \tilde{x}_j(p, \bar{v}) \right]}_{=0} \frac{\partial D_j(p, I)}{\partial I} \right\}.$$

Therefore, we have $[V_{ij}^*] = [\partial V/\partial I] \cdot \{[Y_{ij}] - [\widetilde{D}_{ij}]\}$ at the minimum point. Since $[\partial V/\partial I] > 0$ and $[Y_{ij}]$ is positive semi-definite and $[\widetilde{D}_{ij}]$ is negative semi-definite, then $[V_{ij}^*]$ is positive semi-definite.

Alternative description of the autarkic equilibrium: By the definitions of the expenditure function, the indirect utility function, and the GDP function, we know that $u = V^*(p, \bar{v}) \equiv V(p, Y(p, \bar{v}))$ if and only if

$$E(p, u) = Y(p, \bar{v}). \tag{1.18}$$

By making use of this relation, we can describe the autarkic equilibrium in an alternative way. Totally differentiating Eq. (1.18), we obtain

$$\frac{\partial E(p, u)}{\partial u} du + \sum_{j=1}^{n-1} \left\{ \frac{\partial E(p, u)}{\partial p_j} - \frac{\partial Y(p, \bar{v})}{\partial p_j} \right\} dp_j = 0.$$

As we have already shown, the indirect utility is minimized at the autarkic equilibrium. Accordingly, for any small changes in prices, we must have $du = 0$, which requires that the braced terms in the above expression should be zero: for $j = 1, 2, \ldots, n - 1$,

$$\widetilde{D}_j(p, u) - \tilde{y}_j(p, \bar{v}) = 0. \tag{1.19}$$

The system of n equations comprised of both (1.18) and (1.19) determines the utility level u and the $n - 1$ relative prices of goods in the autarkic equilibrium.

Chapter 2

Basics of Comparative Advantage

When the relative price of a good in one country is lower than in other countries, the first country is said to have a *comparative advantage* in this good over other countries.[1] Differences in the relative prices are, among others, the most important driving force of international trade. A country will export its products to foreign markets where prices are higher than in its own markets and, conversely, import goods and services from foreign markets where prices are lower than in its own markets. In this way, there emerges a *trade pattern* — a description of which country imports or exports what kind of goods and services. Therefore, the first step to examine the structure of international trade is to show how the differences in relative prices across countries are determined. In this chapter, we first introduce a simple trade model called the *Ricardian model*, which highlights the roles of the *differences in production technology* as one of the determinants of comparative advantage. Then, we extend and generalize it into several different directions.

2.1 Technology and Behavior of Firms

Consider a world economy consisting of two countries (*A* and *B*), two goods (good 1 and good 2), and one primary production factor called

---

[1]The notion of comparative advantage dates back to Ricardo (1817), who has clearly shown the roles of comparative advantage in mutually beneficial trade.

labor. Goods are produced by using only labor as inputs under constant-returns-to-scale (CRS) technologies. The production technology characterized by both a single production factor and CRS is called the *Ricardian technology.* Free entry–exit of firms is also assumed.

For the moment, we concentrate on the situation in one of the countries. In general, production functions and other variables introduced below depend not only on the identities of goods but also on the identities of countries to which they belong. Unless necessary, we omit explicit indications of the identities of countries from the variables.

Production function: Assuming the Ricardian technology, we can write production function $F_j : \mathbb{R}_+ \to \mathbb{R}_+$ of good j as follows: for $j = 1, 2, \ldots$

$$y_j = F_j(L_j) \equiv L_j / a_{Lj},$$

where $y_j \geq 0$ and $L_j \geq 0$ are the output of good j and the input of labor, respectively. The constant term $a_{Lj} > 0$ is the *labor input coefficient*, which represents the minimum amount of labor required to produce one unit of good j. The labor input coefficient can be seen as an indicator of the technology level — A smaller a_{Lj} implies a higher technology. The inverse of the labor input coefficient, $1/a_{Lj}$, is the *labor productivity* in good j, which represents the maximum amount of good j obtained from one unit of labor input.

Production possibility set: Let $L > 0$ be the labor endowment of a country. The total amount of labor used to produce goods cannot exceed L, that is, we must have $L_1 + L_2 \leq L$. This inequality and the production functions together define the *production possibility set*

$$\mathscr{Y}(L) \equiv \left\{ y = (y_1, y_2) \in \mathbb{R}_+^2 \mid a_{L1} y_1 + a_{L2} y_2 \leq L \right\},$$

which is a compact and convex subset of $\mathbb{R}_+^2$. In the Ricardian model with two goods, it is easy to verify that a feasible production vector $y = (y_1, y_2)$ is efficient if and only if it satisfies the full employment condition of labor: $a_{L1} y_1 + a_{L2} y_2 = L$.

Let $y = (y_1, y_2)$ be an efficient production vector with $y_1 > 0$. If we decrease good 1 from y, then certain units of labor are released from the

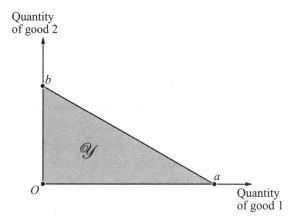

Fig. 2.1   The Production Possibility Set

production of good 1 and, by using the released labor, we can increase good 2. The maximum amount of good 2 that can be increased by decreasing one unit of good 1 is called the *marginal rate of transformation* of good 2 for good 1 (we write MRT_{12} or, simply, MRT). Conversely, if we want to increase one unit of good 1 while sustaining production efficiency, we have to sacrifice the "MRT units" of good 2. In this sense, MRT stands for the *opportunity cost* (in terms of good 2) of producing one additional unit of good 1.

The triangular area *Oab* in Fig. 2.1 illustrates the production possibility set $\mathscr{Y}(L)$ of a country. Segment *ab* represents the set of all efficient production vectors, which we call the *production possibility frontier* or the *transformation curve*. If we decrease one unit of good 1, then a_{L1} units of labor are released from the production of good 1. Further, by using a_{L1} units of labor, we can increase $a_{L1} \times 1/a_{L2}$ units of good 2. Hence, MRT in the Ricardian model is equal to the ratio of the labor input coefficients of good 1 and good 2, a_{L1}/a_{L2}, which is constant and corresponds to the slope of the production possibility frontier.

Profit maximization: Each firm decides whether to enter into or exit from the market and how much good it produces (or how much labor it employs) so as to maximize its own profit. A producer of good j is called "firm j". Given the price p_j of good j and the wage rate w for labor, the profit π_j of firm j can be written as follows: for $j = 1, 2$,

$$\pi_j \equiv p_j y_j - w L_j = p_j F_j(L_j) - w L_j = \{p_j/a_{Lj} - w\} L_j.$$

Because an individual firm cannot control p_j and w in the competitive circumstance, the profit of firm j becomes linear in L_j with the coefficient $p_j/a_{Lj} - w$. Accordingly, firm j's decision depends on the sign of the coefficient. If $p_j/a_{Lj} - w < 0$, the firm can avoid any loss by exiting from the market or by setting $L_j = 0$; in this case, good j is not produced at all. If $p_j/a_{Lj} - w > 0$, the profit tends to infinity as L_j goes infinity; the profit maximizing output of good j does not exit. If $p_j/a_{Lj} - w = 0$, the firm's profit is zero for any non-negative labor input $L_j \geq 0$. A positive finite amount of good j can be produced only in the last case. The demand for labor of firm j can be summarized as follows:

$$L_j = \begin{cases} 0 & \text{if } p_j < w a_{Lj}, \\ \mathbb{R}_+ & \text{if } p_j = w a_{Lj}, \\ +\infty & \text{if } p_j > w a_{Lj}. \end{cases} \tag{2.1}$$

2.2 Production Structure

2.2.1 *Single Country*

Household sector: For simplicity, we assume that the household sector of each country consists of a single household, which owns all the labor forces in the country (i.e., the labor endowment L) and holds all claims to the profits. The household, however, does not consume labor forces as leisure. The household's income I is the sum of the wage and the profits: $I \equiv wL + \pi_1 + \pi_2$. The preference of the household is represented by a monotonically increasing, strictly quasi-concave utility function. Further, we assume that all goods are *indispensable in consumption*.

Labor market: The household supplies labor forces $L > 0$ inelastically to the domestic labor market. On the other hand, the demand for labor is described by Eq. (2.1). The labor market equilibrium condition is

$$L_1 + L_2 = L. \tag{2.2}$$

If $p_j > wa_{Lj}$ for at least one good, the total demand for labor goes infinity; on the other hand, if $p_j < wa_{Lj}$ for all goods, the total demand for labor becomes zero. Neither case satisfies Eq. (2.2). Therefore, the labor market is in equilibrium if a triple of prices and wage rate, (p_1, p_2, w), satisfies the following conditions: for all $j = 1, 2$,

$$p_j \leq wa_{Lj} \tag{2.3}$$

with equality for at least one good. The right-hand side of the above inequality stands for the *average cost* of producing good j. In equilibrium, the average cost of producing one good cannot fall short of the price of the good. Further, if a positive finite amount of good j were to be produced, the price of good j has to coincide with the average cost. It follows from these observations that the equilibrium profits of all firms are zero. In addition, because the labor forces are fully employed, the equilibrium production structure is *efficient* from the viewpoint of the country concerned (i.e., efficient relative to the production possibility set $\mathscr{Y}$).

The autarkic equilibrium price: Without international trade, the demands for all goods in each country must be met by the domestic supplies. It follows that if all goods are indispensable in consumption, they must be produced in some positive amounts in each country. In this case, the triple $(\bar{p}_1, \bar{p}_2, \bar{w})$ of the autarkic equilibrium prices and wage rate has to satisfy Eq. (2.3) with equalities for all goods. Consequently, the autarkic equilibrium relative price of good 1 in terms of good 2, $\bar{p} \equiv \bar{p}_1/\bar{p}_2$, becomes equal to the ratio of the labor input coefficients, that is:

$$\bar{p} = \frac{a_{L1}}{a_{L2}}. \tag{2.4}$$

Although the autarkic equilibrium relative price appears to be determined solely from the characteristics of technology (i.e., the labor input coefficients), a condition on the demand side (i.e., the indispensability of goods) also plays an important role in deriving Eq. (2.4).

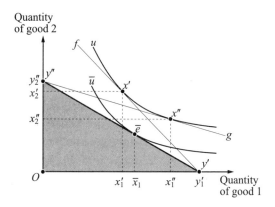

Fig. 2.2   Trade Liberalization and Specialization

The triangular area $Oy'y''$ in Fig. 2.2 illustrates the production possibility set of a country. Equation (2.4) means that the autarkic equilibrium relative price $\bar{p}$ coincides with the slope of the production possibility frontier (i.e., segment $y'y''$). Given the relative price $\bar{p}$, any production vector on the production possibility frontier can satisfy the conditions for the production equilibrium. On the other hand, for the autarkic equilibrium triple $(\bar{p}_1, \bar{p}_2, \bar{w})$, the household's income becomes $\bar{I} \equiv \bar{w}L + \sum_{j=1}^{2} \{\bar{p}_j \bar{y}_j - \bar{w}L_j\} = \bar{p}_1 y_1 + \bar{p}_2 y_2$, where $y = (y_1, y_2)$ is any production vector on the production possibility frontier. In this case, the budget set of the household, $\mathscr{B}(\bar{p}_1, \bar{p}_2, \bar{I})$, happens to coincide with the production possibility set $\mathscr{Y}$. The optimal consumption is attained at point $\bar{e}$ in Fig. 2.2, where an indifference curve $\bar{u}$ is tangent to the budget line $y'y''$. Point $\bar{e}$ also represents the autarkic equilibrium of the country.

Specialization: What will happen to the production structure of a country if the country abandons its isolationist policy and liberalizes trade in goods? (Still, we maintain the assumption that labor forces do not move across countries.) Due to trade liberalization, firms in the country come to face a change in the prices.

Suppose that the world market price is given by $p' \equiv p'_1/p'_2$ and it is higher than the autarkic price $\bar{p}$. That $p' > \bar{p}$ together with Eq. (2.3) implies $p'_1 = w'a_{L1}$ and $p'_2 < w'a_{L2}$, where w' is the wage rate after trade liberalization. Accordingly, firms cease producing good 2 and concentrate on the production of good 1. That is, *complete specialization* in good 1 results under free trade with p' ($>\bar{p}$). Let $y_1' \equiv L/a_{L1}$ be the maximum amount of good 1 that can be produced in the country. Then, the production point for p' will be $y' \equiv (y_1', 0)$ as illustrated in Fig. 2.2. On the other hand, the household's budget line becomes the line segment fy' in Fig. 2.2 and the consumption point of the household will be point $x' \equiv (x_1', x_2')$. In this case, the country exports $y_1' - x_1'$ units of good 1 and imports x_2' units of good 2.

By the same token, if the world market price is given by p'' ($<\bar{p}$), we obtain complete specialization in good 2. The production point is represented by point $y'' \equiv (0, y_2'')$, where $y_2'' \equiv L/a_{L2}$ is the maximum amount of good 2 that can be produced in the country. The budget line becomes the line segment gy'' in Fig. 2.2, and the household chooses x''. In this case, the country imports x_1'' units of good 1 and exports $y_2'' - x_2''$ units of good 2.

Note on the GDP function: Let $Y(p, L) \equiv \max\{py_1 + y_2 \mid (y_1, y_2) \in \mathscr{Y}(L)\}$ be the GDP function for the Ricardian model with two goods.[2] From the above discussion on the specialization patterns, we can easily verify that Y is piecewise linear in p: $Y(p, L) = L/a_{L2}$ if $p \leq \bar{p}$; $Y(p, L) = pL/a_{L1}$ if $p \geq \bar{p}$. Obviously, Y is not differentiable at $p = \bar{p}$. This follows from the fact that the production possibility frontier in the Ricardian model is a straight line and, therefore, the solution to the GDP maximization problem for $p = \bar{p}$ is not unique. Actually, when $p = \bar{p}$, the solution coincides with the production possibility frontier itself.

2.2.2 Trading World

Now let us introduce two countries A and B explicitly and consider international trade between them. To distinguish the identities of countries, we attach superscripts A and B to the corresponding variables.

Comparative advantage: Without loss of generality, we assume the difference in technology between A and B is such that

$$\frac{a_{L1}^A}{a_{L2}^A} < \frac{a_{L1}^B}{a_{L2}^B}. \tag{2.5}$$

---

[2]Here, GDP is measured in terms of good 2.

This means that the marginal rate of transformation in country A is smaller than that in country B: $MRT^A < MRT^B$. Let $\bar{p}^s$ be the autarkic relative price of country s $(=A, B)$ and p be the world relative price that would realize under free trade between two countries. If all goods are indispensable in consumption in both countries, Eqs. (2.4) and (2.5) together imply $\bar{p}^A < \bar{p}^B$, that is, country A has a comparative advantage in good 1 over country B. In turn, country B has a comparative advantage in good 2 over country A.

As for the relationship between p and $\bar{p}^s$, there are three conceivable cases: (i) $\bar{p}^A < \bar{p}^B < p$, (ii) $p < \bar{p}^A < \bar{p}^B$, and (iii) $\bar{p}^A \leq p \leq \bar{p}^B$. In case (i), both countries specialize solely in good 1 as just shown in the last subsection. Good 2 is not available for consumption at all. As we assumed the indispensability of all goods in consumption, case (i) cannot hold in equilibrium. Similarly, in case (ii), both countries specialize in good 2; this cannot hold in equilibrium, either. The only remaining possibility is case (iii). In this case, country A specializes in good 1, exports it, and imports good 2 instead. Conversely, country B specializes in good 2, exports it, and imports good 1. The equilibrium trade pattern becomes such that each country exports the good in which it has a comparative advantage over the other country.

Absolute advantage: When $a_{Lj}^A < a_{Lj}^B$, we say that country A has an *absolute advantage* in (the production of) good j over country B. This means that country A has more advanced production technology in good j than country B. It should be noted that the absolute advantage in good j neither implies nor is implied by the comparative advantage in good j. Actually, we can easily construct an example in which country B has absolute advantages in both goods, still country A has a comparative advantage in good 1 (i.e., both $a_{L1}^A > a_{L1}^B$ and $a_{L2}^A > a_{L2}^B$ hold, but, at the same time, $a_{L1}^A / a_{L2}^A < a_{L1}^B / a_{L2}^B$ holds). As shown above, what determines the production and trade patterns is the comparative advantage; the notion of absolute advantage has nothing to do with their determination (as far as the international labor mobility is assumed away). Therefore, it can be the case that firms with higher technology in one country may lose competition against firms with lower technology in the other country and fail to survive in the trading world.

Net export and net import: To show how the trade equilibrium price is determined, we introduce the concepts of the net export curve and the net import curve. For the moment, we concentrate our attention on country A. We regard that Fig. 2.2 illustrates the situation in country A. From now on, we focus on the quantities of good 1.

If the world market price p happens to be equal to the autarkic equilibrium price $\bar{p}^A$, the consumption point will be $\bar{e}$ and the consumption of good 1 be $\bar{x}_1$ in Fig. 2.2. However, since international trade is allowed, the production point for $p = \bar{p}^A$ may differ from $\bar{e}$; it can be any point on segment $y'y''$. If production occurs at $y' = (y'_1, 0)$, then the production of good 1, y'_1, exceeds the consumption, $\bar{x}_1$. In this case, country A can export $y'_1 - \bar{x}_1$ units of good 1 at the world market price. On the other hand, if production occurs at $y'' = (0, y''_2)$, the consumption of good 1, $\bar{x}_1$, exceeds the production of good 1, which is zero. In this case, country A has to import all of $\bar{x}_1$.

Let $q \equiv y_1 - x_1$ be the *net export* of good 1 of country A. When $p = \bar{p}^A$, the net export of good 1 ranges from $q^a \equiv y'_1 - \bar{x}_1 > 0$ to $q^b \equiv 0 - \bar{x}_1 < 0$. If the world market price rises to p' $(> \bar{p}^A)$ and the budget line becomes fy' as in Fig. 2.2, the consumption of good 1 decreases to x'_1 and, accordingly, the net export of good 1 increases to $q' \equiv y'_1 - x'_1$ $(>q^a)$. If, on the other hand, the world market price goes down to p'' $(< \bar{p}^A)$ and the budget line becomes gy'', the consumption of good 1 increases to x''_1 and, therefore, the net export also decreases to $q'' \equiv 0 - x''_1$ $(<q^b)$.

In Fig. 2.3, the world market price is measured vertically and country A's net export of good 1 is measured horizontally to the right. Curve ℓ with two kinks (at points a and b) illustrates the relationship between the world market price p and country A's net export q. We call this curve the *net export curve* of country A. The flat portion ab of curve ℓ corresponds to the case where $p = \bar{p}^A$. Although the net export curve in Fig. 2.3 is drawn upward-sloping (except when $p = \bar{p}^A$), this may not always be the case. If good 1 is normal, we can show that q is monotonically increasing in the world market price p below $\bar{p}^A$; however, q can become decreasing in p above $\bar{p}^A$. That is, the net export curve may have a "backward-bending" portion in the region above $\bar{p}^A$.

Similarly, we can derive the net export curve of country B. Having assumed Eq. (2.5), we know that country B imports good 1 in equilibrium.

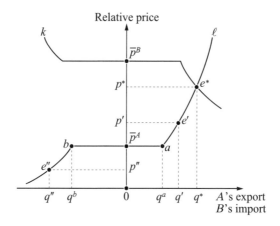

Fig. 2.3   The Import–Demand and Export–Supply Curves

Then, it is convenient to measure both country B's net import of good 1 and country A's net export of good 1 in the same direction. The graph obtained by turning the export supply curve symmetrically with respect to the vertical axis is called the *net import curve*. Curve k in Fig. 2.3 illustrates the net import curve of country B, which is drawn downward-sloping except for the flat portion at the height of the autarkic equilibrium price $\bar{p}^B$.

The trade equilibrium price: Trade equilibrium requires the coincidence of the total supply and the total demand in the world markets for all goods: for $j = 1, 2$,

$$y_j^A + y_j^B = x_j^A + x_j^B. \tag{2.6}$$

Due to the Walras law, it suffices to consider only one of the above conditions. From the market clearing condition for good 1, we have $y_1^A - x_1^A = x_1^B - y_1^B$; that is, the net export of country A is equated to the net import of country B in equilibrium.

The intersection of the net export curve and the net import curve in Fig. 2.3 (i.e., point e^*) represents the trade equilibrium between countries A and B. The trade equilibrium price is p^*, and the equilibrium quantity of trade is q^*. Figure 2.3 illustrates the case of a unique trade equilibrium in which the trade equilibrium price p^* is strictly in-between $\bar{p}^A$ and $\bar{p}^B$

(i.e., $\bar{p}^A < p^* < \bar{p}^B$). In this case, each country completely specializes in the good that the country has a comparative advantage over the other country.

Trade equilibrium may not be unique. We can easily construct some examples with multiple trade equilibria. Further, even if the trade equilibrium is unique, it is possible to have either $p^* = \bar{p}^A$ or $p^* = \bar{p}^B$. In any case, we do not have trade equilibria with $p^* < \bar{p}^A$ or $p^* > \bar{p}^B$. The trade equilibrium price p^* must fall on the closed interval between $\bar{p}^A$ and $\bar{p}^B$.

The world PPS: Before examining the production efficiency of the trade equilibrium, let us introduce the concept of the *world production possibility set* $\mathscr{Y}^W$, which is defined as the vector sum of the production possibility sets of the countries: $\mathscr{Y}^W \equiv \mathscr{Y}^A + \mathscr{Y}^B \equiv \{y \in \mathbb{R}^2_+ | \ y = y^A + y^B, \ y^A \in \mathscr{Y}^A, \ y^B \in \mathscr{Y}^B\}$. Figure 2.4 illustrates the graph of $\mathscr{Y}^W$, which can be drawn as follows. In the figure, the quantity of good 1 is measured horizontally and that of good 2 is measured vertically. The shaded triangular area Oab is the production possibility set of country A; we fix the position of Oab as illustrated in the figure. On the other hand, the shaded triangle $\triangle ocd$ represents the production possibility set of country B with its origin being o (small "ou"). Imagine that $\triangle ocd$ can move freely on the plane with keeping its aspect.

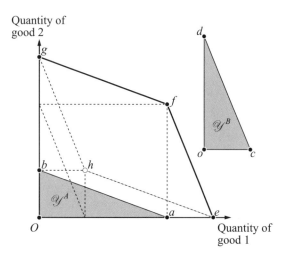

Fig. 2.4   The World Production Possibility Set

Now suppose that point o of $\triangle ocd$ is located at point a, which corresponds to the production point where country A completely specializes in good 1. Then, $\triangle ocd$ overlaps the triangular area aef. Any production vector located in this area can be represented by the sum of country A's production vector corresponding to point a and a certain production vector of country B. Further, as point o moves up along segment ab, $\triangle ocd$ sweeps the parallelogram area $abgf$. Again, any production vector in the area swept by $\triangle ocd$ can be represented by the sum of two production vectors, one in $\mathscr{Y}^A$ and the other in $\mathscr{Y}^B$. In this way, as point o moves over the triangular area Oab (i.e., the production possibility set of country A), $\triangle ocd$ sweeps part of the plane and, eventually, forms a quadrangle area $Oefg$. The area $Oefg$ thus obtained is the graph of $\mathscr{Y}^W$.

The outer boundary efg of the quadrangle area corresponds to the set of efficient world production vectors, that is, the *world production possibility frontier*. Unlike the production possibility frontier of a single country, the world production possibility frontier is not a straight line, but it has a refracting point f. Point e corresponds to the case where both countries completely specialize in good 1; point g corresponds to the case where both countries completely specialize in good 2. The refracting point f corresponds to the case where country A completely specializes in good 1, while country B in good 2. Further, segment ef corresponds to the case where country A completely specializes in good 1, while country B diversifies its production; on the other hand, segment fg corresponds to the case where country A diversifies its production, while country B completely specializes in good 2.

Efficiency of the world production: Let $y^{A*} \in \mathscr{Y}^A$ and $y^{B*} \in \mathscr{Y}^B$ be the equilibrium production vector of the countries for p^*. The world production vector is $y^* = y^{A*} + y^{B*} \in \mathscr{Y}^W$. We know that y^{A*} is efficient relative to $\mathscr{Y}^A$ and also y^{B*} is efficient relative to $\mathscr{Y}^B$. These facts, however, do not automatically guarantee that the world production vector y^* is efficient from the viewpoint of the world as a whole. Here, we show that no matter what the precise value of the trade equilibrium price p^* is, the corresponding world production vector y^* is efficient relative to $\mathscr{Y}^W$.

As shown before, the trade equilibrium relative price p^* must fall on the interval between $\bar{p}^A$ and $\bar{p}^B$. According to the values of p^*, we have three possible production patterns: (i) If $p^* = \bar{p}^A$, country A can diversify its production, while country B has to completely specialize in good 2; (ii) if $\bar{p}^A < p^* < \bar{p}^B$, country A completely specializes in good 1, while country B in good 2; and (iii) if $p^* = \bar{p}^B$, country A completely specializes in good 1, while country B can diversify its production.[3] To prove the equilibrium world production $y^* = (y_1^*, y_2^*)$ is efficient relative to $\mathcal{Y}^W$, it suffices to show that there is no feasible production vector $y' = (y_1', y_2') \in \mathcal{Y}^W$ such that $y_1^* = y_1'$ and $y_2^* < y_2'$. Because the same argument applies as well to cases (ii) and (iii), we only provide a proof for case (i).

If we were to change the world production from y^* keeping the production of good 1 unchanged, we have to decrease the production of good 1 in either one of the countries and increase the same amount of good 1 in the other country. Since, as we assumed case (i), country B has completely specialized in good 2 and its production of good 1 has already reached zero, country B cannot decrease the production of good 1 any more. Therefore, the production of good 1 has to be decreased in country A. Suppose that country A decreases good 1 by one unit and, conversely, country B increases good 1 by one unit. Then, good 2 can be increased by at most "MRT^A units" in country A and it has to be decreased by at least "MRT^B units" in country B. Through these operations, the world production of good 1 can be kept unchanged, but that of good 2 has to be *decreased* by at least "MRT^B − MRT^A units" (note that MRT^B − MRT^A > 0 by assumption). We cannot increase good 2 from y^* with keeping good 1 unchanged. That is, there is no feasible world production vector y' such that $y^* < y'$ — the equilibrium world production vector y^* is efficient relative to $\mathcal{Y}^W$.

---

[3]The following production patterns never occur in equilibrium: (iv) country A completely specializes in good 2, while country B diversifies its production; (v) country B completely specializes in good 1, while country A diversifies its production; and (vi) country A completely specializes in good 2, while country B in good 1. In these cases, even if y^A and y^B are efficient relative to $\mathcal{Y}^A$ and $\mathcal{Y}^B$, respectively, the corresponding world production $y = y^A + y^B$ is not efficient relative to $\mathcal{Y}^W$.

2.2.3 *An Extension*

Now let us consider an extension of the Ricardian model, in which there are three countries (A, B, and C) and three goods (i.e., 1, 2, and 3). The point of this extension is that the numbers of countries and goods are the same.

So far, we have considered the following question: [Q1] *for a given set of the labor input coefficients, what kind of trade pattern will emerge?* or, equivalently, *which good will each country export in equilibrium?* It is relatively easy to answer [Q1] in models with only two goods because there are only two candidates for the production/specialization patterns of each country. However, the number of conceivable production/specialization patterns expands rapidly as the numbers of goods and countries increase simultaneously. For example, in a 3×3 model, country A may completely specialize in only one good (i.e., good 1, or good 2, or good 3); may partially specialize in two of the three goods (i.e., goods 1 and 2, or goods 2 and 3, or goods 1 and 3); or may diversify its production. A similar argument applies to the other countries as well. Consequently, the answer to [Q1] would turn out to be a complicated taxonomy, from which we hardly gain economic insights. Therefore, we investigate here an alternative question: [Q2] *under what conditions on the labor input coefficients will a specified trade pattern emerge in equilibrium?* In particular, we are interested in trade patterns in which each country completely specializes in one and only one good and every good is produced.

Let $M \equiv \{A, B, C\}$ and $N \equiv \{1, 2, 3\}$ be the sets of the countries and the goods, respectively. An *assignment* is a one-to-one mapping γ from M *onto* N. Let Γ denote the set of all assignments. For an assignment $\gamma \in \Gamma$, $\gamma(k) = i$ for $k \in M$ and $i \in N$ means that country k is assigned to produce good i. An ordered array $(\gamma(A), \gamma(B), \gamma(C))$ of the image of γ can be identified with the assignment γ itself. In the 3×3 case, there are six possible assignments: $(1, 2, 3)$, $(1, 3, 2)$, $(2, 1, 3)$, $(2, 3, 1)$, $(3, 1, 2)$, $(3, 2, 1)$. Clearly, an assignment corresponds to a particular production/trade pattern.

McKenzie–Jones theorem: Let us consider the trade/production pattern γ^* such that $(\gamma^*(A), \gamma^*(B), \gamma^*(C)) = (1, 2, 3)$. For γ^* to be the equilibrium trade/production pattern, the prices of goods and the wage rates of the countries have to satisfy the following [in]equalities:

$$\text{(good 1)} \qquad \text{(good 2)} \qquad \text{(good 3)}$$

$$\text{(Country }A\text{) } p_1 = w^A a_{L1}^A, \quad p_2 \leq w^A a_{L2}^A, \quad p_3 \leq w^A a_{L3}^A,$$

$$\text{(Country }B\text{) } p_1 \leq w^B a_{L1}^B, \quad p_2 = w^B a_{L2}^B, \quad p_3 \leq w^B a_{L3}^B, \qquad (2.7)$$

$$\text{(Country }C\text{) } p_1 \leq w^C a_{L1}^C, \quad p_2 \leq w^C a_{L2}^C, \quad p_3 = w^C a_{L3}^C.$$

To eliminate the prices of goods and the wage rates from the above conditions, let us consider the following operation: for each $\gamma \in \Gamma$, choose the [in]equalities corresponding to good $\gamma(k)$ for country $k = A, B, C$. Take $\gamma^* = (1, 2, 3)$ for example. We have three equalities $p_1 = w^A a_{L\gamma^*(A)}^A$, $p_2 = w^B a_{L\gamma^*(B)}^B$, and $p_3 = w^C a_{L\gamma^*(C)}^C$. Multiplying both sides, we obtain $p_1 p_2 p_3 = w^A w^B w^C a_{L\gamma^*(A)}^A a_{L\gamma^*(B)}^B a_{L\gamma^*(C)}^C$. For $\gamma \neq \gamma^*$, we have $p_{\gamma(k)} \leq w^s a_{L\gamma(k)}^s$ for $s = A, B, C$ (actually, one of these inequalities may be equality). Multiplying both sides, we obtain $p_1 p_2 p_3 \leq w^A w^B w^C a_{L\gamma(A)}^A a_{L\gamma(B)}^B a_{L\gamma(C)}^C$. Consequently, we obtain the following conditions:

$$a_{L\gamma^*(A)}^A a_{L\gamma^*(B)}^B a_{L\gamma^*(C)}^C \leq a_{L\gamma(A)}^A a_{L\gamma(B)}^B a_{L\gamma(C)}^C \quad \text{for all } \gamma \in \Gamma.$$

That is, the assignment $\gamma^* \equiv (1, 2, 3)$ will be the equilibrium trade/specialization pattern if the corresponding product of the labor coefficients is the minimum among possible assignments. This result is known as the *McKenzie–Jones theorem*.[4]

Range of the relative prices: Let us take good 3 as the numéraire and set $p_3 = 1$. Then, p_1 and p_2 represent the relative prices of goods 1 and 2 in terms of good 3. By eliminating the wage rates from (2.7), we obtain the following six inequalities:

$$\frac{a_{L1}^A}{a_{L3}^A} \leq p_1, \quad p_1 \leq \frac{a_{L1}^C}{a_{L3}^C},$$

---

[4]See McKenzie (1953) and Jones (1961). The exposition here follows Takayama (1970). As far as the numbers of countries and goods are the same, this result is easily extended to cases with more than three countries/goods.

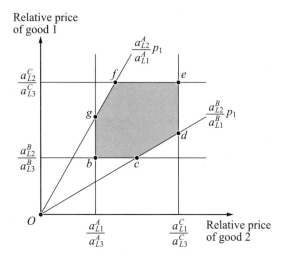

Fig. 2.5   McKenzie–Jones Theorem and the Range of Prices

$$\frac{a_{L2}^{B}}{a_{L3}^{B}} \leq p_2, \quad p_2 \leq \frac{a_{L2}^{C}}{a_{L3}^{C}},$$

$$p_1\frac{a_{L2}^{B}}{a_{L1}^{B}} \leq p_2, \quad p_2 \leq p_1\frac{a_{L2}^{A}}{a_{L1}^{A}}.$$

For $\gamma^* = (1, 2, 3)$ to be the equilibrium production pattern, the solutions for the above system of inequalities with respect to the combinations of relative price (p_1, p_2) must be non-empty. The shaded area *bcdefg* in Fig. 2.5 illustrates the range of the relative prices. As far as the equilibrium relative prices fall on this area, countries A, B, and C come to specialize in good 1, good 2, and good 3, respectively.

2.3   Continuum of Goods

In this section, we extend the model to include (uncountably) many goods and two countries (A and B).[5] Goods are indexed by real numbers in the unit interval $[0, 1] \equiv \{j \in \mathbb{R} \mid 0 \leq j \leq 1\}$.

---

[5]The Ricardian model with a continuum of goods has been developed by Dornbusch, Fischer, and Samuelson (1977); the model is sometimes called the *Dornbusch–Fischer–Samuelson model*.

2.3.1 The Base Model

Relative wage rate: Let $\omega \equiv w^B/w^A$ be the relative wage rate of the countries and let us define $\alpha(j) \equiv a_{Lj}^A/a_{Lj}^B$ for $j \in [0, 1]$. Further, we assume that goods are indexed so that $\alpha(j)$ is monotonically increasing in $j \in [0, 1]$.

Suppose that good i is exported from country A and good j is exported from country B. Then, we have $p_i = w^A a_{Li}^A$, $p_j = w^B a_{Lj}^B$, and $p_k \leq w^s a_{Lk}^s$ for all $k \in [0, 1]$ and for all $s = A, B$. Combining these [in]equalities, we obtain

$$\alpha(i) \leq \omega \leq \alpha(j).$$

That is, the relative wage rate ω determines the ranges of exports/imports of the countries. For a given ω, a good with the index z that solves $\omega = \alpha(z)$ is called the *boundary good*. Goods with lower indices than z are exported from country A (not produced in country B) and, conversely, the other goods with higher indices than z are exported from country B (not produced in country A). Because α is increasing in the indices, the range of country A's exports expands as ω increases.

Demand function: Let x_j^s denote the consumption of good j in country s. We assume that the consumers' preferences of both countries are represented by a common Cobb–Douglas utility function

$$U = \int_0^1 \ln[x_j^s] \mathrm{d}j.$$

Through a usual procedure, we obtain the demand function for good j

$$x_j^s = \frac{w^s L^s}{p_j}, \quad j \in [0, 1], \quad s = A, B, \tag{2.8}$$

where $w^s L^s$ represents the total labor income in country $s = A, B$.

Trade balance condition: For the moment, let us assume that country A is exporting (hence, producing) those goods with lower indices than z. In each country, the value of total production, GDP, coincides with the total labor income $w^s L^s$. Due to the world market equilibrium conditions, the GDP of country A must be equalized to the aggregate expenditure on the goods produced in country A, that is

$$w^A L^A = \int_0^z p_j x_j^A \mathrm{d}j + \int_0^z p_j x_j^B \mathrm{d}j.$$

By making use of Eq. (2.8), the above equation can be converted into

$$(1 - z) w^A L^A = z w^B L^B. \tag{2.9}$$

The left-hand side of Eq. (2.9) represents the value of imports of country A; on the other hand, the right-hand side represents that of country B. That is, Eq. (2.9) implies the *trade balance condition*. Further, by solving Eq. (2.9), we can write $\omega \equiv w^B / w^A$ as a function of z and L^A / L^B.

$$\omega = \beta(z, L^A / L^B) \equiv \left[\frac{1}{z} - 1 \right] \cdot \frac{L^A}{L^B}.$$

Obviously, function β is decreasing in z and increasing in L^A / L^B.

Trade pattern: Function α summarizes the information on the technology (i.e., supply side) of the countries, while function β carries the information on the demand side. Combining these functions, we can find the equilibrium trade pattern

$$\alpha(z) = \beta(z, L^A / L^B).$$

Let z^* be the index that solves the above equation. Good z^* is the equilibrium boundary good. By substituting z^* into β, we obtain the equilibrium relative wage rate $\omega^* \equiv \beta(z^*, L^A / L^B)$.

Figure 2.6 illustrates the determination of the equilibrium trade pattern. In the figure, the index of goods is measured horizontally and the relative wage rate vertically. The upward-sloping curve α represents the graph of function α and the downward-sloping curve β represents the graph of function β. The intersection of these curves determines the equilibrium boundary good z^* and the relative wage rate ω^* simultaneously.

Comparative statics: To see the characteristics of the model, we briefly conduct two comparative statics analyses. First, let us consider a case where an exogenous technological progress occurs solely in country A. Suppose that the labor input coefficients of all goods decrease simultaneously at the same rate — an overall technological progress in country A.

Relative wage rate

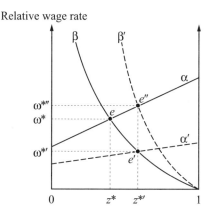

Fig. 2.6   The Ricardian Model with a Continuum of Goods

In this case, curve α in Fig. 2.6 shifts downward uniformly. Then, the index of the boundary good increases from z^* to $z^{*\prime}$, while the relative wage rate decreases from ω^* to $\omega^{*\prime}$. Technological progress in country A expands the range of country A's exports and raises country A's wage rate relative to country B's.

Next, let us consider another case where the population of country A grows exogenously. Suppose L^A increases. Accordingly, curve β moves clockwise with the center at the lower-right corner in Fig. 2.6. Then, the index of the boundary good increases from z^* to $z^{*\prime}$, while the relative wage rate increases from ω^* to $\omega^{*\prime\prime}$. Population growth in country A lowers its wage rate relative to country B and expands the range of country A's exports.

2.3.2   *Transportation Costs and Non-traded Goods*

We introduce transportation costs into the model and examine their implications on the trade structure. Transportation costs here should be understood in a broader sense; they not only include the payments to actual transportation services (e.g., container vessels, cargo planes, freight trains) or other monetary payments such as taxes and tariffs, customs clearance fees, but also include non-monetary impediments to trade such as "time" consumed by administrative procedures and some "difficulties in communication" arising from differences in languages between trading partners.

Transportation costs: Instead of modeling a transportation industry explicitly, we adopt the so-called *iceberg costs*. That is, we assume that a certain portion of traded goods disappears — melts away like an iceberg — on the way from the exporting country to the importing country. To be more specific, suppose that τ units of a good ($\tau > 1$) are required to be dispatched from one country in order to deliver 1 unit of the good to the other country. In other words, ($\tau - 1$)-portion of τ units of the good is lost on the way of transportation. For simplicity, we assume that the transportation costs neither depend on the identities of goods nor on the directions of international transactions (i.e., whether they are exported from country A to country B or vice versa). In addition, we assume that domestic transactions do not incur any transportation costs. For a firm producing good j in country s, the cost of "delivering" 1 unit of good j to the partner country's market is τ times as much as the cost of "producing" 1 unit of good j in the home country, that is, the *unit delivery cost* from country s to the other becomes $\tau w^s a_{Lj}^s$.

The range of non-traded goods: Due to transportation costs, the markets for a good in countries A and B are separated. Therefore, we have to distinguish two prices in two markets for one good. Let p_j^s be the price of good j in country s. Suppose that country A exports good i to country B, while country B exports good j to country A. Then, the unit delivery cost of good i from country A to country B must be equal to the price in country B, that is, $\tau w^A a_{Li}^A = p_i^B$. For firms producing good i in country B, we have $p_i^B \leq w^B a_{Li}^B$. Similarly, we have $\tau w^B a_{Lj}^B = p_j^A$ and $p_j^A \leq w^A a_{Lj}^A$. These [in]equalities together with $\tau > 1$ imply

$$\alpha(i) \leq \omega/\tau < \tau\omega \leq \alpha(j). \tag{2.10}$$

Let $\bar{z}_0$ and $\bar{z}_1$ be the indices that solve $\alpha(z) = \omega/\tau$ and $\tau\omega = \alpha(z)$, respectively. Figure 2.7 illustrates the relationship among $\tau\alpha$, α/τ, ω, $\bar{z}_0$, and $\bar{z}_1$. Because function α is increasing in z, it is easy to verify that (i) $\bar{z}_0$ is increasing in ω and decreasing in τ, (ii) $\bar{z}_1$ is increasing in both ω and τ, and (iii) $\bar{z}_0 < \bar{z}_1$. According to Eq. (2.10), good $\bar{z}_0$ and good $\bar{z}_1$ can be said

Relative wage rate

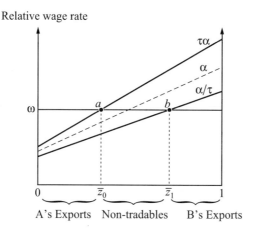

ω

$0 \qquad \bar{z}_0 \qquad \bar{z}_1 \qquad 1$

A's Exports   Non-tradables   B's Exports

Fig. 2.7   Transportation Costs and the Non-traded Goods

to be the boundary goods that determine the ranges of exports of the countries: country A exports those goods with lower indices than $\bar{z}_0$, while country B exports those goods with higher indices than $\bar{z}_1$. Goods with indices between $\bar{z}_0$ and $\bar{z}_1$ emerge as *non-traded goods*, which are produced and consumed in each country, but not traded between countries.

Trade balance and trade pattern: For a given z, let us define z_0 and z_1 so that they satisfy $\alpha(z) = \tau\alpha(z_0) = \alpha(z_1)/\tau$. We have $z_0 = \bar{z}_0$ and $z_1 = \bar{z}_1$ if and only if $\omega = \alpha(z)$. Suppose, for the moment, that country A is exporting goods between 0 and z_0 and country B is exporting goods between z_1 and 1. The total labor income of country A must be equal to the aggregate expenditure on the goods produced in country A, that is

$$w^A L^A = \int_0^{z_1} p_j^A x_j^A \mathrm{d}j + \frac{1}{\tau} \int_0^{z_0} p_j^B x_j^B \mathrm{d}j.$$

As reflected in the second term of the right-hand side of the above equation, the amount that firms in country A can receive from consumers in country B is discounted by the transportation cost τ and becomes less than the actual payment by the consumers in country B. Taking account of Eq. (2.8), we can solve the above equation for ω as

$$\omega = \left[\frac{1 - z_1}{z_0} \right] \cdot \frac{\tau L^A}{L^B}.$$

Because z_0 and z_1 depend on z, we can write the right-hand side of the above equation as a function of z, τ, and L^A/L^B, that is, $\tilde{\beta}(z, \tau, L^A/L^B)$. It is easy to verify that function $\tilde{\beta}$ is decreasing in z and increasing in L^A/L^B; the effects of τ on $\tilde{\beta}$ are ambiguous.

Combining functions α and $\tilde{\beta}$, we obtain the following equilibrium condition:

$$\alpha(z) = \tilde{\beta}(z, \tau, L^A/L^B).$$

Let z^* be the solution to the above equation. Then, the equilibrium relative wage rate $\omega^* \equiv \alpha(z^*)$ and the two boundaries are $\bar{z}_0^*$ and $\bar{z}_1^*$; hence, the equilibrium trade pattern is determined. In equilibrium, country A exports those goods with indices lower than $\bar{z}_0^*$; country B exports those goods with indices higher than $\bar{z}_1^*$; those goods between two boundaries are non-traded goods. Some comparative statics analyses similar to the case with no transportation cost would facilitate the readers' better understanding of the model; they are left for the readers as exercises.

2.4 Remarks and Further Topics

This section deals with three separate topics related to the Ricardian model: the derivation of the gravity equation, the technological leapfrogging, and the roles of time zone differences in trade.

2.4.1 *The Eaton–Kortum Model and the Gravity Equation*

The gravity equation in physics associates the force operating on two objects with the masses of these objects and the distance between them: the force is proportional to the product of two masses and inversely proportional to the square of distance. Analogous relations can be found for bilateral trade. The gravity equation in international economics relates the volume of bilateral trade or other international transactions between two countries to the *magnitudes* of these countries, which can be measured by their respective income levels (i.e., GDP), and the *distance* between them, which includes not only the physical distance but also other impediments to trade such as transportation costs, tariffs, customs procedures, differences in languages, cultural diversities, and so forth. The gravity equation has achieved a great deal of success in empirical studies in international economics on one hand, but it has been criticized for its lack of theoretical foundation on the other.[6]

The basic Ricardian model and its variations examined in the previous sections sharply highlight the roles of technological differences in determining the trade and specialization patterns, but they missed the roles of geographic distances and bilateral trade. By generalizing the two-country continuum-good Dornbusch–Fischer–Samuelson model, Eaton and Kortum (2002) have developed a variation of the Ricardian model with many countries that incorporates the roles of technology and geography. The most salient feature of the Eaton–Kortum model is an assumption that the technology of producing a particular good in each country is represented by the realization of a random variable. In this subsection, we show that the gravity equation can be derived from the Eaton–Kortum model.[7]

Notation: Let M be the set of a finite number of countries. There is a continuum of goods indexed by real numbers in the unit interval $[0, 1] \subset \mathbb{R}$. The labor input coefficient for good k in country i is denoted by a^i_{Lk}. Let w^i be the wage rate in country i. Then, the unit cost of producing good k in country i is $w^i a^i_{Lk}$.[8] To represent the geographic barriers to trade, we introduce iceberg-type transportation costs. Let $\tau^{ij} \geq 1$ be the amount of a good produced in country i necessary to deliver 1 unit of the good to country j. It is possible to have intra-country transportation costs: $\tau^{ii} > 1$ for some $i \in M$.

Let p^{ij}_k be the cost of delivering one unit of good k produced in country i to country j. Then, we have

$$p^{ij}_k = \tau^{ij} w^i a^i_{Lk}.$$

---

[6]The first application of the gravity equation to international trade is Tinbergen (1962).

[7]The gravity equation can be derived from several different theoretical frameworks. In a later chapter, we derive the gravity equation by using a monopolistically competitive model.

[8]Eaton and Kortum (2002) have introduced intermediate goods into their model. To simplify the exposition, we omit intermediate goods here. Therefore, the unit cost of producing a good becomes dependent only on the wage rate, but not on the prices of other goods.

Under perfect competition, consumers in country j can buy good k from the most inexpensive source of the good. Therefore, the price that the consumers in country j actually pay for good k, denoted by p_k^j, becomes as follows:

$$p_k^j = \min \left\{ p_k^{ij} \mid i \in M \right\}.$$

Probabilistic representation of technologies: We assume that the labor productivity for good k in country i, which is equal to the inverse of a_{Lk}^i, is the realization of a random variable Z^i drawn from a country-specific probability distribution $F^i(z) = \text{Prob}[Z^i \leq z]$.[9] The probability distribution F^i represents the fraction of goods for which the labor productivity in country i is below z. Under this assumption, the cost of delivering one unit of a good produced in country i to country j is the realization of the random variable $P^{ij} = \tau^{ij} w^i / Z^i$ and the price that the consumers in country j pay is the realization of $P^j = \min\{ P^{ij} \mid i \in M \}$.

More specifically, we assume that the productivity distribution takes the form of Fréchet: for all $i \in M$,

$$F^i(z) \equiv \exp[-\rho^i z^{-\theta}],$$

where $\rho^i > 0$ and $\theta > 1$. The parameter ρ^i, which is country-specific, is related to the location of the distribution F^i: as ρ^i increases, the geometric mean of the random variable Z^i increases. In contrast, the parameter θ, which is common to all countries, is related to the shape of F^i: as θ increases, the (logarithm of) standard deviation of Z^i decreases. In other words, a higher θ implies a narrower technological heterogeneity across goods. As discussed in Eaton and Kortum (2002), ρ^i and θ can be seen as the indicator of absolute advantage of country i and that of comparative advantage across goods, respectively.[10]

---

[9]Here, F^i denotes a distribution function of a random variable; readers should not confuse this with a production function of a certain good.

[10]It should be noted that the distribution F^i does not depend on the *identities* of goods.

Distribution of prices: Given the distribution F^i of the labor productivity, the distribution of P^{ij} can be written as follows:

$$G^{ij}(p) \equiv \Pr\left[P^{ij} \leq p\right] = 1 - F^i(\tau^{ij}w^i/p)$$

$$= 1 - \exp\left[-\rho^i\left(\tau^{ij}w^i\right)^{-\theta}p^\theta\right].$$

Accordingly, the distribution of prices of the goods that country j actually buys is given by

$$G^j(p) \equiv \Pr\left[P^j \leq p\right] = 1 - \prod_{\ell \in M}\left[1 - G^{\ell j}(p)\right]$$

$$= 1 - \exp\left[-\left(\frac{p}{Q^j}\right)^\theta\right],$$

where

$$Q^j \equiv \left[\sum_{\ell \in M}\rho^\ell\left(\tau^{\ell j}w^\ell\right)^{-\theta}\right]^{-1/\theta}. \tag{2.11}$$

The distribution $G^j(p)$ depends negatively on Q^j. In turn, Q^j depends negatively on ρ^ℓ, and positively on both $\tau^{\ell j}$ and w^ℓ. Roughly speaking, country j is likely to enjoy lower prices when (i) the state of technology is higher, (ii) the transportation costs are lower, and (iii) the production costs are lower.

Expenditure share on bilateral trade: Eaton and Kortum (2002) have shown some important properties of the price distributions: (i) The probability π^{ij} that country i supplies a good at the lowest price to country j is given by

$$\pi^{ij} = \Pr\left[P^{ij} \leq \min\{P^{\ell j} \mid \ell \neq i\}\right] = \int_0^\infty \prod_{\ell \neq i}\left[1 - G^{\ell j}(p)\right] dG^{ij}(p)$$

$$= \rho^i\left(\frac{\tau^{ij}w^i}{Q^j}\right)^{-\theta},$$

which is equivalent to the fraction of goods that country j buys from country i; (ii) The distribution of the price of a good that country j actually buys from any country i is $G^j(p)$, which is independent of the identity of the source country. These properties imply that the fraction of country j's expenditure on goods from country i is equal to π^{ij}, therefore,

$$\frac{X^{ij}}{Y^j} = \pi^{ij} = \rho^i \left(\frac{\tau^{ij} w^i}{Q^j} \right)^{-\theta}, \quad i, j \in M, \tag{2.12}$$

where X^{ij} and Y^j denote the expenditure on goods from country i and the total expenditure of country j, respectively; the latter is equal to the total income of country j.

Multilateral resistance term: The total sales of country i is equal to the total income Y^i of the country. Let $Y^W \equiv \sum_{\ell \in M} Y^\ell$ and $\mu^i \equiv Y^i / Y^W$ be the world total income and the income share of country i, respectively. From Eq. (2.12), we have

$$Y^i = \sum_{\ell \in M} X^{i\ell} = \rho^i (w^i)^{-\theta} \sum_{\ell \in M} \left(\frac{\tau^{i\ell}}{Q^\ell} \right)^{-\theta} Y^\ell.$$

Solving it for $\rho^i (w^i)^{-\theta}$ and substituting the result back into Eq. (2.11), we obtain

$$Q^j = \left[\sum_{\ell \in M} \left(\frac{\tau^{\ell j}}{R^\ell} \right)^{-\theta} \mu^\ell \right]^{-1/\theta}, \quad j \in M, \tag{2.13}$$

where

$$R^\ell \equiv \left[\sum_{k \in M} \left(\frac{\tau^{\ell k}}{Q^k} \right)^{-\theta} \mu^k \right]^{-1/\theta}, \quad \ell \in M. \tag{2.14}$$

Equations (2.13) and (2.14) implicitly define Q^is and R^is as functions of transportation costs of all pairs of countries, $\{\tau^{jk}\}_{j,k \in M}$, and the income shares, $\{\mu^j\}_{j \in M}$. Q^is and R^is are known as the *multilateral resistance terms.*[11] If the transportation costs are symmetric, that is, if $\tau^{ij} = \tau^{ji}$ for all $i, j \in M$, then we have $Q^i = R^i$ for all $i \in M$.[12]

The gravity equation: With the above definitions and assumptions, we can rewrite Eq. (2.12) as follows:

$$X^{ij} = \frac{Y^i Y^j}{Y^W} \left(\frac{\tau^{ij}}{Q^i Q^j} \right)^{-\theta}, \quad i, j \in M. \tag{2.15}$$

The amount of trade between two countries i and j is *proportional* to the product of the total incomes Y^i and Y^j (relative to the world total income Y^W) and *negatively related* (though not inversely proportional) to the transportation cost τ^{ij} between them. This is a reflection of the gravity equation in physics: we can think of the import X^{ij} of country j from country i as the "force" of gravity operating between the two countries; both the total income Y^i and Y^j as the "massess"; and the transportation cost τ^{ij} as the "distance". It should be noted that the bilateral trade between countries i and j depends not only on their bilateral variables, but also on the whole structure of the world trade through the multilateral resistance terms.

2.4.2   *Technological Changes and Leapfrogging*

The long history of international economy has witnessed alternations of the leading countries. For a certain period of time, one country may hold a position of the technological leader in the world economy, who specializes in a growing sector and exports technologically advanced goods. The status of the leader, however, does not last long; in time, another country may come into play and overtake the predecessor to become a new leader — *technological leapfrogging*. Brezis *et al.* (1993) have developed a simple dynamic model in which the technological leapfrogging is determined endogenously through firms' deliberate choice of technology. Although their model is constructed within the framework of the endogenous growth

---

[11]See Anderson and Wincoop (2003, 2004).
[12]Note that the definition of Q^j and R^ℓ are almost symmetric. In the definition of Q^j, the summation is taken over the exporting countries, while in the definition of R^ℓ, the summation is taken over the importing countries.

theory, the majority of their argument can be explained by making use of a static Ricardian model with two countries and two sectors.

Let us consider a world economy consisting of two countries A and B. In each country, there are two sectors: one is a technologically progressive sector and the other is a traditional sector. The traditional sector produces a homogeneous good by using a stagnant technology; the labor input coefficient is assumed to be constant over time and equal to unity. Therefore, as far as a country produces the traditional good, the real wage rate in terms of the homogeneous good in the country is also equal to unity.

Learning-by-doing: The progressive sector can produce a series of generations of the advanced good. Generations are numbered consecutively as k, $k + 1$, and so forth. Each generation is subject to *learning-by-doing*, by which the technology for the existing generation is improved incrementally and gradually as firms acquire their experiences in producing that particular generation. At times, however, there occur *major breakthroughs* that make it possible to create new generations of the advanced good. For simplicity, we assume that all generations of the advanced good are measured in the same physical units and they are perfect substitute with each other.[13]

The production technology of the kth generation is described by the labor input coefficient, $\alpha_k(Z)$, which depends *negatively* on the experience Z in producing the kth generation in a country.[14] The negative dependence of α_k on Z represents the learning-by-doing effect, which is assumed to be completely external to individual firms in the progressive sector and confined within the boundary of each country. Further, we assume that a new generation technology (if available) is more advanced than the former in the sense that $\alpha_{k+1}(Z) < \alpha_k(Z)$ for any experience $Z \geq 0$. It is, however, possible to have $\alpha_{k+1}(Z'') > \alpha_k(Z')$ for different production experiences $Z'' < Z'$.

---

[13]Grossman and Helpman (1995) have provided a comprehensive survey on the interactions of technology and international trade.

[14]The "experience" in producing the advanced good in a country can be measured by the length of time that the country has produced the good or by the cumulative amount of the good produced in the country.

Major innovation: Suppose that the world is in a situation where the kth generation of the advanced good prevails and that country A completely specializes in the advanced good, while country B specializes in the traditional good. Let p', $w^{A'}$, and $w^{B'}$ be the equilibrium relative price of the advanced good and the equilibrium real wage rates in countries A and B, respectively. Further, let $Z^{A'}$ and $Z^{B'}$ be the experiences of countries A and B in producing the advanced good, respectively. Because country A specializes in the advanced good of the k-th generation and, therefore, has some experience, we have $w^{A'} > 1$ and $Z^{A'} > 0$. In contrast, because country B specializes in the traditional good and has no experience in producing the advanced good, we have $w^{B'} = 1$ and $Z^{B'} = 0$. Then, the following conditions must be satisfied in equilibrium:

$$w^{A'} \alpha_k(Z^{A'}) = p' < w^{B'} \alpha_k(Z^{B'}).$$

Without any major breakthrough, country A keeps producing the advanced good and accumulates experiences more, while country B remains unexperienced; the above inequality conditions are strengthened. That is, the learning-by-doing effect only reinforces the comparative advantage of country A in the advanced good.

Now suppose that a major innovation takes place and a new technology becomes available to firms in both countries. If the profit of a firm (evaluated at the price and wage rate just before the innovation) that can be obtained under the new technology is greater than the pre-innovation profit under the old technology, the firm adopts the new one. We consider here a moderate technological jump by this innovation such that $\alpha_k(Z^{A'}) < \alpha_{k+1}(0) < \alpha_k(0)$. Since the wage rate is higher in country A than in country B (i.e., $w^A > 1 = w^B$), it is possible to have the following relation:

$$w^{B'} \alpha_{k+1}(0) < w^{A'} \alpha_k(Z^{A'}) = p' < w^{A'} \alpha_{k+1}(0).$$

In this case, firms in country A do not adopt the new technology, while firms in country B adopt it.[15] The advanced country fails to adopt the new

---

[15] If the innovation is so small that $p' < w^{B'} \alpha_{k+1}(0) < w^{A'} \alpha_{k+1}(0)$, then no firm adopts the new technology. If, on the other hand, the innovation is so large that $w^{B'} \alpha_{k+1}(0) < w^{A'} \alpha_{k+1}(0) < p'$, then

technology just because it has already accumulated a good deal of experiences in the old generation technology and been enjoying a higher wage
rate. On the contrary, the laggard country can profitably adopt the new technology by taking advantage of a lower wage rate due to its laggardness.

Leapfrogging: After a moderate innovation, firms in country B begin to
produce the advanced good with the new technology (the $[k+1]$-th generation) and firms in country A continue to produce it with the old technology
(the kth generation). The supply of the advanced good in the world market increases and the price goes down and, accordingly, the wage rate in
country A decreases. In the new equilibrium immediately after the innovation, country A still specializes in the advanced good, while country B
diversifies. Then, we have

$$w^{B''}\alpha_{k+1}(0) = w^{A''}\alpha_k(Z^{A'}) = p'' < w^{A''}\alpha_{k+1}(0),$$

where p'', $w^{A''} > 1$, and $w^{B''} = 1$ are the relative price of the advanced
good and the wage rates of countries A and B, respectively.

   Now, country B begins to acquire experience in producing the advanced
good (i.e., Z^B begins to increase). If the productivity growth effect due to
learning-by-doing is stronger/faster for the $(k+1)$-th generation than for the
kth generation, there will eventually come the moment at which $\alpha_{k+1}(Z^B)$
in country B falls below $\alpha_k(Z^A)$ in country A. From then on, country A specializes in the traditional good and country B specializes in the advanced
good of the $(k + 1)$-th generation. In this way, country B overtakes country A and occupies the position of a new technological leader in the world
economy until the next major innovation occurs.[16]

---

all firms in both countries adopt the new technology and, therefore, both countries come to share the
same technology.

[16]By using a two-country oligopolistic model of international trade incorporating endogenous choice
of technology by firms, Motta *et al.* (1997) have provided a quite different view of the leapfrogging.
They have shown that there can be multiple equilibria: one where the leader firm maintains its position
and the other where the leapfrogging can occur *without any exogenous change in the technology.* Also,
they have shown that the latter equilibrium cannot pass the risk dominance criterion of equilibrium
selection; this result suggests that the leapfrogging equilibrium is hard to observe.

2.4.3   *Time Zone Differences*

Trade in services has become an active area in the modern international economy. In addition, recent advancement of the information-communication technology (ICT) such as the Internet has brought about revolutionary changes in the ways through which international services transactions are made. To explain the phenomenon of the rapid growth of trade in services in relation to the revolutionary advancement of the communication technology, the notion of *time zone difference* has recently attracted a great deal of attention.

Continuity effect: A well-known example of trade in services taking advantage of the time zone differences is a computer software industry in the US and India (Cairncross, 1997).[17] Engineers of a US software company draft a "source cord" of a computer program in a business day, but may not be able to complete it by the end of business hour of the day. Then the US company sends the in-process cord (in the form of an electronic file) to its affiliate company in India through the Internet as an attachment to an e-mail; the Indian engineers take over the job of cord processing. While the US engineers are sleeping in the nighttime in the US, the Indian engineers can add and rewrite lines, run some preliminary tests, and debug the program in the daytime in India. When the US engineers come back to the office and begin to work in the next morning, they can receive an improved source cord from India. The US company *imports* the cord processing services from India; equivalently, it *outsources* the cord processing to India. The US company can obtain the final product or an improved in-process product *earlier* than when it carries out all the tasks by itself. In this way, the US company can truncate the length of time of production. Head

---

[17]Other examples include a semiconductor chip manufacturer that keeps 24-hour chip design systems by locating design teams separately in the US, India, and Europe (Brown and Linden, 2009); call centers located in Ireland in order to cope with complaints and questions raised by customers in the US or in European countries (Gupta and Seshasai, 2007; Cairncross, 1997); medical diagnoses services (e.g., X-ray reading) during the night in the US that are outsourced to other English-speaking countries in different time zones such as Australia, Malaysia, India, South Africa (Wachter, 2006).

et al. (2009) called this kind of time-saving effect of the time-zone-related trade in services as the *continuity effect.*

Vertical division of labor and discounting: To show how the time zone difference and its continuity effect facilitate international trade, Marjit (2007) has constructed a simple Ricardian model emphasizing the roles of *vertical division of labor* in production and *discounting* in consumption.[18] There are two *small* countries A and B embedded in a larger world economy. Countries A and B are *symmetric*, except that they are located in different time zones with completely opposite daytime and nighttime. One day (i.e., 24 hours) is comprised of daytime and nighttime of equal time length; workers work only in the daytime. Each country can produce a time-zone-related good 1 and a regular good 2. Let a_{Lj} be the labor input coefficient for good $j = 1, 2$. The production process of one unit of good 1 is divided into two vertically related consecutive stages I and II; each stage requires $a_{L1}/2$ units of labor and takes 1 working day; in addition, stage I must be precedent to stage II. Therefore, without outsourcing, production of good 1 takes 2 working days. In contrast, production of good 2 is instantaneous and only requires 1 working day.

Market transactions are made at the beginning of every day; markets open every 24-hour. Suppose that production of the goods starts on Monday morning in country A. Without trade in services (i.e., outsourcing of either one of stages), production of good 1 completes in the Tuesday evening; good 1 will be sold at price p_1 in the Wednesday morning market. In contrast, if a good 1 firm outsources stage II after finishing stage I in the daytime of Monday to a company located in country B, then stage II is processed in country B during country A's nighttime; good 1 will be available in the next morning in country A and sold at price p_1 in the Tuesday morning market. From the perspective of a firm, the revenue of p_1 on Wednesday is different from that of p_1 on Tuesday; to make a meaningful comparison, the former should be discounted by the factor δ $(0 < \delta < 1)$, which might arise from the consumers' impatience.

---

[18] Kikuchi (2006, 2009) have constructed a monopolistically competitive model of time-zone-related trade in intermediate business services. He assumed differentiated intermediate business services, which require two successive production stages as in Marjit (2007)'s model. In his model, trade pattern of the intermediate business services is reciprocal.

Specialization and trade gains: The conditions that both countries A and B specialize in the regular good *before* liberalization of trade in services are $\bar{w}^s a_{L1} > \delta p_1$ and $\bar{w}^s a_{L2} = p_2$, where $\bar{w}^s$ denotes the pre-liberalization wage rate in country $s = A, B$. On the other hand, the conditions that both countries specialize in the time-zone-related good *after* liberalization of trade in services are $w^A a_{L1}/2 + w^B a_{L1}/2 = p_1$ and $w^s a_{L2} > p_2$, where w^s denotes the post-liberalization wage rate in country $s = A, B.$[19] Combining these conditions, we obtain

$$\frac{1}{\delta}\left(\frac{a_{L1}}{a_{L2}}\right) > \left(\frac{p_1}{p_2}\right) > \left(\frac{a_{L1}}{a_{L2}}\right).$$

Under this condition, trade in services between countries A and B can occur. Although country A outsources stage II to country B in our example above, it is also possible country B outsources stage II to country A — trade pattern between A and B is not determined uniquely. In addition, by liberalizing trade in services, the pair of countries A and B comes to have a comparative advantage in the time-zone-related good.

The real wage rate *before* liberalization of trade in services is $\bar{w}^s/p_2 = 1/a_{L2}$. From the specialization conditions *after* liberalization, we have

$$\frac{w^A/p_2}{2} + \frac{w^B/p_2}{2} = \frac{p_1/p_2}{a_{L2}} > \frac{1}{a_{L2}} = \frac{\bar{w}^s}{p_2}, \quad s = A, B.$$

By symmetry, we have $w^A = w^B$. The above inequality implies $w^s > \bar{w}^s$. Workers in both countries clearly gain from liberalization of trade in services.

Synchronization effect: The time zone difference has not only positive impacts on international activities of firms (i.e., the continuity effect), but also some negative impacts. Consider a multinational firm whose head-quarter and a foreign subsidiary are located in different time zones. If the time zone difference is large enough, it is difficult for the headquarter and the subsidiary to communicate smoothly and/or frequently because some employees have to come to the office earlier or stay in the office later

---

[19]Recall the continuity effect of time-zone-related trade, which in effect increases the revenue from δp_1 to p_1 by truncating the length of production time. In addition, through outsourcing of either one of stages, the unit cost of producing good 1 becomes $w^A a_{L1}/2 + w^B a_{L1}/2$.

than the regular business hour in respective time zones; this requires some extra payments to the employees and makes international activities of the multinational firm more expensive. The larger the time zone difference is, the more difficult it is to coordinate and/or synchronize the activities by the headquarter and the subsidiary. Head *et al.* (2009) called this negative impact of the time zone difference as the *synchronization effect.*

24-hour operation and shift-working: Matsuoka and Fukushima (2010) have considered another situation where the time-zone-related good is produced in two successive stages that must be processed without interruption; in other words, the good requires 24-hour continuous operations. If we were to produce this good only in one country, it is necessary to carry out the nighttime operation in this country and, accordingly, to employ some night-shift workers, who will be paid a higher wage rate with nighttime premia. If, however, trade in services or outsourcing of stages is allowed, firms can reduce the production cost by eliminating night-shift workers. This can be an alternative source of gains from time-zone-related trade.[20]

---

[20]Kikuchi and Long (2011) and Nakanishi and Long (2015) have investigated the allocational as well as distributional effects of time-zone-related trade and shift-working. Mandal *et al.* (2017) have examined the roles of the international movement of educational capital across different time zones. Focusing on the roles of trade in intermediate business services over different time zones, Kikuchi and Marjit (2011) and Marjit and Mandal (2017) have dealt with the growth issues within the framework of the AK endogenous growth model. Further, Nakanishi and Long (2018) have examined the effects of R&D offshoring over different time zones on both the growth rate and the wage rate within the framework of the Schumpeterian endogenous growth model.

Chapter 3

Factor Endowments

The knowledge of production technologies can be diffused all over the world through, for example, spillover effects, migration of skilled workers, or learning efforts by firms. The technology differences among countries may disappear in the long run and, if so, they cannot be a source of comparative advantage any longer. Instead of technology differences, the *Heckscher–Ohlin–Samuelson (HOS) model* and the *Specific Factors (SF) model* focus on the roles of the *factor endowments*, which can vary from one country to another because each country has its own historical background, geographic characteristics, demographic structure, and other features. One country may have a large amount of capital stock because it succeeded in an earlier start of industrialization than the other countries, while another country may be rich in labor forces because it has enjoyed a higher birthrate. Even if the production technologies are the same among countries, those differences in the factor endowments generate differences in the autarkic prices — the structure of comparative advantages.

Unlike the Ricardian model, both the HOS model and the SF model assume two or more factors of production. The industries are distinguished by the way how these factors are used in the production of each good. In the HOS model, all factors are used in every industry, but in different proportions. In the SF model, each industry is assumed to have one particular factor pertaining to this industry (i.e., specific factor), which is indispensable in the production of the corresponding good, but useless in the production of the other goods. Because these models contain many factors, we can use them to examine the implications of international trade on the (functional) *income distribution* within a country.

3.1   The Roles of General Factors

Let us begin with the simplest HOS model with two countries (A and B), two goods (1 and 2), and two factors of production called *capital* and *labor*.[1] Both capital and labor are *general factors* in the sense that they are used in the production of both goods and freely mobile across industries. We assume that both countries share the same production technologies, but the (ratio of) factor endowments of them are different. For the moment, we concentrate on the situation in one country and omit the indices that stand for "countries" from the notation.

3.1.1   *Technology*

Let $K_j \geq 0$ and $L_j \geq 0$ be the inputs of capital and labor for the production of good $j = 1, 2$, respectively. Production technology of good j is described by a neoclassical production function $F_j(K_j, L_j)$, which is differentiable, monotonically increasing, linearly homogeneous, and concave in (K_j, L_j).

Production possibility set: Let $K > 0$ and $L > 0$ be the endowments of capital and labor of a country, respectively. Total amounts of capital and labor used in the production of both goods must satisfy the resource constraints: $K_1 + K_2 \leq K$ and $L_1 + L_2 \leq L$. Production vector is denoted by $y = (y_1, y_2)$. Then, the production possibility set (PPS) is defined as follows:

$$\mathscr{Y}(K, L)$$
$$\equiv \left\{ y = (y_1, y_2) \in \mathbb{R}^2_+ \left| \begin{array}{l} y_j \leq F_j(K_j, L_j), \ K_j, L_j \geq 0, \ j = 1, 2, \\ K_1 + K_2 \leq K, \ L_1 + L_2 \leq L \end{array} \right. \right\},$$

---

[1] Ohlin (1933) has focused on the roles of differences in the factor endowments as a source of comparative advantage. The original contributions by Heckscher and Ohlin (published in the 1910s and 1920s) were written in Swedish; the English-translated versions of their early works can be found in Heckscher and Ohlin (1991). Because their arguments have been mathematically sophisticated by P.A. Samuelson's various contributions (e.g., Samuelson, 1953–1954), a formal general equilibrium model that incorporates two or more factors of production has come to be often called the Heckscher–Ohlin–Samuelson model.

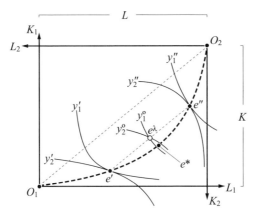

Fig. 3.1 Production Box Diagram

which is a compact convex subset of $\mathbb{R}_+^2$. As shown in Chapter 1, a factor allocation, $\{(K_1, L_1), (K_2, L_2)\}$, is efficient if (i) the resource constraints are satisfied with equalities and (ii) the marginal rates of technical substitution of capital for labor in both industries coincide with each other:

$$\left[\frac{\partial F_1(K_1, L_1)}{\partial L_1}\right] \bigg/ \left[\frac{\partial F_1(K_1, L_1)}{\partial K_1}\right] = \left[\frac{\partial F_2(K_2, L_2)}{\partial L_2}\right] \bigg/ \left[\frac{\partial F_2(K_2, L_2)}{\partial K_2}\right].$$

Production box diagram: Figure 3.1 illustrates the *production box diagram* of a country. From the lower-left corner O_1, the capital input for good 1 is measured upward; the labor input to the right. From the upper-right corner O_2, the capital input for good 2 is measured downward; the labor input to the left. The height and width of the rectangular area are set equal to the endowments of capital K and labor L, respectively. Then, each point in the rectangular area represents a particular factor allocation that satisfies the resource constraints with equalities. Thus, the rectangular area can be identified with the set of all factor allocations satisfying the full employment conditions for both factors.

Efficient locus: In Fig. 3.1, curves labeled y'_1 and y''_1 are *isoquants* of good 1, while curves labeled y'_2 and y''_2 are those of good 2. With a slight abuse of notation, we identify the labels for the curves y'_1, y''_1, y'_2, and y''_2 with the quantities of goods, respectively. Then, we have $y'_1 < y''_1$ and $y'_2 > y''_2$. Isoquants y'_1 and y'_2 are tangent at point e', meaning that the marginal rates of technical substitution of both industries coincide with each other. That is, the factor allocation e' and the corresponding production vector $y' = (y_1', y_2')$ are efficient; the same is true for points e'' and $y'' = (y_1'', y_2'')$. The dotted line $O_1 e' e'' O_2$ is the graph of the tangency points of isoquants and it represents the set of all efficient factor allocations — the *efficient locus*.

The ratio of the inputs of capital and labor in good j, K_j/L_j, is called the *capital intensity* of good j. At any point in the box diagram, the capital intensity of good 1 is represented by the angle of the line segment connecting the point and O_1, while the capital intensity of good 2 is represented by the angle of the line segment connecting the point and O_2. When $K_1/L_1 < K_2/L_2$, we say that good 2 is more *capital intensive* than good 1; equivalently, good 1 is more *labor intensive* than good 2. The angle of the diagonal line $O_1 O_2$ is equal to the ratio of the endowments of capital and labor, K/L.

With our assumptions on the production functions, we can prove that the efficient locus never crosses the diagonal line $O_1 O_2$ at an interior point. This means that either one of the following three cases holds: except for two end points O_1 and O_2, (i) the efficient locus is located entirely below the diagonal; (ii) it is located entirely above the diagonal; or (iii) it completely coincides with the diagonal line.

Production possibility frontier: The production possibility frontier (PPF) or the transformation curve is the projection of the efficient locus onto the y_1–y_2 plane. Moving from O_1 to O_2 along the efficient locus, good 1 monotonically increases from zero up to a certain positive amount (i.e., $F_1(K, L)$), while good 2 monotonically decreases from a certain positive amount (i.e., $F_2(K, L)$) down to zero. Points Q_1 and Q_2 in Fig. 3.2 correspond to O_1 and O_2 in Fig. 3.1, respectively. Therefore, the PPF must be a downward-sloping curve that connects Q_1 and Q_2 on the y_1–y_2 plane.

The *marginal rate of transformation* of good 2 for good 1 (MRT_{12} or, simply, MRT) is the maximum amount of good 2 that can be increased when good 1 is decreased by one unit from an efficient production vector. Graphically, MRT is represented by (the absolute value of) the slope of the PPF. As shown in Chapter 1, MRT is equal to the ratio of the marginal

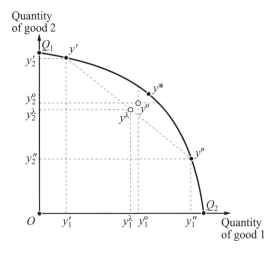

Fig. 3.2   Production Possibility Frontier

products of capital in both industries; it is also equal to the ratio of the marginal products of labor in both industries.

$$\text{MRT} \equiv -\left.\frac{dy_2}{dy_1}\right|_{K,L:\text{ given}} = \left[\frac{\partial F_2}{\partial K_2}\right]\Big/\left[\frac{\partial F_1}{\partial K_1}\right]$$

$$= \left[\frac{\partial F_2}{\partial L_2}\right]\Big/\left[\frac{\partial F_1}{\partial L_1}\right]. \tag{3.1}$$

Concavity of the PPF: Now let us take arbitrary efficient factor alloca-
tions $e' \equiv \{(K_1', L_1'), (K_2', L_2')\}$ and $e'' \equiv \{(K_1'', L_1''), (K_2'', L_2'')\}$ as in Fig. 3.1.
Let y' and y'' be the production vectors that correspond to e' and e'',
respectively. They are represented by the corresponding points y' and y''
in Fig. 3.2, respectively. Of course, the PPF has to go through points
y' and y''.

Let us consider the downward-sloping line segment $y'y''$ in Fig. 3.2. We
show that the PPF has to be located above this line segment (except for two
end points). For an arbitrary real number λ with $0 < \lambda < 1$, let us define
$y^\lambda \equiv \lambda y' + [1-\lambda]y''$, which corresponds to a point on the line segment $y'y''$.
The concavity of the production functions implies the following relations:

for $j = 1, 2$,

$$y_j^\lambda \equiv \lambda y_j' + [1 - \lambda] y_j'' = \lambda F_j(K_j', L_j') + [1 - \lambda] F_j(K_j'', L_j'')$$
$$\leq F_j\left(\lambda K_j' + [1 - \lambda] K_j'', \lambda L_j' + [1 - \lambda] L_j''\right).$$

Define a factor allocation $e^\lambda \equiv \{(\lambda K_j' + [1 - \lambda] K_j'', \lambda L_j' + [1 - \lambda] L_j'')\}_{j=1,2}$, which corresponds to the entry of F_j in the last term of the above equation. Obviously, we have $e^\lambda = \lambda e' + [1 - \lambda] e''$, which is represented by point e^λ in Fig. 3.1. Because e^λ is feasible, the production vector y^λ is also feasible. This means that the set of production vectors corresponding to the line segment $y'y''$ in Fig. 3.2 must be contained in the production possibility set.

However, the factor allocation e^λ is not efficient (i.e., not on the efficient locus in Fig. 3.1). This inefficiency of e^λ is caused by the difference in the factor intensities of both industries. Let y° be the production vector that corresponds to e^λ. We have $y^\circ \geq y^\lambda$ by definition. Because e^λ is not efficient, y° is not efficient, either. Accordingly, there exists an *efficient* production vector y^* such that $y^* > y^\circ$; *a fortiori*, we have $y^* > y^\lambda$. Graphically, point y^* is located to the "northeast" of y^λ as illustrated in Fig. 3.2. The PPF has to go through points y', y'', and y^*.

The above results apply equally well to any pair of efficient production vectors and any convex combination of them. Therefore, the PPF has to be concave to the origin. The bold curve $Q_1 y' y^* y'' Q_2$ in Fig. 3.2 represents the PPF that corresponds to the efficient locus $O_1 e' e^* e'' O_2$ in Fig. 3.1. Intuitively, the curvature of the PPF is related to the difference in the factor intensities. If the factor intensities of both goods are the same (i.e., if the efficient locus coincides with the diagonal of the production box diagram), the PPF becomes a straight line. On the other hand, if the factor intensities diverge, the PPF bends concave to the origin.

3.1.2 *Production Equilibrium*

Given the prices of goods and the factor endowments, a production equilibrium is determined through the behavior of firms and the functioning of factor markets.

Behavior of a firm: Let r and w be capital rental and wage rate, respectively. The minimum cost function of good j is defined as follows: for $j = 1, 2$,

$$C_j(r, w, y_j) \equiv \min_{K_j, L_j} \left\{ rK_j + wL_j \mid F_j(K_j, L_j) \geq y_j \right\}.$$

As shown in Chapter 1, the relative wage rate, w/r, and the marginal rate of technical substitution of capital for labor are equalized at the cost minimizing point:

$$\frac{w}{r} = \left[\frac{\partial F_j(K_j, L_j)}{\partial L_j} \right] \Big/ \left[\frac{\partial F_j(K_j, L_j)}{\partial K_j} \right]. \tag{3.2}$$

The solution to the cost minimization problem yields the *conditional demand functions* for capital and labor: $\tilde{K}_j(r, w, y_j)$ and $\tilde{L}_j(r, w, y_j)$. Under the CRS technology, the minimum cost function becomes multiplicatively separable:

$$C_j(r, w, y_j) \equiv c_j(r, w) y_j.$$

Due to Shephard's lemma, the input coefficients of capital and labor, a_{Kj} and a_{Lj}, can be written as functions of (r, w): for $j = 1, 2$,

$$a_{Kj}(r, w) \equiv \frac{\partial c_j(r, w)}{\partial r} \quad \text{and} \quad a_{Lj}(r, w) \equiv \frac{\partial c_j(r, w)}{\partial w}.$$

The profit of firm j is $\pi_j \equiv \{p_j - c_j(r, w)\} y_j$. If $p_j - c_j(r, w) > 0$, firm j can earn infinitely large profits by increasing outputs infinitely[2]; the profit maximizing output does not exit. If $p_j - c_j(r, w) < 0$, firm j ceases to supply good j; the profit maximizing output is zero. A positive finite supply of good j is possible only if $p_j - c_j(r, w) = 0$. Therefore, in equilibrium, we must have

$$p_j - c_j(r, w) \leq 0, \quad y_j \geq 0, \quad \{p_j - c_j(r, w)\} y_j = 0.$$

In any case, the equilibrium profit of firm j is zero.

---

[2] Because of the resource constraint, this is not possible in the long run.

Factor markets: Since firm j's demand for capital is $a_{Kj}(r,w)y_j$, the total demand for capital becomes $a_{K1}(r,w)y_1 + a_{K2}(r,w)y_2$. It is not possible in equilibrium that the total demand for capital exceeds the supply of capital (i.e., the capital endowment K). If the total demand for capital falls short of K, then the capital service becomes free (i.e., $r = 0$). For the capital service to be traded at a positive rental rate, the total demand for capital must meet the supply K. Therefore, in equilibrium, we have

$$a_{K1}(r,w)y_1 + a_{K2}(r,w)y_2 - K \leq 0, \quad r \geq 0,$$

$$r \cdot \{a_{K1}(r,w)y_1 + a_{K2}(r,w)y_2 - K\} = 0.$$

By the same token, similar conditions must hold for the labor market:

$$a_{L1}(r,w)y_1 + a_{L2}(r,w)y_2 - L \leq 0, \quad w \geq 0,$$

$$w \cdot \{a_{L1}(r,w)y_1 + a_{L2}(r,w)y_2 - L\} = 0.$$

The interior production equilibrium: In almost all cases, we are interested in *interior* equilibria where all goods and services are produced and utilized in positive amounts at positive prices. Suppose that the prices of goods and the factor endowments are positive and given exogenously. Then, the production equilibrium conditions are summarized as follows[3]:

$$\text{(Price system)} \quad \begin{cases} c_1(r,w) = p_1, \\ c_2(r,w) = p_2, \end{cases} \tag{3.3}$$

$$\text{(Quantity system)} \quad \begin{cases} a_{K1}(r,w)y_1 + a_{K2}(r,w)y_2 = K, \\ a_{L1}(r,w)y_1 + a_{L2}(r,w)y_2 = L. \end{cases} \tag{3.4}$$

For a given set of exogenous parameters $\{p_1, p_2, K, L\}$, the above system of four equations determine four endogenous variables: rental r, wage rate w, and the supplies of goods y_1 and y_2.

Carefully examining the above system, we recognize that the whole system can be separated into two subsystems. Equation (3.3), which we call

---

[3]This formulation of the production equilibrium conditions in the basic HOS model is due to Jones (1965).

the price system, consists of two equations containing only price variables: r, w, p_1, and p_2. For given prices of goods, the price system determines r and w, which are apparently independent of the factor endowments. We can write the equilibrium factor prices as functions of the good prices: $\tilde{r}(p_1, p_2)$ for rental and $\tilde{w}(p_1, p_2)$ for wage rate. It is easy to verify that if a quadruplet $\{r, w, p_1, p_2\}$ solves the price system (3.3), then another quadruplet $\{\lambda r, \lambda w, \lambda p_1, \lambda p_2\}$ for any positive $\lambda > 0$ also solves it. Therefore, the functions of the equilibrium factor prices, $\tilde{r}$ and $\tilde{w}$, become linearly homogeneous in (p_1, p_2).

Once r and w have been determined through the price system, the input coefficients of capital and labor become definite. Then, Eq. (3.4) can be seen practically as a system of *linear* equations of y_1 and y_2, which we call the quantity system. For given factor endowments, the quantity system determines y_1 and y_2. In this case, we can write the equilibrium supplies of goods as functions of the good prices and the factor endowments: $\tilde{y}_j(p_1, p_2, K, L)$ for $j = 1, 2$. Because the equilibrium factor prices are linearly homogeneous in (p_1, p_2), any proportional changes in the prices of both goods do not affect the input coefficients in the quantity system. Accordingly, they do not affect the solution to Eq. (3.4), either. Therefore, the equilibrium supply $\tilde{y}_j$ is homogeneous of degree zero in (p_1, p_2). It is again easy to verify that, for a given (p_1, p_2), if a quadruplet $\{y_1, y_2, K, L\}$ solves the quantity system, another quadruplet $\{\lambda y_1, \lambda y_2, \lambda K, \lambda L\}$ for any positive $\lambda > 0$ solves it, too. This means that $\tilde{y}_j$ is linearly homogeneous in the factor endowments (K, L).

As far as the interior equilibrium is concerned, the price system determines the factor prices first, and then the quantity system determines the supplies of goods — this *recursive structure* is one of the distinctive features of the basic HOS model.

Value marginal product: In the production equilibrium, the reward rate of a production factor is equalized to the value marginal product of that factor: for $j = 1, 2$, we have

$$r = p_j \frac{\partial F_j(K_j, L_j)}{\partial K_j} \quad \text{and} \quad w = p_j \frac{\partial F_j(K_j, L_j)}{\partial L_j}. \tag{3.5}$$

First, note that Eq. (3.2) implies there exists a certain value λ_j common to both factors such that $r = \lambda_j[\partial F_j/\partial K_j]$ and $w = \lambda_j[\partial F_j/\partial L_j]$.[4] It suffices to show that $p_j = \lambda_j$. The definition of cost function and the linear homogeneity of F_j together imply the following relation:

$$c_j(r, w)y_j \equiv r\tilde{K}_j(r, w, y_j) + w\tilde{L}_j(r, w, y_j)$$

$$= \lambda_j \frac{\partial F_j(K_j, L_j)}{\partial K_j} K_j + \lambda_j \frac{\partial F_j(K_j, L_j)}{\partial L_j} L_j$$

$$= \lambda_j \left[\frac{\partial F_j(K_j, L_j)}{\partial K_j} K_j + \frac{\partial F_j(K_j, L_j)}{\partial L_j} L_j \right]$$

$$= \lambda_j F_j(K_j, L_j) = \lambda_j y_j.$$

If $y_j > 0$ as we assumed, then $c_j(r, w) = \lambda_j$. Therefore, Eq. (3.3) implies $p_j = \lambda_j$. It should be noted that Eq. (3.5) is not directly derived from the first-order conditions for the profit maximization of a firm, but derived from the conditions for the long-run (zero profit) interior production equilibrium.

Relative price and the production point: The quantity system (3.4) means that both factors are fully employed in equilibrium. In addition, Eq. (3.2) implies the equalization of the marginal rates of technical substitution of both goods. Therefore, for a given set of parameters $\{p_1, p_2, K, L\}$, the solution to the system (3.3)–(3.4) implies an efficient factor allocation, meaning that the production point is on the production possibility frontier (PPF).

Further, the production point is characterized by the equality of the relative price, $p \equiv p_1/p_2$, and the MRT. From Eqs. (3.1) and (3.5), we have

$$p \equiv \frac{p_1}{p_2} = \left[\frac{\partial F_2}{\partial K_2} \right] \bigg/ \left[\frac{\partial F_1}{\partial K_1} \right] = \left[\frac{\partial F_2}{\partial L_2} \right] \bigg/ \left[\frac{\partial F_1}{\partial L_1} \right] = \text{MRT}.$$

$$(3.6)$$

Because the PPF is downward-sloping and concave to the origin, Eq. (3.6) implies that if p increases, the production point moves toward good 1 along the PPF. In other words, $\tilde{y}_1$ is increasing in p, while $\tilde{y}_2$ is decreasing in p.

---

[4]Here, λ_j is nothing but the Lagrange multiplier for the cost minimization problem.

The ratio of the quantities of production, y_1/y_2, can be written as a function of p and the factor endowments ratio K/L:

$$S(p, K/L) \equiv \frac{\tilde{y}_1(p_1, p_2, K, L)}{\tilde{y}_2(p_1, p_2, K, L)} = \frac{\tilde{y}_1(p, 1, K/L, 1)}{\tilde{y}_2(p, 1, K/L, 1)}.$$

The latter equality follows from the fact that $\tilde{y}_j$ is homogeneous of degree zero in (p_1, p_2) and of degree one in (K, L). We call S the *relative supply function*. Of course, S is increasing in p.

3.1.3 *Commodity Prices and Factor Prices*

By examining the price system (3.3), we can infer the relationship between good prices and factor prices. Suppose that p_1 increases, while p_2 remains constant. From $c_1(r, w) = p_1$, we know that at least one of r and w has to rise. However, if both r and w rise simultaneously, the other equation $c_2(r, w) = p_2$ will be violated. To keep $c_2(r, w)$ constant at p_2, either r or w has to fall. Hence, we must have $\partial \tilde{r}(p_1, p_2)/\partial p_j > 0$ if and only if $\partial \tilde{w}(p_1, p_2)/\partial p_j < 0$. An increase in the price of a good affects different factors in opposite directions.

Factor intensity: The above argument does not specify the signs of $\partial \tilde{r}(p_1, p_2)/\partial p_j$ and $\partial \tilde{w}(p_1, p_2)/\partial p_j$. To specify which factor price is to rise or fall against an increase in the price of a good, we need detailed information how the factors are used in the production of goods. The production activities in two industries are distinguished by their capital intensities. In the following, we assume that good 1 is more labor intensive than good 2, equivalently, that good 2 is more capital intensive than good 1:

$$\frac{K_1}{L_1} < \frac{K_2}{L_2} \quad \Leftrightarrow \quad \frac{a_{K1}(r, w)}{a_{L1}(r, w)} < \frac{a_{K2}(r, w)}{a_{L2}(r, w)}. \tag{3.7}$$

With this assumption, we can call good 1 and good 2 as the *labor intensive good* and the *capital intensive good*, respectively.

Distributive share: An alternative way of describing the difference in the factor intensities is to use the notion of the *distributive share*. Let θ_{Kj} be the distributive share of capital in the production of good j, that is, $\theta_{Kj} \equiv r a_{Kj}(r, w)/c_j(r, w)$. Similarly, the distributive share of labor in the production of good j is denoted by $\theta_{Lj} \equiv w a_{Lj}(r, w)/c_j(r, w)$. By definition, we have $0 \leq \theta_{Kj}, \theta_{Lj} \leq 1$ and $\theta_{Kj} + \theta_{Lj} = 1$.[5] Further, we have Eq. (3.7) if and only if $\theta_{K2} - \theta_{K1} = \theta_{L1} - \theta_{L2} > 0$. Differences in the distributive shares correspond to differences in the factor intensities.

We are now in a position to state one of the fundamental theorems derived from the HOS model.

Proposition 3.1 (Stolper and Samuelson, 1941). *An exogenous increase in the price of one good brings about* (i) *an increase in the reward rate of one factor used intensively in the production of that good and* (ii) *a decrease in the reward rate of the other factor. The rate of increase in the reward rate of the former factor is greater than that in the price of the good.*

Since the latter part of the assertion has become widespread due to the contribution by Jones (1965), it is called *Jones' magnification effect*.

Proof. By totally differentiating the price system (3.3) and rearranging the results, we obtain the following relations: for $j = 1, 2$,

$$a_{Kj}\, dr + a_{Lj}\, dw = dp_j \quad \Leftrightarrow \quad \theta_{Kj}\hat{r} + \theta_{Lj}\hat{w} = \hat{p}_j, \qquad (3.8)$$

where $\hat{r} \equiv dr/r$, $\hat{w} \equiv dw/w$, and $\hat{p}_j \equiv dp_j/p_j$.[6] The above relations mean that the percentage change in each price is represented by a weighted average of the percentage changes in rental and wage rate. That is, if $\hat{r} \neq \hat{w}$, then $\hat{p}_j$ comes in between $\hat{r}$ and $\hat{w}$. By solving the above relations for $\hat{r}$ and $\hat{w}$, we obtain

$$\hat{r} = -\frac{\theta_{L2}}{|\Theta|}\hat{p}_1 + \frac{\theta_{L1}}{|\Theta|}\hat{p}_2 \quad \text{and} \quad \hat{w} = \frac{\theta_{K2}}{|\Theta|}\hat{p}_1 - \frac{\theta_{K1}}{|\Theta|}\hat{p}_2,$$

where $|\Theta| \equiv \theta_{K2}\theta_{L1} - \theta_{K1}\theta_{L2} = \theta_{K2} - \theta_{K1} = \theta_{L1} - \theta_{L2} > 0$ by Eq. (3.7). Further, subtracting both sides, we obtain

$$\hat{w} - \hat{r} = \frac{\hat{p}_1 - \hat{p}_2}{|\Theta|}.$$

---

[5] In almost all cases, we assume that both θ_{Kj} and θ_{Lj} are strictly positive, meaning that both factors are indispensable in the production of both goods.

[6] We denote the percentage change of a variable x by attaching a hat symbol over the variable, that is, $\hat{x} \equiv dx/x$. The "hat" notation has become popular among trade theorists after Jones (1965).

Now suppose that only p_1 increases, while p_2 remains constant: $\hat{p}_1 > 0 = \hat{p}_2$. Then, $\hat{w} > \hat{r}$. Since the percentage changes in the good prices come in between $\hat{r}$ and $\hat{w}$, we have

$$\hat{w} > \hat{p}_1 > 0 = \hat{p}_2 > \hat{r}.$$

An increase in the price of the labor intensive good ($\hat{p}_1 > 0$) brings about both an increase in the wage rate ($\hat{w} > 0$) and a decrease in the rental ($\hat{r} < 0$). Further, the rate of increase in the wage rate is greater than that in the price of the labor intensive good ($\hat{w} > \hat{p}_1$).[7]   □

According to the Stolper–Samuelson theorem, when the price of the labor intensive good increases, the real wage rate surely increases and the real rental decreases (no matter which good is used to measure the "real" reward rates). In other words, laborers (owners of labor) will gain, while capitalists (owners of capital) will lose.[8] In this way, any change in the (relative) prices of goods gives rise to a conflict among owners of different factors within a country.

Factor price frontier: For a given price p_j, the *factor price frontier* of good j is the graph of combinations of rental and wage rate, (r, w), that satisfies the price–cost equality $c_j(r, w) = p_j$.[9] In Fig. 3.3, wage rate is measured vertically and rental is measured horizontally. Because the unit cost function is increasing and concave in (r, w), the corresponding factor price frontier is downward-sloping and convex to the origin. In addition, due to Shepard's lemma, the slope of the curve represents the factor intensity of the good. Two curves f and g in Fig. 3.3 are the factor price frontier of good 1 for p_1 and that of good 2 for p_2, respectively. The intersection of these curves, point e, represents the equilibrium of the price system; the equilibrium rental and wage rate are r and w in the figure. Reflecting the assumption on the factor intensities (3.7), the factor price frontier of good 1 is drawn flatter than that of good 2 at point e.

Suppose that the price of good 1 (i.e., the labor intensive good) increases from p_1 to p_1'. Then, the factor price frontier of good 1 shifts outward from f to f' in proportion to the change in the price. The new

---

[7]If $\hat{p}_1 < \hat{p}_2$, we have $\hat{w} < \hat{p}_1 < \hat{p}_2 < \hat{r}$. Further, if $\hat{p}_1 = \hat{p}_2$, we have $\hat{w} = \hat{p}_1 = \hat{p}_2 = \hat{r}$. Even if the nominal prices of the goods change proportionally, real variables such as the real wage rates

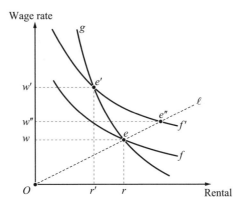

Fig. 3.3   Factor Price Frontiers

equilibrium is point e'. The rental falls down to r' and the wage rate rises up to w'. The magnification effect can be verified as follows. Draw a straight line ℓ from the origin O passing through the (old) equilibrium point e. Let e'' be the intersection of ℓ and f' and let w'' be the wage rate corresponding to e''. Then, the rate of price increase is represented by the ratio of the length of segments ee'' and Oe, that is, $\hat{p}_1 = |ee''|/|Oe|$.[10] Because triangles Oew and $Oe''w''$ are similar figures, we have $|ee''|/|Oe| = |ww''|/|Ow|$. On the other hand, the actual rate of wage increase is equal to the ratio of the length of segments ww' and Ow, that is, $\hat{w} = |ww'|/|Ow|$. Obviously, $|ww'| > |ww''|$. Combining these facts, we obtain $\hat{w} > \hat{p}_1$.

3.1.4 *Factor Endowments and the Production Structure*

Let us turn to the quantity system (3.4). By totally differentiating the quantity system and rearranging the results, we obtain

$$\begin{cases} a_{K1}dy_1 + a_{K2}dy_2 = dK \\ a_{L1}dy_1 + a_{L2}dy_2 = dL \end{cases} \Leftrightarrow \begin{cases} \lambda_{K1}\hat{y}_1 + \lambda_{K2}\hat{y}_2 = \hat{K} \\ \lambda_{L1}\hat{y}_1 + \lambda_{L2}\hat{y}_2 = \hat{L} \end{cases}$$

$(w/p_1$ and $w/p_2)$ and the real rental rates $(r/p_1$ and $r/p_2)$ will not be affected at all. Only the relative price p_1/p_2 matters.

[8]If the price of the capital intensive good increases, the situation is reversed: laborers lose and capitalists win.

[9]Mussa (1979) has introduced the notion of factor price frontier.

[10]For a line segment connecting points a and b in a figure, the expression $|ab|$ means the length of the segment.

where $\lambda_{Kj} \equiv a_{Kj}y_j/K$ and $\lambda_{Lj} \equiv a_{Lj}y_j/L$ denote the proportion of the capital services and that of the labor forces used in the production of good j, respectively. By definition, $\lambda_{K1} + \lambda_{K2} = 1$ and $\lambda_{L1} + \lambda_{L2} = 1$. Assumption (3.7) implies $\lambda_{L1} - \lambda_{K1} = \lambda_{K2} - \lambda_{L2} > 0$. We can show that the following relations[11]:

$$\hat{y}_1 = -\frac{\lambda_{L2}}{|\Lambda|}\hat{K} + \frac{\lambda_{K2}}{|\Lambda|}\hat{L}, \quad \hat{y}_2 = \frac{\lambda_{L1}}{|\Lambda|}\hat{K} - \frac{\lambda_{K1}}{|\Lambda|}\hat{L},$$

$$\hat{y}_1 - \hat{y}_2 = \frac{\hat{L} - \hat{K}}{|\Lambda|},$$

where $|\Lambda| \equiv \lambda_{K2}\lambda_{L1} - \lambda_{K1}\lambda_{L2} = \lambda_{L1} - \lambda_{K1} = \lambda_{K2} - \lambda_{L2} > 0$. Therefore,

$$\hat{y}_1 \gtreqless \hat{L} \gtreqless \hat{K} \gtreqless \hat{y}_2.$$

This establishes the *Rybczynski theorem*.

Proposition 3.2 (Rybczynski, 1955). *An exogenous increase in the endowment of one factor brings about* (i) *an increase in the quantity of one good that is intensive in that factor and* (ii) *a decrease in the quantity of the other good. The rate of increase in the former good is greater than that of the increase in the factor endowment.*

Similar to the Stolper–Samuelson theorem, the latter part of the assertion of the Rybczynski theorem is known as Jones' magnification effect. The Rybczynski theorem shows that, under the assumption of (3.7), the equilibrium supply function $\tilde{y}_1$ is decreasing in K but increasing in L, while $\tilde{y}_2$ is increasing in K but decreasing in L. Then, the relative supply function S becomes decreasing in K/L.

Figure 3.4 illustrates the Rybczynski theorem. Straight lines k and ℓ represent the full employment conditions for capital and labor, respectively. By Eq. (3.7), ℓ is drawn steeper than k. The initial production equilibrium for p is attained at the intersection of these lines (i.e., point e). The PPF in this case is the curve aeb and the MRT at e is equal to the given relative price p. If the labor endowment L increases, ℓ shifts outward proportionally. Following the increase in the labor endowment, the PPF also shifts

---

[11]We omit the proof here, because it can be done similar to the proof of the Stolper–Samuelson theorem.

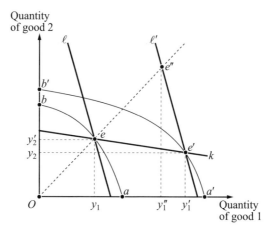

Fig. 3.4   The Rybczynski Theorem and the Production Possibility Frontier

outward, but this is biased toward the labor intensive good. The new production equilibrium for p is established at point e'. Again, the MRT at e'
is equal to p. Consequently, good 1 (the labor intensive good) increases,
while good 2 (the capital intensive good) decreases.

Jones' magnification effect is also verified as follows. Draw a straight
line from the origin O passing through e and let e'' be its intersection with
ℓ' and y_1'' be the output of good 1 corresponding to e''. Then, the rate of
increase in the labor endowment is represented by the ratio of $|ee''|/|Oe|$,
which is equal to the ratio $|y_1 y_1''|/|Oy_1|$. The actual rate of increase in good 1
is equal to $|y_1 y_1'|/|Oy_1|$, which is obviously greater than $|ee''|/|Oe|$.

Activity vector: Let us look at the Rybczynski theorem from a different
angle by rewriting the quantity system (3.4) as follows:

$$\begin{pmatrix} a_{K1} \\ a_{L1} \end{pmatrix} y_1 + \begin{pmatrix} a_{K2} \\ a_{L2} \end{pmatrix} y_2 = \begin{pmatrix} K \\ L \end{pmatrix}. \tag{3.9}$$

We call $a_{\bullet j} \equiv (a_{Kj}, a_{Lj})^{\mathrm{t}}$ an *activity vector* of good j and interpret y_j
as activity level of the good j production. With this new expression of
Eq. (3.9), the quantity system together with $y_j \geq 0$ for $j = 1, 2$ means
that the endowment vector (K, L) is represented by a non-negative linear
combination of the activity vectors. In other words, the endowment vector

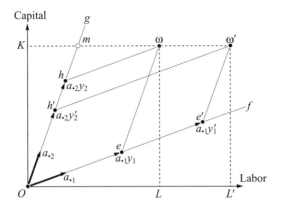

Fig. 3.5 Activity Vectors, the Diversification Cone, and the Rybczynski Theorem

(K, L) is included in the convex cone spanned by the set of activity vectors $\{a_{\bullet 1}, a_{\bullet 2}\}$.[12]

Figure 3.5 illustrates this alternative interpretation of the quantity system; labor is measured horizontally and capital is measured vertically. Two bold arrows originated from O represent the activity vectors $a_{\bullet 1}$ and $a_{\bullet 2}$, respectively. The convex cone spanned by $\{a_{\bullet 1}, a_{\bullet 2}\}$ is represented by the wedge-shaped area fOg. The (initial) endowment vector (K, L) is represented by point ω in the figure. Because the endowment vector is located in the wedge-shaped area, there exist activity levels $y_1, y_2 \geq 0$ such that $a_{\bullet 1} y_1 + a_{\bullet 2} y_2 = (K, L)$.

The activity levels can be found in the figure as follows. Draw a straight line from point ω parallel to line Og and let e be its intersection with line Of; similarly, draw a straight line from point ω parallel to line Of and let h be its intersection with line Og. Then, we obtain a parallelogram $Oe\omega h$. It immediately follows from the parallelogram rule of the vector summation that $\overrightarrow{Oe} + \overrightarrow{Oh} = \overrightarrow{O\omega}$. That is, $\overrightarrow{Oe}$, $\overrightarrow{Oh}$, and $\overrightarrow{O\omega}$ correspond to $a_{\bullet 1} y_1$, $a_{\bullet 2} y_2$, and (K, L), respectively. Therefore, the length of $\overrightarrow{Oe}$ and that of $\overrightarrow{Oh}$ can be identified with the activity levels y_1 and y_2, respectively.

---

[12] A set $S \subset \mathbb{R}^n$ is a *cone* if $\xi \in S$ implies $\lambda \xi \in S$ for any non-negative real number $\lambda \geq 0$. A set $S \subset \mathbb{R}^n$ is a *convex cone* if $\xi, \xi' \in S$ implies $\lambda \xi + \lambda' \xi' \in S$ for any non-negative real numbers $\lambda, \lambda' \geq 0$. The convex cone spanned by a set $S \subset \mathbb{R}^n$ is the smallest convex cone that contains S.

Now, suppose that the labor endowment increases from L to L'. Then, the point corresponding to the new endowment vector (K, L') becomes ω' in Fig. 3.5. It should be noted that ω' is still located in the wedge-shaped area fOg — the convex cone spanned by $\{a_{\bullet 1}, a_{\bullet 2}\}$. Accordingly, there exist activity levels $y_1', y_2' \geq 0$ such that $a_{\bullet 1} y_1' + a_{\bullet 2} y_2' = (K, L')$. Similar to parallelogram $Oe\omega h$, we can draw a new parallelogram $Oe'\omega'h'$, where $\overrightarrow{Oe'}$ and $\overrightarrow{Oh'}$ correspond to $a_{\bullet 1} y_1'$ and $a_{\bullet 2} y_2'$, respectively. As is obvious from the figure, $\overrightarrow{Oe'}$ is longer than $\overrightarrow{Oe}$, while $\overrightarrow{Oh'}$ is shorter than $\overrightarrow{Oh}$. Hence, we obtain $y_1 < y_1'$ and $y_2 > y_2'$. This proves the former part of the Rybczynski theorem. Further, the rate of increase in the labor endowment is represented by the ratio $|LL'|/|OL|$. On the other hand, the rate of increase in good 1 is represented by the ratio $|ee'|/|Oe|$, which is equal to $|\omega\omega'|/|m\omega|$. Because $|OL| > |m\omega|$ and $|LL'| = |\omega\omega'|$, we have $|\omega\omega'|/|m\omega| > |\omega\omega'|/|m\omega|$. That is, the rate of increase in good 1 is greater than that of the labor endowment. This confirms Jones' magnification effect.

Diversification cone: If the quantity system were to be satisfied when the endowment vector is located outside of the cone spanned by $\{a_{\bullet 1}, a_{\bullet 2}\}$, either one of y_1 and y_2 must be negative — the conditions for an interior equilibrium are violated and, therefore, the economy must specialize in one of the goods. For a given price vector p, an interior equilibrium is possible if and only if the endowment vector is included in the convex cone spanned by the activity vectors $\{a_{\bullet 1}, a_{\bullet 2}\}$ corresponding to p. Hence, we call it the *diversification cone*.

3.1.5   *Factor Endowments and Comparative Advantage*

Let us introduce two countries A and B explicitly into the model. We assume that (i) the production technologies of both countries are identical; (ii) the household sector of each country consists of a single household who possesses all factors of production in the country and supplies them inelastically to the domestic factor markets; and (iii) the households of both countries share the same homothetic preference. The only difference of these countries is their factor endowments.

Factor abundance: Let K^s and L^s denote the endowments of capital and labor of country $s = A, B$, respectively. We say that country A is *relatively* *labor abundant* (*capital scarce*) than country B or, equivalently, country B is *relatively capital abundant* (*labor scarce*) than country A if and only if

$$\frac{K^A}{L^A} < \frac{K^B}{L^B}. \tag{3.10}$$

The autarkic equilibrium price: The demand function derived from a homothetic preference is linear in income. This implies that the *income–consumption path* becomes a straight line passing through the origin and that the ratio of consumption of goods, x_1/x_2, depends only on the relative price of good 1, but not on the income level. Then, we can write the ratio of consumption of the goods as a decreasing function of p: $x_1/x_2 = \mathcal{D}(p)$, which we call the *relative demand function*. Due to our assumption of the identical homothetic preference, the relative demand functions of both countries become the same.

Let $\bar{p}^s$ be the autarkic equilibrium relative price in country $s = A, B$. The autarkic equilibrium price in country s with the endowment ratio K^s/L^s is determined by the following equality: for $s = A, B$,

$$\mathcal{D}(p) = \mathcal{S}(p, K^s/L^s). \tag{3.11}$$

Because $\mathcal{D}$ is decreasing in p and $\mathcal{S}$ is increasing in p and decreasing in K/L, we obtain $\bar{p}^A < \bar{p}^B$ under the assumption of Eq. (3.7). The relative price of the labor intensive good (good 1) is cheaper in the labor abundant country A than in the capital abundant country B. That is, the labor abundant country has a comparative advantage in the labor intensive good. Conversely, the capital abundant country has a comparative advantage in the capital intensive good.

Proposition 3.3 (Ohlin, 1933; Heckscher and Ohlin, 1991). *Suppose that two countries have the same CRS technologies and homothetic preferences, but different relative factor endowments. Then, a country has a comparative advantage in the good that is produced by using relatively abundant factor intensively.*

3.1.6 *Factor Price Equalization*

We have shown that the difference in factor endowments of two countries can be a cause of the difference in the autarkic prices of goods, which, in turn, is a driving force of international trade in "goods" between these countries. Now we examine what will happen to the income distributions (i.e., factor prices) in these countries if free trade in goods is allowed. Note that each country has its own price system: for $s = A, B$,

$$\begin{cases} c_1(r^s, w^s) = p^s, \\ c_2(r^s, w^s) = 1, \end{cases}$$

where good 2 is taken as the numéraire and its price is fixed at unity. Because countries A and B share the identical CRS technologies, the *functional forms* of their price systems are the same, but, depending on whether they are in autarky or under free trade, the relative prices that the countries face are different. Given the relative price p^s, the price system determines the factor prices (r^s, w^s) in country $s = A, B$.

If both countries are in autarky, their autarkic relative prices are different. Under our assumption on the factor abundance, we have $\bar{p}^A < \bar{p}^B$ by the Heckscher–Ohlin theorem. Further, under our assumption on the factor intensities, we have both $\bar{r}^A > \bar{r}^B$ and $\bar{w}^A < \bar{w}^B$ by the Stolper–Samuelson theorem. In contrast, if both countries engage in international trade in goods and if there is no impediments to trade such as tariffs and transportation costs, the relative prices that the countries face converge to a certain common value, say, $p^* = p^A = p^B$. Then, the price systems of both countries become identical and their solutions would be the same: $(r^*, w^*) = (r^A, w^A) = (r^B, w^B)$. That is, even if the production factors themselves do not move across countries, the factor prices can be equalized through free trade only in goods. This remarkable result is known as the *Factor Price Equalization (FPE) theorem*.

The above argument for the FPE theorem depends on two implicit assumptions: (i) *incomplete specialization* prevails in both countries and (ii) there exists a *unique* solution to the price system for any p^s. Unfortunately, neither of these assumptions necessarily holds true. For a given combination of the factor endowments of country s, we can show that there exist two threshold prices, $p_{\min}^s$ and $p_{\max}^s$, such that (i) $y_1^s = 0$ for all $p \leq p_{\min}^s$ and (ii) $y_2^s = 0$ for all $p \geq p_{\max}^s$. Therefore, it may be the case that for some range of relative prices, one country completely specializes in one good, while the other diversifies. In this case, the price system does not hold in the completely specializing country, neither do the FPE theorem. In addition, even if both countries diversify in equilibrium, the price system may admit multiple solutions. Then, depending on the factor endowments of A and B, it is possible that under free trade in goods, one of the solutions is realized in one country, while another solution is realized in the other country. Again, the FPE theorem fails.

Remark on the global univalence: A classical approach to the FPE theorem can be found in the literature concerning the *global univalence* (see, for example, Nikaido, 1968). Let us consider a general n-good n-factor HOS model (i.e., the numbers of goods and factors are the same). The array of unit cost functions $c = (c_1, c_2, \ldots, c_n)$ naturally defines a mapping from the factor price space $\mathbb{R}^n_+$ to the good price space $\mathbb{R}^n_+$. For a given price vector $p \in \mathbb{R}^n_+$, the price system becomes $c(w) = p$, where $w \in \mathbb{R}^n_+$ denotes a factor price vector. If the mapping c is *one-to-one* and its range covers the goods price space, then we can define the inverse c^{-1} on the goods price space. Because all countries come to face the same equilibrium price vector p^* under free trade in goods, the factor price vector will be given by $c^{-1}(p^*)$ and become the same across countries; this would establish the FPE theorem. Based on this argument, the global univalence literature had tried to seek the conditions under which the mapping c is globally invertible.[13] The conditions found in the literature put some restrictions on the sign patterns of the Jacobian of c and its minors and, therefore, they are apparently related to the notion of "factor intensities" in general settings. Unfortunately, economic implications of these conditions are not clear. Moreover, Kemp (1969) has pointed out that the global univalence is neither sufficient nor necessary for the FPE theorem. So, we shall not pursue this line of research any further.

3.1.7 *Integrated Economy*

The notion of "integrated economy" introduced by Dixit and Norman (1980) sheds a new light on the FPE theorem. The integrated economy

---

[13]The well-known *inverse function theorem* guarantees the *local* invertibility of c. Suppose $c(\bar{w}) = \bar{p}$ for some $\bar{p} \in \mathbb{R}^n_+$. If the Jacobian of c evaluated at $\bar{w}$ does not vanish, then there exists an inverse c^{-1} defined on some *neighborhood* of $\bar{p}$.

is based on a very simple idea, but it turns out to be a useful as well as powerful analytical tool with which we can investigate not only the features of the HOS model but also other trade models.[14]

The basic HOS model begins by assuming that each country has its own factor endowments that are mobile across industries but not across countries, while the integrated economy approach begins with an integrated equilibrium of the world economy in which not only goods but also production factors are freely mobile across countries as well as across industries. Given the integrated equilibrium, we consider under what conditions it is possible to *divide* the world endowments of production factors between countries so that the total production and consumption as well as the prices of goods and factors remain the same as the integrated equilibrium.

The world production box diagram: K^W and L^W denote the world factor endowments of capital and labor, respectively. Let $(p^*, x^*, y^*, \{(K_j^*, L_j^*)\}_{j=1,2}, (r^*, w^*))$ be an integrated equilibrium of the world economy, where $p^* = (p_1^*, p_2^*)$ is the goods price vector, $x^* = (x_1^*, x_2^*)$ is the total demand vector, $y^* = (y_1^*, y_2^*)$ is the total production vector, (K_j^*, L_j^*) is the factor input vector for good j, and (r^*, w^*) is the factor price vector. Of course, we have $x^* = y^*$, $y_j^* = F_j(K_j^*, L_j^*)$, $K_1^* + K_2^* = K^W$, $L_1^* + L_2^* = L^W$, and $p^*x^* = p^*y^* = r^*K^W + w^*L^W$. Let $a_{\bullet j}^* \equiv (a_{Kj}(r^*, w^*), a_{Lj}(r^*, w^*))$ be the unit activity vector of good j in equilibrium. Then, we have $(K_j^*, L_j^*) = a_{\bullet j}^* y_j^*$ for $j = 1, 2$. Obviously, y^* solves $\sum_j a_{\bullet j}^* y_j^* = (K^W, L^W)$.

Figure 3.6 illustrates the "world" production box diagram. The height and width of the rectangular area correspond to K^W and L^W, respectively. The lower-left corner O is the origin for country A; the upper-right corner O' for country B. Looking at from O, the upper-right corner O' can be identified with the world endowment vector (K^W, L^W); symmetrically, the same also applies to O'. The rectangular area represents the set of all possible divisions (or assignments) of the world endowments between countries, that is, $\{(K^s, L^s)\}_{s=A,B}$ such that $K^A + K^B = K^W$ and $L^A + L^B = L^W$.

---

[14]For the application of the integrated economy to the monopolistically competitive trade model, see Helpman and Krugman (1985).

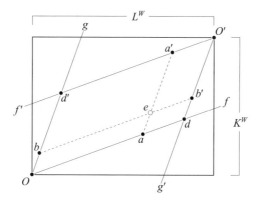

Fig. 3.6 Integrated Economy

Similar to Fig. 3.5, the angle of line Of ($O'f'$) represents the capital intensity of good 1 and that of line Og ($O'g'$) represents the capital intensity of
good 2.[15] Therefore, the wedge-shaped areas fOg and $f'O'g'$ represent the
diversification cones of countries A and B. The lengths of the line segments
Od ($= O'd'$) and Od' ($= O'd$) can be identified with y_1^* and y_2^*.

FPE set: In Fig. 3.6, the intersection of the diversification cones of the
countries forms a parallelogram area $OdO'd'$, which we call the FPE set.[16]
Now let us consider a division $\{(K^s, L^s)\}_{s=A,B}$ of the world endowments in
this area as point e in the figure. Then, we can show that the *disintegrated
equilibrium* in trade in goods between the separated countries, where the
endowment of country s is given by (K^s, L^s), generates same outcomes as
the integrated equilibrium — the total quantities of production and consumption of goods will remain the same and the factor markets in each
country be in equilibrium under (r^*, w^*). Naturally, FPE will be realized.

To prove this, let us assume that p^* and (r^*, w^*) prevail in the disintegrated trading world. Because (K^s, L^s) is in the diversification cone of
country s, there exists a production vector $y^{s*} = (y_1^{s*}, y_2^{s*}) \geq 0$ that solves
$(K^s, L^s) = \sum_j a_{\bullet j}^* y_j^{s*}$, meaning that (r^*, w^*) is actually the equilibrium

---

[15]We are assuming $a_{K1}^*/a_{L1}^* < a_{K2}^*/a_{L2}^*$.

[16]Deardorff (1994) has introduced the notion of *lens*, which generalizes the parallelogram here, and
investigated the conditions for FPE when the numbers of goods and countries are more than two. For
more relations between the FPE theorem and Deardorff's lens, see Demiroglu and Yun (1999), Kemp
(2006), and Qi (2003, 2010).

factor price vector in country s. By definition, we have $(K^W, L^W) = \sum_s (K^s, L^s) = \sum_s \sum_j a^*_{\bullet j} y^{s*}_j = \sum_j a^*_{\bullet j} \{y^{A*}_j + y^{B*}_j\}$. By the definition of y^*, we have $\sum_j a^*_{\bullet j} \{y^{A*}_j + y^{B*}_j - y^*_j\} = 0$. Therefore, if the set of activity vectors $\{a^*_{\bullet 1}, a^*_{\bullet 2}\}$ is *linearly independent*, we obtain $y^* = y^{A*} + y^{B*}$.[17]

As we assumed that countries A and B share the same homothetic preference, the total demand for goods depends only on the total income of the countries but not on the distribution of income between countries. As far as the factor price vector (r^*, w^*) prevails in each of the countries (as we have just shown), the total demand for goods remains the same as x^*. Under p^*, the world markets for goods are in equilibrium, meaning that p^* is indeed the equilibrium price of goods in the disintegrated trading world.

Factor contents of trade: One unit of production of good j requires a^*_{Kj} units of capital and a^*_{Lj} units of labor in equilibrium — one unit of good j embodies $a^*_{\bullet j} \equiv (a^*_{Kj}, a^*_{Lj})$ units of factors. In turn, when a household chooses a certain consumption vector, we can say that the household is *indirectly* consuming certain units of factors embodied in the goods. Accordingly, for $s = A, B$, we can associate a consumption vector $x^s = (x^s_1, x^s_2)$ of goods with an *indirect* consumption vector of factors (K^s_x, L^s_x) through the relation $(K^s_x, L^s_x) = \sum_j a^*_{\bullet j} x^s_j$. Given the endowments of factors (K^s, L^s), the price vector p^*, and the factor price vector (r^*, w^*), the budget constraint of country s is written as $p^* x^s = r^* K^s + w^* L^s$. Taking account of the price system, we can rewrite it as follows: for $s = A, B$,

$$r^* K^s_x + w^* L^s_x = r^* K^s + w^* L^s.$$

In Fig. 3.7, the above indirect budget constraint can be represented by line II' passing through point e that corresponds to the division of the world endowments $\{(K^s, L^s)\}_{s=A,B}$. The slope of II' is equal to w^*/r^*.

Let (K^{s*}_x, L^{s*}_x) be the equilibrium indirect consumption of factors of country s. Since we assume identical homothetic preferences, the ratios of consumption of goods of both countries are the same. This implies that the ratios of indirect consumption of factors are the same, too.

---

[17]In our two-good two-factor model, the difference in the factor intensities between goods ensures that the set $\{a^*_{\bullet 1}, a^*_{\bullet 2}\}$ is linearly independent.

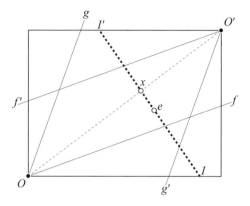

Fig. 3.7   Factor Contents of Trade

Furthermore, these ratios must be equal to the world endowment ratio in equilibrium: $K_x^{A*}/L_x^{A*} = K_x^{B*}/L_x^{B*} = K^W/L^W$. Therefore, the indirect consumption division $\{(K_x^{S*}, L_x^{S*})\}_{S=A,B}$ must occur at the intersection of the diagonal OO' and the budget line II' in Fig. 3.7 (i.e., point x).

Since (K_x^{S*}, L_x^{S*}) and (K^s, L^s) correspond to the actual consumption x^* and production y^*, respectively, then the actual net import $x^{s*} - y^{s*}$ can be translated into the *indirect net import* of factors $(K_x^{S*}, L_x^{S*}) - (K^s, L^s)$, which measures the *factor contents* of trade in goods. The notion of factor content trade sheds a new light on the Heckscher–Ohlin theorem. In Fig. 3.7, point e is located below the diagonal. This means that country A is more labor abundant (capital scarce) than country B. On the other hand, both countries indirectly consume factors in the same proportion. Then, as illustrated in the figure, country A indirectly consumes more capital and less labor than its endowments, while country B indirectly consumes more labor and less capital than its endowments. Each country indirectly exports its abundant factor and imports its scarce factor — this is exactly a reflection of the Heckscher–Ohlin theorem in terms of the factor contents.

3.2   The Roles of Specific Factors

In the HOS model, capital and labor are assumed to be *general factors*. In contrast, a factor that is indispensable and used only in the production of a certain good, but immobile across industries is called a *specific factor*.

It should be noted that the specificity of a factor depends not only on the physical characteristics of the factor itself but also on how we assume or interpret the "time frame" of the model. Some specific factors are intrinsic to certain goods by nature; these factors do not move to other industries simply because they are useless there. Other factors may be of use in many industries but cannot move across industries quickly — it may take a long time for these factors to move from one sector to another. In this case, the specificity of factors is attributable to the time frame of the model. These factors are specific to certain goods and immobile across industries *in the short run*, but becomes general and mobile *in the long run*. In this section, we consider the *Specific-Factors model* (SF model) in which there are two goods (1 and 2) and good j is produced by using both its own specific factor (i.e., *factor j*) and a general factor.[18] For simplicity, we interpret factor j as a sector-specific *capital* and the general factor as *labor*.[19]

3.2.1 *Technology and Behavior of Firms*

The production technology of good j is described by a neoclassical production function $F_j(K_j, L_j)$, where K_j and L_j are the inputs of factor j and labor, respectively. Factor j is specific to good j and all the existing amount of factor j is put into the production of good j. That is, K_j here is fixed and equal to the endowment of factor j. We assume positive, diminishing marginal productivity of labor: $\partial F_j(K_j, L_j)/\partial L_j > 0$ and $\partial^2 F_j(K_j, L_j)/\partial L_j^2 < 0$. Sometimes the Inada conditions are required: $\lim_{L_j \downarrow 0} \partial F_j(K_j, L_j)/\partial L_j = +\infty$ and $\lim_{L_j \uparrow +\infty} \partial F_j(K_j, L_j)/\partial L_j = 0$.

Production possibility set: The production possibility set (PPS) for the SF model is defined as follows:

$$\mathscr{Y}(K_1, K_2, L)$$

$$\equiv \left\{ y = (y_1, y_2) \in \mathbb{R}_+^2 \,\middle|\, \begin{array}{l} y_j \leq F_j(K_j, L_j), \ j = 1, 2, \\ K_1, K_2 \text{: given}, \ L_1 + L_2 \leq L \end{array} \right\},$$

---

[18]For early contributions to the Specific-Factors model, see Ikemoto (1969), Jones (1971), and Samuelson (1971).

[19]In reality, labor is not necessarily a general factor. In particular, some kinds of skilled labor such as medical doctors, lowers, and professional baseball players and others can be regarded as specific factors to the industries concerned.

where $K_j > 0$ and $L > 0$ are the endowments of factor j and labor, respectively. Because the production functions are continuous and concave in labor inputs, the PPS for the SF model becomes a compact convex subset of $\mathbb{R}^2_+$. Since the specific factors are always fully employed in their respective industries, the production efficiency is achieved if and only if labor is fully employed. The marginal rate of transformation (MRT) can be represented by the ratio of the marginal productivities of labor in both industries:

$$\mathrm{MRT} \equiv - \left. \frac{dy_2}{dy_1} \right|_{K_1,K_2,L:\text{given}}$$

$$= \left[\frac{\partial F_2(K_2, L_2)}{\partial L_2} \right] \Big/ \left[\frac{\partial F_1(K_1, L_1)}{\partial L_1} \right]. \tag{3.12}$$

Profit maximization and labor demand: Given the price p_j of good j and the wage rate w for labor, the profit π_j of a firm producing good j (i.e., firm j) is written as follows: for $j = 1, 2$,

$$\pi_j \equiv p_j F_j(K_j, L_j) - w L_j.$$

The first-order condition for profit maximization is

$$\frac{\partial \pi_j}{\partial L_j} = 0 \iff p_j \frac{\partial F_j(K_j, L_j)}{\partial L_j} = w. \tag{3.13}$$

By solving the above equation, we can write the labor demand of firm j as a function of w, p_j, and K_j: $L_j = \psi_{Lj}(w, p_j, K_j)$. It is easy to verify that ψ_{Lj} is decreasing in w, increasing in both p_j and K_j, and homogeneous of degree zero in (w, p_j). Since the derivative $\partial F_j / \partial L_j$ is homogeneous of degree zero in (K_j, L_j), we can rewrite Eq. (3.13) as follows:

$$\frac{\partial F_j(1, L_j/K_j)}{\partial L_j} = \frac{w}{p_j}.$$

By solving the above equation for L_j/K_j, we obtain an alternative expression for the labor demand function:

$$L_j = \psi_{Lj}(w, p_j, K_j) \equiv \phi_{Lj}(w/p_j) K_j.$$

Obviously, ϕ_{Lj} is decreasing in w/p_j. In the following, we use these alternative expressions, ψ_{Lj} and $\phi_{Lj} K_j$, interchangeably.

The maximized profit of a firm can be written as a function of p_j, w, and K_j: for $j = 1, 2$,

$$\tilde{\pi}_j(w, p_j, K_j) \equiv p_j F_j(K_j, \psi_{Lj}(w, p_j, K_j)) - w\psi_{Lj}(w, p_j, K_j)$$
$$= p_j F_j(1, \phi_{Lj}(w/p_j))K_j - w\phi_{Lj}(w/p_j)K_j.$$

If we assume the Inada conditions, we have $\tilde{\pi}_j(w, p_j, K_j) \geq 0$ for any $w \geq 0$ and $p_j \geq 0$. The maximized profit $\tilde{\pi}_j$ satisfies $\partial\tilde{\pi}_j(w, p_j, K_j)/\partial w = -\psi_{Lj}(w, p_j, K_j)$ and $\partial\tilde{\pi}_j(w, p_j, K_j)/\partial p_j = F_j(K_j, \psi_{Lj}(w, p_j, K_j))$. These facts are known as *Hotelling's lemma* (Hotelling, 1932).

3.2.2 Labor Market and the Production Structure

The equilibrium wage rate: Substituting the labor demand functions into the labor market equilibrium condition $L = L_1 + L_2$, we obtain

$$L = \sum_j \psi_{Lj}(w, p_j, K_j) \equiv \sum_j \phi_{Lj}(w/p_j)K_j, \qquad (3.14)$$

which determines the equilibrium wage rate $\tilde{w}(p_1, p_2, K_1, K_2, L)$. Unlike the HOS model, the equilibrium wage rate explicitly depends upon the endowments of production factors. Since the labor demand functions are homogeneous of degree zero in (w, p_j), then $\tilde{w}$ becomes linearly homogeneous in (p_1, p_2). Further, we can show that if (w, p_1, p_2) solves Eq. (3.14) for (K_1, K_2, L), then (w, p_1, p_2) also solves Eq. (3.14) for $(\lambda K_1, \lambda K_2, \lambda L)$ for any $\lambda > 0$. Hence, $\tilde{w}$ is homogeneous of degree zero in (K_1, K_2, L). By totally differentiating Eq. (3.14), we obtain the following results: for $j = 1, 2$,

$$\frac{\partial\tilde{w}}{\partial L} = \frac{-1}{\Delta} < 0, \qquad \frac{\partial\tilde{w}}{\partial p_j} = \frac{1}{\Delta} \cdot \frac{\partial\psi_{Lj}}{\partial p_j} > 0,$$
$$\frac{\partial\tilde{w}}{\partial K_j} = \frac{1}{\Delta} \cdot \frac{\partial\psi_{Lj}}{\partial K_j} > 0,$$

where $\Delta \equiv -\sum_i \partial\psi_{Li}/\partial w > 0$. An increase in the labor endowment lowers the wage rate, while an increase in the price of a good or in the endowment of a specific factor raises the (nominal) wage rate. Further, the elasticity of equilibrium wage rate with respect to the price of good j, denoted by ε_{wj}, can be calculated as follows: for $j = 1, 2$,

$$\varepsilon_{wj} \equiv \frac{\partial \tilde{w}}{\partial p_j} \cdot \frac{p_j}{w} = \frac{1}{w\Delta} \cdot \frac{\partial \psi_{Lj}}{\partial p_j} p_j = \frac{-1}{\Delta} \cdot \frac{\partial \psi_{Lj}}{\partial w} < 1.$$

The third equality follows from Euler's theorem for homogeneous functions and the zero-degree homogeneity of ψ_{Lj} in (w, p_j). Since ε_{wj} is positive but less than unity, the nominal wage rate *increases* but the real wage rate in terms of good j *decreases* when p_j increases.

Rental for a specific factor: Factor j receives the profit π_j of good j. Let $r_j \equiv \pi_j/K_j$ be the rental rate for factor j, which can be written as a function of exogenous parameters:

$$r_j = \tilde{r}_j(p_1, p_2, K_1, K_2, L) \equiv \frac{\tilde{\pi}_j(\tilde{w}(\cdot), p_j, K_j)}{K_j}$$
$$= p_j F_j(1, \phi_{Lj}(\tilde{w}(\cdot)/p_j)) - \tilde{w}(\cdot)\phi_{Lj}(\tilde{w}(\cdot)/p_j)$$
$$= p_j \frac{\partial F_j(1, \phi_{Lj}(\tilde{w}(\cdot)/p_j))}{\partial K_j}. \tag{3.15}$$

From the last expression, we recognize that the rental rate for factor j is equal to the value marginal product of factor j and that the endowments of specific factors affect the rental rate only through the *indirect* channel of the (changes in) wage rate. Since $\tilde{w}$ is linearly homogeneous in (p_1, p_2), then $\tilde{r}_j$ becomes linearly homogeneous in (p_1, p_2), too. Simple calculation yields the following results: for $i, j = 1, 2$ and $i \neq j$,

$$\frac{\partial \tilde{r}_j}{\partial p_j} = F_j(1, \psi_{Lj}) - \frac{\partial \tilde{w}}{\partial p_j} \cdot \psi_{Lj} = \frac{p_j y_j - \varepsilon_{wj} w L_j}{p_j K_j} > \frac{\pi_j}{p_j K_j} \geq 0,$$
$$\frac{\partial \tilde{r}_j}{\partial p_i} = -\frac{\partial \tilde{w}}{\partial p_i} \cdot \psi_{Lj} < 0, \quad \frac{\partial \tilde{r}_j}{\partial L} = -\frac{\partial \tilde{w}}{\partial L} \cdot \psi_{Lj} > 0,$$
$$\frac{\partial \tilde{r}_j}{\partial K_j} = -\frac{\partial \tilde{w}}{\partial K_j} \cdot \psi_{Lj} < 0, \quad \frac{\partial \tilde{r}_j}{\partial K_i} = -\frac{\partial \tilde{w}}{\partial K_i} \cdot \psi_{Lj} < 0.$$

The first line follows from $0 < \varepsilon_{wj} < 1$, which implies $p_j y_j - \varepsilon_{wj} w L_j > p_j y_j - w L_j = \pi_j \geq 0$. This also implies that the elasticity of the rental rate for factor j with respect to the price of good j, denoted by ε_{rj}, is more than unity: for $j = 1, 2$,

$$\varepsilon_{rj} \equiv \frac{\partial \tilde{r}_j}{\partial p_j} \cdot \frac{p_j}{r_j} > 1.$$

Accordingly, when the price of good j increases, not only the nominal rental rate for factor j but also the real rental rate in terms of good j increase.

Production structure: Given the price vector (p_1, p_2) and the factor endowments (K_1, K_2, L), the production structure is determined through the labor market equilibrium. Because the labor is fully employed and Eq. (3.12) is satisfied via firms' profit maximization, the equilibrium production point turns out to be efficient. By substituting the labor demand function into the production function, we can express the equilibrium production of good j as a function of the prices of goods and the endowments of factors: for $j = 1, 2$,

$$
\begin{aligned}
y_j &= \tilde{y}_j(p_1, p_2, K_1, K_2, L) \\
&\equiv F_j(K_j, \psi_{Lj}(\tilde{w}(p_1, p_2, K_1, K_2, L), p_j, K_j)).
\end{aligned}
$$

Because the equilibrium price $\tilde{w}$ is linearly homogeneous in (p_1, p_2) and the labor demand ψ_{Lj} is homogeneous of degree zero in (w, p_j), the equilibrium production $\tilde{y}_j$ becomes homogeneous of degree zero in (p_1, p_2). Simple calculation yields the following results: for $i, j = 1, 2$ and $i \neq j$,

$$
\begin{aligned}
\frac{\partial \tilde{y}_j}{\partial p_j} &= \frac{\partial F_j}{\partial L_j} \left\{ \frac{\partial \psi_{Lj}}{\partial p_j} + \frac{\partial \psi_{Lj}}{\partial w} \cdot \frac{\partial \tilde{w}}{\partial p_j} \right\} \\
&= \frac{\partial F_j}{\partial L_j} \cdot \frac{\partial \psi_{Lj}}{\partial p_j} \left\{ 1 - \varepsilon_{wj} \right\} > 0, \\
\frac{\partial \tilde{y}_j}{\partial K_j} &= \frac{\partial F_j}{\partial K_j} + \frac{\partial F_j}{\partial L_j} \left\{ \frac{\partial \psi_{Lj}}{\partial K_j} + \frac{\partial \psi_{Lj}}{\partial w} \cdot \frac{\partial \tilde{w}}{\partial K_j} \right\} \\
&= \frac{\partial F_j}{\partial K_j} + \frac{\partial F_j}{\partial L_j} \cdot \frac{\partial \psi_{Lj}}{\partial K_j} \left\{ 1 - \varepsilon_{wj} \right\} > 0, \\
\frac{\partial \tilde{y}_j}{\partial L} &= \frac{\partial F_j}{\partial L_j} \cdot \frac{\partial \psi_{Lj}}{\partial w} \cdot \frac{\partial \tilde{w}}{\partial L} > 0,
\end{aligned}
$$

$$\frac{\partial \tilde{y}_j}{\partial p_i} = \frac{\partial F_j}{\partial L_j} \cdot \frac{\partial \psi_{Lj}}{\partial w_j} \cdot \frac{\partial \tilde{w}}{\partial p_i} < 0,$$

$$\frac{\partial \tilde{y}_j}{\partial K_i} = \frac{\partial F_j}{\partial L_j} \cdot \frac{\partial \psi_{Lj}}{\partial w} \cdot \frac{\partial \tilde{w}}{\partial K_i} < 0.$$

The implications of the above results are clear and intuitive. When the price of good j rises or when the endowment of factor j increases, the supply of good j increases while that of the other good decreases. When the labor endowment increases, the supplies of both goods increase simultaneously.

Similar to the HOS model, we can define the relative supply function:

$$S(p, K_1, K_2, L) \equiv \frac{\tilde{y}_1(p_1, p_2, K_1, K_2, L)}{\tilde{y}_2(p_1, p_2, K_1, K_2, L)}$$

$$= \frac{\tilde{y}_1(p_1/p_2, 1, K_1, K_2, L)}{\tilde{y}_2(p_1/p_2, 1, K_1, K_2, L)}.$$

The relative supply function S is increasing in both $p \equiv p_1/p_2$ and K_1 but decreasing in K_2. Although an increase in L brings about increases in both goods, the effect on the relative supply is ambiguous.[20]

3.2.3 *Specific Factor and Comparative Advantage*

Let us introduce countries A and B explicitly into the model. As in the HOS model, we assume that they share the same technologies and the same homothetic preference. A triple (K_1^s, K_2^s, L^s) denotes the factor endowments of country s. The relative demand for goods, x_1/x_2, is described by the function $\mathcal{D}(p)$, which is decreasing in p. Combining S and $\mathcal{D}$, we obtain the condition for the autarkic equilibrium: for $s = A, B$,

$$\mathcal{D}(p) = S(p, K_1^s, K_2^s, L^s),$$

which determines the autarkic price $\bar{p}^s$. Suppose that countries A and B are identical except for the endowments of factor 1. Specifically, let us assume country A has more factor 1 than country B: $K_1^A > K_1^B, K_2^A = K_2^B$,

---

[20]This depends on the relative magnitudes of the elasticities of labor demand in both sectors.

and $L^A = L^B$. Because S is increasing in K_1 and p, but $\mathcal{D}$ is decreasing in p, we have $\bar{p}^A < \bar{p}^B$. That is, the factor-1 abundant country A has a comparative advantage in good 1 over country B.[21]

Proposition 3.4   (Specific Factor and Comparative Advantage). *A country that is abundant in specific factor j has a comparative advantage in good j.*

Under free trade in goods, countries A and B face a common equilibrium price. However, as shown by the results of the comparative statics, the rental for factor j is lower in the factor-j abundant country than in the other country. Obviously, FPE fails to hold.

3.2.4   *Foreign Direct Investment*

The SF model can be used to examine the industry-level foreign direct investment (FDI). Here, we assume that the specific factors of different industries are completely different physical objects and intrinsic to the corresponding industries; they cannot move across "industries" even in the long run, but can move across "countries" if they are allowed to do so.

Countries A and B have the same technologies and the same homothetic preferences. Let K_j^s and L^s be the endowments of factor j and labor in country s ($j = 1, 2$; $s = A, B$). We assume that countries A and B are different only in the endowments of factor 1. Without loss of generality, we set $K_1^A > K_1^B$, $K_2^A = K_2^B$ ($= K_2$), and $L^A = L^B$ ($= L$).

Free trade in goods: First, let us consider a situation where only trade in goods is allowed. As shown above, country A has a comparative advantage in good 1 under our assumptions; in the free trade equilibrium in goods, country A exports good 1 and both countries face the same prices of goods. Let p° be the equilibrium relative price of good 1 under free trade in goods. The rental rate for factor 1 in country s ($= A, B$) is given by Eq. (3.15). Further, because $\tilde{r}_1$ is decreasing in the endowment of factor 1, the rental

---

[21]Because the effect of the labor endowment on the relative supply is ambiguous, we cannot theoretically predict the structure of comparative advantage solely from the difference in the labor endowments.

rate for factor 1 in country A is lower than that in country B:

$$r_1^A = \tilde{r}_1(p^\circ, 1, K_1^A, K_2, L) < \tilde{r}_1(p^\circ, 1, K_1^B, K_2, L) = r_1^B. \tag{3.16}$$

Factor movements: The above difference in the rental rates between countries A and B provides the owners of factor 1 with an incentive to shift factor 1 from country A to country B — FDI. Now suppose that factor 1 becomes able to move freely across countries, while factor 2 and labor do not. Let I be the amount of FDI (i.e., factor 1 that moves from country A to country B), which is determined endogenously so that the rental rates in both countries are equalized:

$$\tilde{r}_1(p^*, 1, K_1^A - I, K_2, L) = \tilde{r}_1(p^*, 1, K_1^B + I, K_2, L), \tag{3.17}$$

where p^* denotes the equilibrium relative price of good 1 under FDI. By the symmetry assumption, we have $K_1^A - I = K_1^B + I$ in equilibrium; therefore, $I = (K_1^A - K_1^B)/2$. A half of the difference in the endowments of factor 1 is invested from country A to country B. Consequently, in each country a half of the world total endowment of factor 1 is employed.

FPE: As shown in Eq. (3.15), changes in the endowments of specific factors do not *directly* affect the rental rates, they do only through the *indirect* channel of wage changes. Then, the equalization of the rental rates for factor 1 in both countries implies the equalization of the wage rates there, which in turn implies the equalization of the rental rates for factor 2. Therefore, FPE is realized.

Repatriation and GNP: Because both countries come to use the same amounts of all factors of production under FDI, they have (effectively) the same production possibility set: $\mathscr{Y}(K_1^A - I, K_2, L) = \mathscr{Y}(K_1^B + I, K_2, L)$. Then, they realize the same production vectors in equilibrium. Let $y^* = (y_1^*, y_2^*)$, r_j^*, and w^* be the production vector, the rental rate for factor j, and the wage rate, which are common to both countries in the equilibrium under FDI. Both countries share the same *gross domestic product* (GDP): $p^* y_1^* + y_2^*$, which is equal to $r_1^*(K_1^A - I) + r_2^* K_2 + w^* L$ (for country A) and to $r_1^*(K_1^B + I) + r_2^* K_2 + w^* L$ (for country B). The income that factor 1 receives in country B via FDI is $r_1^* I$, which is repatriated to country A. Let Y^s denote the *gross national product* (GNP) of country s, which is equal to the total factor income that accrues to the household sector of each country. Then, we have $Y^A = p^* y_1^* + y_2^* + r_1^* I$ and $Y^B = p^* y_1^* + y_2^* - r_1^* I$. The household of country A enjoys a higher disposable income than that of country B.

3.3   Remarks and Further Topics

In this section, we take up three topics relating to the HOS model and the SF model: the first topic is the relationship between the HOS model and the SF model; the second one is extensions of the Stolper–Samuelson theorem that include more than two goods and factors, with particular attention to the notion of factor intensity; and the last one is a generalization of the HOS model to include a continuum of goods.

3.3.1   *The SF Model as a Short-run HOS Model*

Suppose that the specific factors of different industries consist of physically the same objects, but it takes long time for them to move from one sector to another. In other words, the specificity of a factor is caused by its "short-run immobility" across industries.[22] In the short run, the rental rate in one industry can be different from that in the other industry. If, for example, the rental in industry 1 is higher than in industry 2, then the capital employed in industry 2 begins to move toward industry 1. As capital moves, the differential in the rental rates shrinks and, eventually, they converge to a common value. In the long run, capital can be regarded as a general factor. The endowment of capital is allocated between industries so that the rental rates in both industries are equalized. The full employment condition for capital is $K = K_1 + K_2$, where K is the capital endowment in an economy. The movement of capital across industries can be described by the following differential equation: for given p_1, p_2, K, and L,

$$\frac{dK_1}{dt} = \tilde{r}_1(p_1, p_2, K_1, K - K_1, L) - \tilde{r}_2(p_1, p_2, K_1, K - K_1, L),$$

where t denotes the "time" variable. In the long run, we must have $dK_1/dt = 0$, implying $r_1 = r_2 = r$ for some r.

---

[22]See Mussa (1974) and Neary (1978).

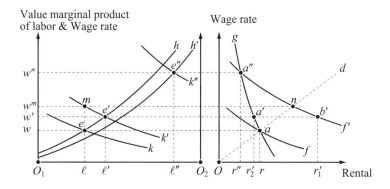

Fig. 3.8 The SF Model as a Short-run HOS Model

Let us examine the long-run effects of a price change. To be concrete, we assume that good 1 is more labor intensive in the long run: $K_1/L_1 < K_2/L_2$. Curves k and h in the left panel of Fig. 3.8 represent the graphs of the value marginal product of labor in the good 1 production and that in the good 2 production (i.e., VMP_{L1} and VMP_{L2}), respectively. On the other hand, curves f and g in the right panel represent the factor price frontiers of good 1 and good 2, respectively. The initial long-run equilibrium is described by point e in the left panel and by point a in the right panel. The initial wage rate is w and the rental is r ($= r_1 = r_2$).

Suppose that the relative price of good 1 increases from p_1 to p'_1. In proportion to the price increase, VMP_{L1} increases and, accordingly, curve k shifts up to curve k'. At the same time, the factor price frontier for good 1 shifts up from curve f to curve f'. The rate of increase in p_1 is equal to the ratios $|em|/|\ell e|$ in the left panel and $|an|/|Oa|$ in the right panel. The new short-run equilibrium becomes point e' in the left panel. The nominal wage rate increases from w to w', while the real wage rate in terms of good 1, w/p_1, decreases. Labor allocation changes from ℓ to ℓ': L_1 increases, while L_2 decreases. The rental rate in good 1 increases from r to r'_1, which satisfies $c_1(r'_1, w') = p'_1$ as represented by point b' in the right panel. On the other hand, the rental rate in good 2 decreases from r to r'_2, which satisfies $c_2(r'_2, w') = p_2$ as point a'. The short-run discrepancy of the rental rates in two industries (i.e., $r'_1 > r'_2$) gives the capital employed in the good-2 sector incentives to move toward the good-1 sector.

As capital moves across industries, VMP_{L1} increases, while VMP_{L2} decreases. Since good 1 is less capital intensive than good 2, the positive effect of an increase in K_1 on VMP_{L1} is greater (in absolute terms) than the negative effect of a decrease in K_2 on VMP_{L2}. Therefore, curve k' shifts up to curve k'' and curve h shifts down to curve h'. The new long-run equilibrium becomes point e'', which corresponds to the intersection of the factor price frontiers f' and g (i.e., point a'').

When the price of the labor-intensive good increases, the wage rate increases and the rental rate in the capital-intensive sector decreases both in the short run and in the long run, while the rental rate in the labor-intensive sector once increases in the short run, but eventually decreases in the long run. These observations indicate that the interests of factor owners can be in conflict with each other, depending on (i) the industry where the factor is employed or on (ii) how the factor owners take the future events into account.

3.3.2 Extensions of the Stolper–Samuelson Theorem

Friends and enemies: In a general setting with more than two goods and factors, the Stolper–Samuelson theorem can be decomposed into several distinct assertions: (a) an increase in the price of a good leads to a decrease in at least one of factor prices; (b) an increase in the price of a good leads to an increase in at least one of the other factor prices; (c) the rate of increase in the latter factor price is greater than the rate of increase in the good price (i.e., Jones' magnification effect). When an increase in the price of good j brings about an increase (a decrease) in the real reward rate of factor i, good j is said to be a *friend* (an *enemy*, respectively) of factor i. Every good is a friend of at least one factor and an enemy of another factor.[23]

The *friend-and-enemy* version of the Stolper–Samuelson theorem can be proved under very mild conditions. Let us consider a model with m factors and n goods, where $n, m \geq 2$; we maintain here the assumptions of

---

[23] Jones and Scheinkman (1977) have introduced the notions of "friends" and "enemies" and proved this version of generalization of the Stolper–Samuelson theorem. For several other directions of the generalization, see the commentary article by Deardorff (1994).

the constant returns to scale, perfect competition, and no joint production. Let $w = (w_1, \ldots, w_i, \ldots, w_m)$ and $p = (p_1, \ldots, p_j, \ldots, p_n)$ denote factor price vector and price vector, respectively. Further, let $c_j : \mathbb{R}_+^m \to \mathbb{R}_+$ be the unit cost function of good j. Then, similar to the 2×2 case, the price system can be written as follows:

$$c_j(w_1, \ldots, w_i, \ldots, w_m) = p_j, \quad j = 1, 2, \ldots, n. \tag{3.18}$$

Without loss of generality, we concentrate on only two goods, good k and good ℓ, and consider a case where the price of good k increases with keeping the other good prices unchanged. By totally differentiating the price-cost equations of both goods, we have

$$\theta_{1k}\hat{w}_1 + \cdots + \theta_{ik}\hat{w}_i + \cdots + \theta_{mk}\hat{w}_m = \hat{p}_k > 0, \quad \text{(good } k) \tag{3.19}$$

$$\theta_{1\ell}\hat{w}_1 + \cdots + \theta_{i\ell}\hat{w}_i + \cdots + \theta_{m\ell}\hat{w}_m = 0, \quad \text{(good } \ell) \tag{3.20}$$

where $\theta_{ij} \equiv w_i a_{ij}(w)/c_j(w)$ denotes the distributive share of factor i in the production of good j. We assume that $\theta_{ik} > 0$ and $\theta_{i\ell} > 0$ for all i.[24] Let us define $\hat{w}_{i_0} \equiv \min\{\hat{w}_1, \ldots, \hat{w}_m\}$ and $\hat{w}_{i_1} \equiv \max\{\hat{w}_1, \ldots, \hat{w}_m\}$. Since $\sum_{i=1}^m \theta_{ij} = 1$ for all j by definition, Eq. (3.19) means that the positive percentage change in the good k price is represented by a weighted average of the percentage changes in factor prices, which implies $\hat{w}_{i_1} > 0$. Together with this, Eq. (3.20) implies $\hat{w}_{i_0} < 0$. Therefore, we have

$$\hat{w}_{i_0} < 0 < \hat{p}_k < \hat{w}_{i_1}.$$

This proves statements (a) through (c). That is, good k is a friend of factor i_1, but an enemy of factor i_0.

Weak and strong theorems: The above argument does not specify *which* factor price will actually increase in response to an increase in the price of a good. In order to associate each factor with one particular good, we need to assume that the numbers of goods and factors are equal: $m = n \geq 2$. Hereafter, we associate factor i with good i for $i = 1, 2, \ldots, n$.

---

[24] In order for the argument here to be valid, it is not necessary $\theta_{ik} > 0$ and $\theta_{i\ell} > 0$ *for all* i. What is needed is that both good k and good ℓ use the same subset of (no less than two) factors in strictly positive amounts. In addition, we need to assume that good k and good ℓ are produced both before and after the price change.

Chipman (1969) has shown two directions of generalization of the Stolper–Samuelson theorem in the case with equal numbers of goods and factors:

The Weak Stolper–Samuelson theorem (WSS). An increase in the price of good *i* leads to a *more-than-proportionate* increase in the reward rate of the corresponding factor *i*.

The Strong Stolper–Samuelson theorem (SSS). An increase in the price of good *i* leads to simultaneous decreases in the reward rates of all factors other than factor *i*.

WSS says nothing about changes in w_j ($j \neq i$). Even if WSS holds, w_j may increase or decrease in response to an increase in p_i. Mitra and Jones (1999) added a condition that "the rate of increase in the reward rate for factor *i* in response to an increase in the price of good *i* is the highest among all changes in the factor prices" to WSS and called the extended theorem as the *strong version* of WSS. On the other hand, SSS strengthens the condition in point (a), which involves only one (unspecified) factor price, to the one that involves *all* factor prices but factor *i*.

Apparently, SSS does not refer to changes in the reward rate of factor *i*. However, it is easy to show that SSS implies WSS. Let $\hat{p} = (\hat{p}_1, \ldots, \hat{p}_n)$ and $\hat{w} = (\hat{w}_1, \ldots, \hat{w}_n)$ be vectors of percentage changes in good and factor prices, respectively. Define the distributive share matrix $\Theta \equiv [\theta_{ij}]_{i,j=1,\ldots,n}$, which is an $n \times n$ stochastic matrix with its column sums being equal to unity.[25] Then, for a unit vector $u \equiv (1, 1, \ldots, 1)$, we have $u = u\Theta$. If there exists the inverse of Θ, we have $u\Theta^{-1} = u\Theta\Theta^{-1} = u$, which implies that every column sum of the inverse Θ^{-1} is also equal to unity. Similar to Eq. (3.8), total differentiation of the price–cost equations (3.18) yields $\hat{p} = \hat{w}\Theta$ in matrix form. By solving it, we obtain $\hat{w} = \hat{p}\Theta^{-1}$. Suppose $\hat{p}_i > 0$ and $\hat{p}_k = 0$ for all $k \neq i$. Then, we have

$$\hat{w}_j = \hat{p}_i\gamma_{ij}, \quad j = 1, 2, \ldots, n,$$

where γ_{ij} denotes (i, j)-element of Θ^{-1}. Therefore, SSS holds true if and only if all off-diagonal elements of Θ^{-1} is negative: $\gamma_{ij} < 0$ for all i, j with

---

[25] A nonnegative square matrix $B \equiv [b_{ij}]_{i,j=1,\ldots,n}$ is said to be a *stochastic matrix* if every column sum (or every row sum) is equal to 1: $\sum_{i=1}^{n} b_{ij} = 1$ for all $j = 1, \ldots, n$; or $\sum_{j=1}^{n} b_{ij} = 1$ for all $i = 1, \ldots, n$.

$i \neq j$. Moreover, since $\sum_{i=1}^{n} \gamma_{ij} = 1$ for all j as shown above, SSS implies $\gamma_{ii} = 1 - \sum_{k \neq i} \gamma_{kj} > 1$. Hence, we have $\hat{w}_i = \hat{p}_i \gamma_{ii} > \hat{p}_i$ for all i, implying the strong version of WSS.

Various definitions of factor intensity: For the statement that "good i is produced by using factor i intensively" to be meaningful, we have to introduce an operational definition of the notion of factor intensity in a general setting. Several variations have been introduced to prove WSS and/or SSS.

Remember that in the 2×2 model, good 1 is said to be labor intensive than good 2 if $\theta_{L1} > \theta_{L2}$. By the same token, Chipman (1969) has introduced the following definition of factor intensity: good i is said to be factor i intensive in the sense of Chipman if

$$\theta_{ii} > \theta_{ij} \quad \text{for all } j \neq i; \ i = 1, 2, \ldots, n. \tag{CH}$$

This definition says that the distributive share of factor i in (the production of) good i is higher than those of factor i in other goods, but it says nothing about the distributive shares of the other factors in good i. Even if CH is satisfied, it is possible that another factor k has a higher distributive share in good i than factor i, that is, $\theta_{ii} < \theta_{ki}$. In this case, it may be more appropriate to say that factor k, rather than factor i, is intensive in good i.

Taking account of the distributive shares of factors other than factor i in good i, Kemp and Wegge (1969) have introduced a stronger condition for factor intensity: good i is said to be factor i intensive in the sense of Kemp and Wegge if

$$\frac{\theta_{ii}}{\theta_{ki}} > \frac{\theta_{ij}}{\theta_{kj}}, \quad j \neq i, \ k \neq i; \ i = 1, 2, \ldots, n. \tag{KW}$$

KW implies CH. The inequality in KW can be rewritten as $\theta_{ii}\theta_{kj} > \theta_{ij}\theta_{ki}$. Summing both sides over $k \neq i$ and rearranging the result appropriately, we obtain CH as follows: for $j \neq i$,

$$\sum_{k \neq i} \theta_{ii}\theta_{kj} > \sum_{k \neq i} \theta_{ij}\theta_{ki} \Rightarrow \theta_{ii} \sum_{k \neq i} \theta_{kj} > \theta_{ij} \sum_{k \neq i} \theta_{ki}$$

$$\Rightarrow \quad \theta_{ii}(1 - \theta_{ij}) > \theta_{ij}(1 - \theta_{ii}) \Rightarrow \theta_{ii} > \theta_{ij}.$$

KW is based on the pairwise comparison of the ratios of distributive shares of factors i and k in the production of goods i and j. In this comparison, the information about distributive shares of factors other than i and k is not used. Therefore, even if factor i has the largest cost share (in the sense of KW) comparing to any other *single* factor, factor i may have a smaller cost share than the *collective* cost share of other factors. Making use of full information about cost shares of all factors, Jones *et al.* (1993) proposed a stronger definition of factor intensity: good i is said to be factor i intensive in the sense of Jones–Marjit–Mitra if

$$\frac{\theta_{ii}}{\theta_{ki}} - \frac{\theta_{ij}}{\theta_{kj}} > \sum_{s \neq i, j, k} \left| \frac{\theta_{si}}{\theta_{ki}} - \frac{\theta_{sj}}{\theta_{kj}} \right|, \quad j \neq i, \ k \neq i; \ i = 1, 2, \ldots, n. \quad \textbf{(JMM)}$$

Since the right-hand side of the above inequality is non-negative, JMM implies KW. With a similar reasoning, Mitra and Jones (1999) have proposed another definition of factor intensity, which strengthens CH: good i is said to be "factor i intensive" in the sense of Mitra and Jones if

$$\theta_{ii} - \theta_{ij} > \sum_{s \neq i} \left| \theta_{si} - \theta_{sj} \right|, \quad j \neq i; \ i = 1, 2, \ldots, n. \quad \textbf{(MJ)}$$

Based on various definitions of factor intensity, the Stolper–Samuelson theorem has been extended to cases with more than two goods and factors. Provided that the numbers of goods and factors are the same, the relationship among the intensity conditions (KW, CH, JMM, and MJ) and the versions of the Stolper–Samuelson theorem (WSS and SSS) is illustrated by Fig. 3.9. In the figure, arrows indicate the direction of logical implication; solid arrows do not require restrictions on the common number of goods

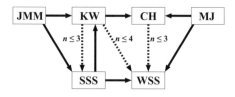

Fig. 3.9   Logical Relationship among the Intensity Conditions and the Variations of the Theorem

and factors, but broken arrows require restrictions on the upper bound of the common number of goods and factors.[26]

3.3.3 *The HOS Model with a Continuum of Goods*

Following Dornbusch *et al.* (1980), we extend the two-factor, two-country HOS model to include a continuum of goods. Goods are indexed by real numbers in the unit interval $[0, 1] \subset \mathbb{R}$. We assume that both countries share the same CRS production technology and, also, the same Cobb–Douglas preference represented by the utility function $U = \int_0^1 \ln[x_j] dj$, which generates the demand function for good j:

$$x_j = \frac{Y}{p_j}, \tag{3.21}$$

where Y and p_j denote the income level and the price of good j. The endowments of capital and labor of a country are denoted by K and L. Then, the income of the country becomes $Y = rK + wL$. The capital–labor endowment ratio is denoted by $k \equiv K/L$.

Technology: Let $c_j(r, w) \equiv r a_{Kj}(r, w) + w a_{Lj}(r, w)$ be the unit cost function of good j, where $a_{Kj}(r, w)$ and $a_{Lj}(r, w)$ denote the input coefficients of capital and labor for good j, respectively. The capital intensity of good j can be written as a function of the wage–rental ratio $\omega \equiv w/r$:

$$k_j(\omega) \equiv \frac{a_{Kj}(r, w)}{a_{Lj}(r, w)} = \frac{a_{Kj}(1, \omega)}{a_{Lj}(1, \omega)}. \tag{3.22}$$

The latter equality follows from the zero-homogeneity of the input coefficients with respect to (r, w). As usual, $k_j(\omega)$ is increasing in ω. Further, we assume that goods are numbered so that $k_j(\omega)$ is increasing in j for any ω.

The autarkic wage–rental ratio: Let y_j, K_j, and L_j be the production of good j, the capital and labor used in good j, respectively. The zero profit

---

[26]We omit here the proofs of the implications illustrated in the figure. Readers may consult the original articles: Chipman (1969), Kemp and Wegge (1969), Jones *et al.* (1993), Mitra and Jones (1999).

condition for good j can be written as

$$y_j = \frac{rK_j + wL_j}{p_j}. \qquad (3.23)$$

Note that we have $K_j/L_j = k_j(\omega)$. Putting these relations into the market equilibrium conditions in autarky, that is, $x_j = y_j$ for all $j \in [0, 1]$, we have

$$\frac{L_j}{L} = \frac{\omega + k}{\omega + k_j(\omega)}. \qquad (3.24)$$

Substituting the above result into the full employment conditions, $\int_0^1 K_j \mathrm{d}j = K$ and $\int_0^1 L_j \mathrm{d}j = L$, and rearranging the results appropriately, we obtain

$$G(\omega, k) \equiv \int_0^1 \frac{(\omega + k)\{k_j(\omega) - k\}}{\omega + k_j(\omega)} \mathrm{d}j = 0. \qquad (3.25)$$

This determines the autarkic wage–rental ratio as a function of the capital–labor endowment ratio. By simple calculation, we can show that

$$\frac{\partial G(\omega, k)}{\partial \omega} = \int_0^1 \frac{1}{\{\omega + k_j(\omega)\}^2}$$

$$\times \left[\{k_j(\omega) - k\}^2 + (\omega + k)^2 \frac{\partial k_j(\omega)}{\partial \omega} \right] \mathrm{d}j > 0,$$

$$\frac{\partial G(\omega, k)}{\partial k} = - \int_0^1 \frac{\omega + k}{\omega + k_j(\omega)} \mathrm{d}j < 0,$$

where the latter derivative is evaluated at the equilibrium. Therefore, the autarkic wage–rental ratio is increasing in the capital–labor endowment ratio. In other words, the capital-rich country has a higher wage–rental ratio.

The autarkic equilibrium price: Given the Cobb–Douglas preference, we have the price–cost equation for all goods in the autarkic equilib-rium: $p_j = c_j(r, w)$ for all $j \in [0, 1]$. Then, the price of good i rel-ative to good j can be written as a function of the wage–rental ratio:

$p_i/p_j = c_i(r, w)/c_j(r, w) = c_i(1, \omega)/c_j(1, \omega)$. Simple calculation yields

$$\frac{\mathrm{d}\ln[p_i/p_j]}{\mathrm{d}\omega} = \frac{\theta_{Li}(1, \omega) - \theta_{Lj}(1, \omega)}{w}, \qquad (3.26)$$

where $\theta_{Li}(\omega)$ denotes the distributive share of labor in good i. It is easy to show that $\theta_{Li}(\omega) > \theta_{Lj}(\omega)$ if and only if $k_i(\omega) < k_j(\omega)$. Therefore, the above result implies that an increase in the wage–rental ratio leads to increases in the relative prices of labor intensive goods. Since a country with a higher capital–labor endowment ratio has a higher wage–rental ratio, the country has comparative advantages in capital intensive range of goods.

Free trade with FPE: Similar to the basic 2×2 HOS model, if the capital–labor endowment ratios, $k^A \equiv K^A/L^A$ and $k^B \equiv K^B/L^B$, are close enough, FPE obtains. More precisely, if the division $\{(K^s, L^s)\}_{s=A,B}$ of the world endowments (K^W, L^W) is included in the FPE set, the disintegrated equilibrium of trade in goods generates the same outcomes as the integrated equilibrium. Figure 3.10 illustrates the world production box diagram and the FPE set, which is represented by the shaded lens-shaped area. If, for example, the division of the world endowments between countries is given by point e as illustrated in the figure, free trade in goods will realize the FPE.

The autarkic wage–rental ratio of country $s = A, B$, denoted by ω^s, is the solution to $G(\omega, k^s) = 0$. On the other hand, the free trade wage–rental ratio ω^* is the solution to $G(\omega, k^W) = 0$, where $k^W \equiv K^W/L^W$.

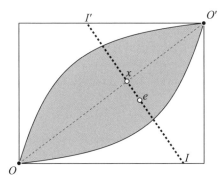

Fig. 3.10   The FPE Set of the HOS Model with a Continuum of Goods

If we assume $k^A < k^B$ as illustrated by point e in Fig. 3.10, we have $k^A < k^W < k^B$ and, accordingly, $\omega^A < \omega^* < \omega^B$. That is, comparing to the autarkic equilibrium, free trade in goods raises the wage–rental rate in the labor-rich country, while lowers that in the capital-rich country.

Although the consumption pattern of each country in the free trade equilibrium is determined uniquely, the production pattern of each country is not. This is because the model with infinitely many goods and only two factors admits a very high degree of freedom in production.[27] Therefore, the trade pattern *in terms of goods* between countries A and B cannot be made definite. However, the trade pattern *in terms of factor contents* will be made definite; the labor-rich country indirectly exports labor and indirectly imports capital, while the capital-rich country vice versa. The argument is precisely the same as in the case of the factor content trade in the basic HOS model.

Free trade without FPE: If the capital–labor endowment ratios of the countries are far apart, FPE cannot obtain. In this case, there is a threshold index z that determines the boundary of exports of the countries: the labor-rich country exports the labor intensive range of goods with indices lower than z (i.e., $0 \leq j \leq z$) and the capital-rich country exports the capital intensive range of goods with indices higher than z (i.e., $z \leq j \leq 1$).

The boundary good z and the wage–rental ratios of both countries are determined endogenously through the trade balance condition and the factor market equilibrium conditions in both countries. The expenditure of country A on the capital intensive range of goods is equal to the import of country A; similarly, the expenditure of country B on the labor intensive range of goods is equal to the import of country B. Therefore, the trade balance condition requires $\int_z^1 p_j x_j^A \mathrm{d}j = \int_0^z p_j x_j^B \mathrm{d}j$. Taking account of the demand function and the price–cost equality for the boundary good z, we

---

[27]Consider a model with (finitely many) n goods and m factors and suppose that $n > m$. Then, the degree of freedom in production becomes $n - m$. That is, given that the situation is in an *interior equilibrium*, we can change the production of $n - m$ goods arbitrarily (but small in size) without violating any of the equilibrium conditions.

obtain

$$\frac{z}{1-z} = \frac{L^A}{L^B} \cdot \frac{a_{Lz}(\omega^B)}{a_{Lz}(\omega^B)} \cdot \frac{\omega^A + k^A}{\omega^A + k_z(\omega^A)} \cdot \frac{\omega^B + k_z(\omega^B)}{\omega^B + k^B}. \tag{3.27}$$

The factor market equilibrium condition in each country can be written as follows:

$$G^A(\omega^A, k^A, z) \equiv \int_0^z \frac{k_j(\omega^A) - k^A}{\omega^A + k_j(\omega^A)} \mathrm{d}j = 0, \tag{3.28}$$

$$G^B(\omega^B, k^B, z) \equiv \int_z^1 \frac{k_j(\omega^B) - k^B}{\omega^B + k_j(\omega^B)} \mathrm{d}j = 0. \tag{3.29}$$

For each $s = A, B$, function G^s is increasing both in ω^s and z and decreasing in k^s. An increase z means that labor-rich country A produces more capital intensive goods; while capital-rich country B produces less labor intensive goods.[28] Therefore, an increase in z leads to simultaneous decreases in the wage–rental ratios in both countries. Trade equilibrium is described by the system (3.27)–(3.29), which determines z, ω^A and ω^B simultaneously.[29]

---

[28] Note that the boundary good z is the most capital intensive among those goods produced in country A, but the least capital intensive in country B.

[29] Although we can conduct comparative statics analysis based on the system, we omit it here because the most of the results are somewhat ambiguous.

Chapter 4

Free Trade and Welfare

How does international trade affect the welfare of people? By participating in international trade, can everyone improve their standard of living? If some (though not all) people were to suffer from trade liberalization, what can we do for them? These are long-standing questions in international trade to which a great deal of theoretical efforts have been devoted and a vast number of results has been accumulated under the title of *gains-from-trade propositions*. This chapter addresses the gains-from-trade propositions and related issues in the competitive circumstance. We first introduce some welfare criteria and investigate their implications for the existence of so-called *social utility functions*. Based on a social utility function, we prove the basic gains-from-trade proposition. Roughly, we can say that "free trade is better than no trade". Then, we turn to the cases where trade liberalization would bring about conflicts of interests among people in a country. We show that the conflict among people can be dissolved or mitigated if trade liberalization is accompanied by some appropriate redistribution policies. We also introduce some useful analytical tools such as the *trade utility function*, *trade indifference curve*, and the *offer curve*.

4.1 Welfare Criteria

In what sense can we say that free trade is "better" than no trade? For a single person or a single household who possesses a well-defined utility function, the answer is simple and straightforward: one state of the world (e.g., free trade) is "better" than another (e.g., autarky) if the former gives rise to a higher utility than the latter. For a country consisting of many households, the situation is different and complicated. In order to make meaningful statements about the effects of trade liberalization on the welfare of a country, we have to clarify what is meant by the "welfare of a country" or in what case and on what ground we can say that a group of households (i.e., a country) is made better-off. In this section, we introduce and examine several welfare criteria. We are particularly interested in the relations of those criteria to the notion of *social utility function*, which is introduced in several different contexts. If we can presume a meaningful social utility function (based on certain welfare criteria), we can treat the "welfare of a country" in the same way as the welfare of a single household and, therefore, can make things considerably simple.

Notation: We consider an economy consisting of finitely many households.[1] Let H be the (finite) set of households. We assume that the consumption space is $\mathbb{R}^n_+$ for all households. A consumption vector of household h is denoted by $x_h \equiv (x_{h1}, x_{h2}, \ldots, x_{hn}) \in \mathbb{R}^n_+$. Household h possesses a well-behaved utility function $U_h : \mathbb{R}^n_+ \to \mathbb{R}$, which is continuous, monotonic, and quasi-concave as usually assumed. The utility index of household h is denoted by u_h $(= U_h(x_h))$. An array of the consumption vectors of the households, $X \equiv \{x_h\}_{h \in H}$, is called a *consumption allocation*. For an aggregate consumption vector x, the *feasible set of consumption allocations* of x is defined by $\mathscr{A}(x) \equiv \{\{x_h\}_{h \in H} | \ x = \sum_{h \in H} x_h\}$. For a subset Z of the consumption space, we write $\mathscr{A}(Z) \equiv \bigcup_{x \in Z} \mathscr{A}(x)$. A vector consisting of utility indices $\mu \equiv (u_h)_{h \in H}$ is called a *utility vector*. A utility vector that corresponds to a consumption allocation $X = \{x_h\}_{h \in H}$ is denoted by $\mu(X) \equiv (U_h(x_h))_{h \in H}$.

4.1.1 *Pareto Criterion*

If a change in the situation in an economy with many households makes no one worse-off, while someone better-off, then people in this economy may

---

[1]The range of an "economy" here depends on the context under consideration: it can be a single country or the world economy as a whole.

agree to say that "this change is socially desirable" or that "the resulting situation is socially preferable to the initial situation". The Pareto criterion is a social value judgment based on unanimous agreements (in a weak sense):

Definition 4.1 (Pareto-Superiority and Pareto Criterion). For two consumption allocations $X' = \{x'_h\}_{h \in H}$ and $X'' = \{x''_h\}_{h \in H}$, we say that X' is Pareto-superior to X'' or that X' Pareto-dominates X'' if the following two conditions are satisfied:

(i) $U_h(x'_h) \geq U_h(x''_h)$ for all $h \in H$, and
(ii) $U_k(x'_k) > U_k(x''_k)$ for some $k \in H$.

When X' Pareto-dominates X'', we write $X' >_P X''$.[2] The "Pareto criterion" is such a social value judgment that a consumption allocation is considered to be "socially preferable" to another if the former Pareto-dominates the latter.[3]

Given a subset Z of the consumption space, a feasible consumption allocation $X' \in \mathscr{A}(Z)$ is said to be *Pareto-efficient* (relative to Z) if there is no feasible $X'' \in \mathscr{A}(Z)$ that Pareto-dominates X'.

In vector form, two conditions in the definition of Pareto-superiority are equivalent to $\mu(X') > \mu(X'')$. When a consumption allocation changes to another that Pareto-dominates the former, we call such a change in the situation as a *Pareto improvement*. As is obvious from the definition, the binary relation $>_P$ is *transitive*: if $X' >_P X''$ and $X'' >_P X'''$ for three consumption allocations, then we have $X' >_P X'''$. Successive Pareto-improvements from an initial consumption allocation give rise to an eventual Pareto-improvement. The binary relation $>_P$, however, fails to be *complete*. That is, there can be a pair of two consumption allocations X' and X'' such that neither $X' >_P X''$ nor $X'' >_P X'$. If this is the case, the Pareto criterion

---

[2] When (i) is satisfied, we say that X' is *Pareto-non-inferior* to X'', or that X' *weakly Pareto-dominates* X'', and write $X' \geqslant_P X''$.

[3] Strictly speaking, the definition of Pareto-superiority here is the one for the *weak Pareto-superiority*; the social value judgment based on the weak Pareto-superiority is called the *strong Pareto criterion*. On the other hand, when $U_h(x'_h) > U_h(x''_h)$ for all $h \in H$, we say that X' is *strongly Pareto-superior* to X'' or that X' *strongly Pareto-dominates* X''. The social value judgment based on the strong Pareto-superiority is called the *weak Pareto criterion*. See Boadway and Bruce (1984).

tells nothing about which consumption allocation is more desirable from the point of view of the economy as a whole.

What can be said about the welfare effects of trade liberalization based on the Pareto criterion? Does trade liberalization bring about a Pareto improvement for the country? Unfortunately, the answer is not necessarily positive. It suffices to consider the Stolper-Samuelson theorem. Suppose that the price of the capital intensive good increases due to trade liberalization. Since the real rental rate increases and the real wage rate decreases, the utility indices of capital owners definitely increase, while those of laborers decrease. In this case, the change in the consumption allocations due to trade liberalization cannot be ranked by the Pareto criterion. The Pareto criterion is too strong a condition to be applied to evaluate the welfare effects of trade liberalization of a country with many (heterogeneous) households.

4.1.2 *Social Utility Function*

Single-household assumption: In international trade theories, it is frequently assumed that the household sector of a country consists of a single household or an individual, who owns all the resources of the country. Let U be the utility function of "the household" of a country; U is assumed to satisfy usual properties of continuity, monotonicity, and quasi-concavity. With the single-household assumption, the well-being of a "country" as a whole is identified with that of "the household". That is, if $U(x') > U(x'')$ for two aggregate consumption bundles x' and x'', we say that x' is *socially preferable* to x'' or that the country is better-off at x' than at x''. In this sense, the utility function U of "the household" can be called the *social utility function*. The single-household assumption is equivalent to assuming the existence of the social utility function. The welfare judgment based on the social utility function is both *transitive* and *complete*.

Under the single-household assumption, the demand structure of a country is described by the *social demand function* D derived from U, which depends on the prices of goods and the "total income" of the country: $D(p, I)$, where p and I denote the price vector and the total income, respectively. The social demand function behaves exactly the same as the demand function of an individual; that is, D is continuous and homogeneous of degree zero in (p, I) and the Slutzky matrix derived from D is symmetric and negative semi-definite.[4]

Behavior of the aggregate demand function: Without the assumption of social utility function, the demand structure of a country with many households is described by the *aggregate demand function* $D^\sharp$ obtained by adding up the individual demand functions of the households in the country: $D^\sharp(p, \{I_h\}_{h \in H}) \equiv \sum_{h \in H} D_h(p, I_h)$, where D_h and I_h denote the demand function and income of household h, respectively. In general, the behavior of the aggregate demand function $D^\sharp$ is different from a demand function of an individual, because it depends on the "income distribution" among households — even if the total income $I \equiv \sum_{h \in H} I_h$ is fixed, the total demand for goods can change when the income distribution $\{I_h\}_{h \in H}$ changes. The aggregate demand function cannot be regarded as if it were derived from the maximization of a social utility function. Thinking of it in the other way around, if the aggregate demand function $D^\sharp$ behaves in the same way as a demand function of an individual, we can presume the existence of a *fictitious social utility function* that generates $D^\sharp$. Further, if this is the case, it might be possible to attach some welfare implications to this fictitious social utility function.

If the aggregate demand function $D^\sharp$ were to be equivalent to the social demand function derived from a social utility function, it has to be independent of income distributions among households. In other words, the total demand must not be affected by any changes in income distribution that keep the total income unchanged. By totally differentiating the definition of the aggregate demand function $D^\sharp$ with respect to income distribution with keeping the total income unchanged (i.e., $dI = 0 = dI_1 + \sum_{h \in H \setminus \{1\}} dI_h$), we obtain

$$\sum_{h \in H \setminus \{1\}} \left\{ \frac{\partial D_h(p, I_h)}{\partial I_h} - \frac{\partial D_1(p, I_1)}{\partial I_1} \right\} dI_h = 0.$$

Because, for any $h \in H \setminus \{1\}$, the sign of dI_h can be set either positive or negative arbitrarily, then every parenthesized term in the above equation

---

[4]It is well known that these restrictions on the demand function and the Slutzky matrix are all that can be derived from the utility maximization hypothesis.

must be zero. Therefore, we have

$$\frac{\partial D_1(p, I_1)}{\partial I_1} = \frac{\partial D_h(p, I_h)}{\partial I_h} \quad \text{for all } h \in H \backslash \{1\}. \tag{4.1}$$

This means that, for any p and any income distribution $\{I_h\}_{h \in H}$, the "income effects" of all the households must be identical.

Two sufficient conditions for Eq. (4.1) are known. One is that all the households share the same homothetic preference. In this case, the individual demand function can be written as a linear function of income: for $h \in H$,

$$D_h(p, I_h) \equiv \phi(p) I_h.$$

The income effects are identical for all households: $\partial D_h(p, I_h) / \partial I_h = \phi(p)$. Clearly, the aggregate demand function becomes independent of the income distribution: $D^\sharp(p, \{I_h\}_{h \in H}) = \phi(p) \{\sum_{h \in H} I_h\} = \phi(p) I$.

The other sufficient condition is that the utility functions of all the households are quasi-linear in a common good (say, good n): for $h \in H$,

$$U_h(x_1, x_2, \ldots, x_{n-1}, x_n) \equiv U_h^\circ(x_1, x_2, \ldots, x_{n-1}) + x_n,$$

where U_h° is the sub-utility function of household h defined over the non-numéraire goods. In this case, the demand function of household h becomes as follows: for $h \in H$,

$$D_{hj}(p, I_h) \equiv \begin{cases} \phi_{hj}(\tilde{p}) & \text{for } j = 1, 2, \ldots, n-1, \\ \{I_h - \sum_{i \neq n} p_i \phi_{hi}(\tilde{p})\} / p_n & \text{for } j = n, \end{cases}$$

where $\tilde{p}$ denotes $(n-1)$-vector of the relative prices in terms of good n for the non-numéraire goods. Therefore, the income effects become as follows: for $h \in H$,

$$\frac{\partial D_h(p, I_h)}{\partial I_h} = (\underbrace{0, 0, \ldots, 0}_{n-1 \text{ zeros}}, 1/p_n).$$

In both cases, we can (re)write the aggregate demand function as a function of the price vector and the total income: $D^\sharp(p, \{I_h\}_{h \in H}) \equiv D^\sharp(p, I)$, where $I \equiv \sum_{h \in H} I_h$.

Fictitious social utility function: In the theory of consumer behavior, the problem of recovering the utility function from a given demand system is known as the "integrability problem" — if the Slutzky matrix derived from a demand function is symmetric and negative semi-definite, then there exists a quasi-concave utility function that generates the demand function.[5] With this result, we can establish the following theorem:

Proposition 4.1. *There exists a fictitious social utility function that generates the aggregate demand function* $D^{\sharp}$ *if either one of the following conditions is satisfied:*

(i) *all the households share the same homothetic preference[6]; or*
(ii) *the utility functions of all the households are quasi-linear in a common good.[7]*

Proof. It suffices to show that the Slutzky matrix

$$S^{\sharp} \equiv \left[\frac{\partial D_i^{\sharp}}{\partial p_j} + x_j \frac{\partial D_i^{\sharp}}{\partial I} \right]_{i,j=1,\ldots,n}$$

derived from the aggregate demand function $D^{\sharp}(p, I)$ is symmetric and negative semi-definite. Let

$$S_h \equiv \left[\frac{\partial D_{hi}}{\partial p_j} + x_{hj} \frac{\partial D_{hi}}{\partial I_h} \right]_{i,j=1,\ldots,n}$$

be the Slutzky matrix derived from the individual demand function $D_h(p, I_h)$. For each $h \in H$, because D_h is derived through the usual procedure of utility maximization by household h, S_h is symmetric and negative semi-definite. Under one of the conditions in the theorem, it is easy to verify that $S^{\sharp} = \sum_{h \in H} S_h$. Therefore, $S^{\sharp}$ is also symmetric and negative semi-definite. □

Let $U^{\sharp}$ be the fictitious social utility function recovered from the aggregate demand function $D^{\sharp}$. What welfare implications can we infer from $U^{\sharp}$?

---

[5]For a rigorous treatment of the integrability problem, see Hurwicz and Uzawa (1971).
[6]See Gorman (1953). For more modern treatment on this problem based on the duality theory, see Diewert (1980).
[7]See Kawamata (1991, Chapter 6).

We now show the following lemma that characterizes the fictitious social utility function:

Lemma 4.1. *Suppose the conditions in Proposition 4.1 are satisfied and, therefore, there exists a fictitious social utility function $U^{\sharp}$. Then, the utility index that $U^{\sharp}$ assigns to an aggregate consumption vector x represents the maximum sum of the utility indices of households that can be attained by distributing x among the households in a Pareto-efficient way.*

Proof. (Since the same argument applies to both cases as well, we only consider the case where all the households share the same homothetic preference.) Let U be the homothetic utility function common to all the households. Without loss of generality, we can assume U is linearly homogeneous. Then, for each $h \in H$, the individual demand function and the individual expenditure function can be written as follows: $D_h(p, I_h) \equiv \phi(p)I_h$ and $E_h(p, u_h) \equiv e(p)u_h$, where u_h is the utility index of household h. On the other hand, the aggregate demand function becomes $D^{\sharp}(p, I) \equiv \sum_{h \in H} D_h(p, I_h) \equiv \phi(p)I$, where $I \equiv \sum_{h \in H} I_h$ is the total income. Since the functional forms of D_h and $D^{\sharp}$ are identical, the fictitious social utility function $U^{\sharp}$ that generates $D^{\sharp}$ takes the same form as the common utility function U. Therefore, the (social) expenditure function that corresponds to $U^{\sharp}$ also takes the same form as the individual expenditure function: $E^{\sharp}(p, u) \equiv e(p)u$, where u is the (social) utility index.

Let $\bar{u}$ be an arbitrary (social) utility index and let us take an arbitrary aggregate consumption vector $\bar{x}$ from the boundary of an *upper contour set* $\{x \mid U^{\sharp}(x) \geq \bar{u}\}$ with respect to the fictitious social utility function. We have $\bar{u} = U^{\sharp}(\bar{x})$. Due to the supporting-hyperplane theorem,[8] there exists a shadow price vector $\bar{p}$ such that $\bar{p}\bar{x} = \bar{I} \equiv E^{\sharp}(\bar{p}, \bar{u}) \equiv e(\bar{p})\bar{u}$. By duality, we have $\bar{x} = D^{\sharp}(\bar{p}, \bar{I}) \equiv \phi(\bar{p})\bar{I}$. Let us consider an arbitrary income distribution $\{I_h\}_{h \in H}$ that satisfies $\bar{I} = \sum_{h \in H} I_h$. We have $\sum_{h \in H} D_h(\bar{p}, I_h) = \phi(\bar{p}) \sum_{h \in H} I_h = \phi(\bar{p})\bar{I} = \bar{x}$, which means that the income distribution gives rise to a *Pareto-efficient* consumption allocation of the given $\bar{x}$ among the households.[9] For $\{I_h\}_{h \in H}$, the equality $I_h = E_h(\bar{p}, u_h)$ determines the utility

---

[8]For the supporting-hyperplane theorem, see Takayama (1985).

[9]The converse is also true: for any Pareto-efficient consumption allocation of $\bar{x}$, there exists an income distribution satisfying $\sum_{h \in H} I_h = \bar{I}$ that realizes the consumption allocation.

index u_h of household h; by summing this relation over all households, we have $\bar{I} = \sum_{h \in H} I_h = \sum_{h \in H} E_h(\bar{p}, u_h) \equiv e(\bar{p}) \sum_{h \in H} u_h$. Combining these results, we obtain $\bar{u} = \sum_{h \in H} u_h$. That is, for any $\bar{x} \in \{x \mid U^\sharp(x) = \bar{u}\}$, the maximum sum of the utility indices of households that can be attained by allocating $\bar{x}$ efficiently among the households is equal to $\bar{u}$. □

What can be said about the social desirability (based on the Pareto criterion) of two aggregate consumption vectors x' and x'' by making use of the information obtained from the fictitious social utility function? Let $X' = \{x'_h\}_{h \in H}$ and $X'' = \{x''_h\}_{h \in H}$ be Pareto-efficient consumption allocations associated with x' and x'', respectively; we have $x' = \sum_{h \in H} x'_h$ and $x'' = \sum_{h \in H} x''_h$. In addition, let us define $u'_h = U_h(x'_h)$ and $u''_h = U_h(x''_h)$ for all $h \in H$. Then, by Lemma 4.1, we have $U^\sharp(x') = \sum_{h \in H} u'_h$ and $U^\sharp(x'') = \sum_{h \in H} u''_h$. If X' is Pareto-superior to X'', we have $\sum_{h \in H} u'_h > \sum_{h \in H} u''_h$, which is equivalent to $U^\sharp(x') > U^\sharp(x'')$. However, $U^\sharp(x') > U^\sharp(x'')$ does not necessarily imply the Pareto-superiority of X' over X''; it can be the case that $u'_h > u''_h$ for some $h \in H$, while $u'_k < u''_k$ for other $k \in H$. Therefore, even if $U^\sharp(x') > U^\sharp(x'')$ holds true, we cannot say (based on the Pareto criterion) that x' is socially preferable to x''.

By the way, if $U^\sharp(x') > U^\sharp(x'')$ holds true, it is always possible, even in the case where X' and X'' cannot be ranked by the Pareto criterion, to show that there exists a consumption allocation $X^\circ \in \mathscr{A}(x')$ that Pareto-dominates X'' and that there is *no* consumption allocation in $\mathscr{A}(x'')$ that Pareto-dominates X'. The fictitious social utility function carries information about the *possibilities* that an aggregate consumption vector can be reallocated among the households so that the resulting consumption allocation will be Pareto-superior to a consumption allocation associated with another aggregate consumption vector. In this sense, the fictitious social utility function can be considered an indicator of the *potential Pareto-superiority* of an aggregate consumption vector over another (as far as it is defined well).

4.1.3 *Revealed Preference in the Aggregate*

Suppose that, in the competitive circumstance, household h actually chooses x'_h when price vector p' prevails. If $p'x'_h \geq p'x''_h$ for another consumption vector x_h'', we say that x_h' is *revealed preferred* to x_h'' by household h. If x_h' is revealed preferred to x_h'', we can infer that $U_h(x_h') \geq U_h(x_h'')$.[10] By extending this argument to the relation among aggregate consumption vectors, we can establish another welfare criterion.

Definition 4.2 (Revealed Preference in the Aggregate). Let $X' \equiv \{x_h'\}_{h \in H}$ be an consumption allocation realized when the price vector is given by p', and $X'' \equiv \{x_h''\}_{h \in H}$ be another consumption allocation. Further, let x' and x'' be the aggregate consumption vectors associated with X' and X'', respectively. If

$$p'x' \geq p'x'', \tag{4.2}$$

we say that x' is "socially preferable" to x'' in the sense of the revealed preference in the aggregate.[11]

For X' and X'', if $p'x_h' \geq p'x_h''$ for all $h \in H$ with at least one strict inequality, Eq. (4.2) holds true (with strict inequality) and, moreover, we can say that X' is Pareto-superior to X''. However, even if Eq. (4.2) holds true with strict inequality, it is possible to have $p'x_h' < p'x_h''$ for some $h \in H$; in this case, X' may fail to be Pareto-superior to X''. The welfare comparison based on Eq. (4.2) involves a stronger value judgment than the Pareto criterion, which is related to how we evaluate the *possibilities of potential Pareto-improvements*. We can show the following theorem:

Proposition 4.2. *Suppose that Eq. (4.2) holds for two aggregate consumption vectors x' and x'' associated with two consumption allocations X' and X'', respectively. Then, there is no consumption allocation in $\mathscr{A}(x'')$ that Pareto-dominates X'.*

Proof. Suppose, in negation, that there exists a consumption allocation $\{x_h\}_{h \in H} \in \mathscr{A}(x'')$ that Pareto-dominates X'. Then, we must have $p'x_h \geq p'x_h'$ for all $h \in H$ with at least one strict inequality. Summing these inequalities over $h \in H$, we obtain $p'x'' = p'(\sum_{h \in H} x_h) > p'x'$ — a contradiction.   □

---

[10]If $p'x_h' > p'x_h''$, we can infer that $U_h(x_h') > U_h(x_h'')$.
[11]Ohyama (1972) have introduced this criterion and used to examine various issues such as gains from trade, economic growth, customs unions, and so forth.

It should be noted that the criterion (4.2) of the revealed preference in the aggregate has nothing to do with the existence of a fictitious social utility function. If, however, there exists a fictitious social utility function $U^\sharp$ that generates the social demand function, Eq. (4.2) implies $U^\sharp(x') \geq U^\sharp(x'')$.

4.1.4 *The Compensation Principle*

People in an economy may easily agree to say that "a change in the situation is socially desirable" if the change entails a Pareto-improvement. In this sense, the Pareto criterion involves a *weak* value judgment. However, in many practical cases, the conditions for Pareto-improvement are hardly met — changes in the situation tend to make some people better off and the others worse off. The Pareto criterion is not applicable to those cases. As far as we stick to the Pareto criterion, we can seldom make a meaningful judgment about whether a particular change in the situation (e.g., trade liberalization) is socially desirable or not.

The Pareto criterion directly compares two consumption allocations. In contrast, the compensation principle *indirectly* compares two consumption allocations by taking account of the possibility of reallocating available aggregate consumption bundle(s) among households and, thereby, extend the applicability of the Pareto criterion. To define the compensation principle formally, we need to introduce some new concepts. A *state* is a subset of available aggregate consumption vectors, denoted by A, B, and so forth. For a given state $A \subset \mathbb{R}^n_+$, a consumption allocation $X = \{x_h\}_{h \in H}$ is said to be "feasible in A" if there exists $x \in A$ such that $\sum_{h \in H} x_h = x$. The set of all consumption allocations that are feasible in A is denoted by $\mathscr{A}(A)$. A *situation* is a pair (A, X) of a state A and a feasible consumption allocation $X \in \mathscr{A}(A)$. If a particular consumption allocation is (known to be) realized when the set of available aggregate consumption bundles is A, we write the consumption allocation as $X^A = \{x_h^A\}_{h \in H}$. Moreover, we call the pair (A, X^A) as "situation A" for simplicity. The set of all possible situations is denoted by $\mathscr{S}$.

The compensation principle is described by binary relations on $\mathscr{S}$. Depending on the differences in the feasibility of reallocations of aggregate consumption bundles, there are several variations of the compensation principle.

Definition 4.3 (Kaldor Criterion: Kaldor, 1939). For $(A, X^A), (B, X^B) \in$ $\mathscr{S}$, we say that situation A is socially preferable to situation B in the Kaldor sense if there exists a consumption allocation $X \in \mathscr{A}(A)$ that Pareto-dominates X^B. In this case, we write $(A, X^A) >_K (B, X^B)$.

Suppose that situation B is the status quo of an economy and that the economy is moving from situation B toward situation A. Some households are going to be better-off and others worse-off by the transition from situation B to situation A; in other words, there are some "winners" and "losers" of this transition. The Kaldor criterion says that if it is *possible* for the winners to compensate the losers for their losses by transferring some of the resources/goods in situation A and make everyone better-off than in situation B, then (even if the compensation is not actually carried out) the transition from situation B to situation A is socially desirable.

The next criterion is close to the Kaldor criterion in its spirit.

Definition 4.4 (Hicks Criterion: Hicks, 1940). For $(A, X^A), (B, X^B) \in \mathscr{S}$, we say that situation A is socially preferable to situation B in the Hicks sense if there is no consumption allocation $X \in \mathscr{A}(B)$ that Pareto-dominates X^A. In this case, we write $(A, X^A) >_H (B, X^B)$.

The Hicks criterion says that if it is *not possible* for the losers of the transition from situation B to situation A to dissuade the winners to give up the transition by transferring some of the resources/goods in situation B, then the transition from situation B to situation A is socially desirable. As is obvious from the definitions of the Kaldor and Hicks criteria, we have $(A, X^A) >_K (B, X^B)$ if and only if $(B, X^B) >_H (A, X^A)$ is *not* satisfied.

Both of the Kaldor and Hicks criteria can make a contradictory judgment. For example, it is possible to have two situations that satisfy $(A, X^A) >_K (B, X^B)$ and $(B, X^B) >_K (A, X^A)$ simultaneously. That is, the Kaldor criterion does not necessarily satisfy the *asymmetry*; this is known as the *Scitovsky paradox* (Scitovsky, 1941). The same argument also applies to the Hicks criterion. To avoid this inconsistency, Scitovsky (1941) has proposed another criterion:

Definition 4.5 (Scitovsky Criterion: Scitovsky, 1941). For (A, X^A), $(B, X^B) \in \mathscr{S}$, we say that situation A is socially preferable to situation B in the Scitovsky sense if both $(A, X^A) \succ_K (B, X^B)$ and $(A, X^A) \succ_H (B, X^B)$ are satisfied. In this case, we write $(A, X^A) \succ_{Sc} (B, X^B)$.

Unfortunately, the Scitovsky criterion may fail to be *transitive*; that is, there can be three situations such that $(A, X^A) \succ_{Sc} (B, X^B)$, $(B, X^B) \succ_{Sc} (C, X^C)$, and $(C, X^C) \succ_{Sc} (A, X^A)$. This is known as the *Gorman paradox* (Gorman, 1955). The inconsistencies in the Kaldor, Hicks, and Scitovsky criteria are caused by the asymmetric treatment of the situations under consideration. When, for example, we judge which of the situations (A, X^A) and (B, X^B) is socially desirable according to the Kaldor criterion, we fix the consumption allocation X^B as a reference point and compare it with other consumption allocations that are feasible in situation A. The possibility of reallocations of the resources in only one of the situations is taken account, while that in the other situation is ignored. The Kaldor, Hicks, and Scitovsky criteria are based on one-to-many comparisons of consumption allocations. The following criterion treats the situations symmetrically and is based on many-to-many comparisons of consumption allocations:

Definition 4.6 (Samuelson Criterion: Samuelson, 1950). For (A, X^A), $(B, X^B) \in \mathscr{S}$, we say that situation A is socially preferable to situation B in the Samuelson sense if for any $X' \in \mathscr{A}(B)$, there exists a consumption allocation $X'' \in \mathscr{A}(A)$ that Pareto-dominates X'. In this case, we write $(A, X^A) \succ_{Sm} (B, X^B)$.[12]

Although the Kaldor–Hicks criteria can be applied to many practical cases to which the Pareto criterion cannot be applied, they are the least consistent in that they may fail to be asymmetric. The Scitovsky criterion is asymmetric, but may fail to be transitive. The Samuelson criterion is logically consistent, but its applicability is narrow in scope. Obviously, there is a trade-off between the consistency of various criteria in the compensation principle and their applicability.

---

[12]The condition for $(A, X^A) \succ_{Sm} (B, X^B)$ can be weakened as follows: (i) for any $X' \in \mathscr{A}(B)$, there exists $X'' \in \mathscr{A}(A)$ that *weakly* Pareto-dominates X' and (ii) there exists at least one $X \in \mathscr{A}(B)$ that is Pareto-dominated by a consumption allocation in $\mathscr{A}(A)$.

Utility possibility frontier: To facilitate the understanding of the compensation principle, let us introduce the notion of *utility possibility frontier*. Given an aggregate consumption bundle $x \in \mathbb{R}_+^n$, we can define the *utility possibility set* for x, which is denoted by $\mathscr{U}(x) \equiv \{\mu(X) \mid X \in \mathscr{A}(x)\}$. The outer boundary of $\mathscr{U}(x)$ is called the *utility possibility surface (curve)* for x, which corresponds to the Pareto-efficient consumption allocations relative to x. Similarly, for a given subset $A \subset \mathbb{R}_+^n$ of aggregate consumption bundles, we can define the utility possibility set $\mathscr{U}(A) \equiv \bigcup_{x \in A} \mathscr{U}(x)$ for A. The outer boundary of $\mathscr{U}(A)$ is called the *utility possibility frontier* for A, which is nothing but the outer envelop of utility possibility surfaces for x in A.

Figure 4.1 illustrates some examples of the utility possibility frontiers in an economy with two households ($h = 1, 2$). The utility level of household 1 is measured horizontally, while that of household 2 vertically. Solid curves aa', bb', and cc' represent the utility possibility frontiers for situations (A, X^A), (B, X^B), and (C, X^C), respectively. Further, points μ^A, μ^B, and μ^C represent the utility vectors that correspond to the *actual* consumption allocations in the three situations: $\mu^k \equiv \mu(X^k)$ for $k = A, B, C$. (For the moment, ignore the broken curves in the figure.)

Since the utility possibility frontier bb' for situation B passes through the "northeast" of point μ^A, we can say that situation B is socially

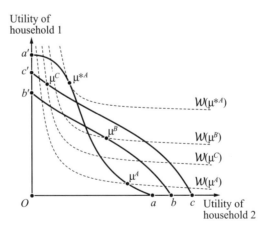

Fig. 4.1   Utility Possibility Frontiers and the Social Welfare Function

preferable to situation A according to the Kaldor criterion: $(B, X^B) \succ_{\mathrm{K}}$ (A, X^A). Also, we have $(B, X^B) \succ_{\mathrm{H}} (A, X^A)$, because the utility possibility frontier aa' for situation A *does not* go through the northeast of point μ^B. Combining these results, we obtain $(B, X^B) \succ_{\mathrm{Sc}} (A, X^A)$. Because aa' and bb' intersect with each other, the Samuelson criterion cannot be applied to the comparison of situations A and B. On the other hand, the utility possibility frontier cc' for situation C is located uniformly above bb', we have $(C, X^C) \succ_{\mathrm{Sm}} (B, X^B)$. Further, since aa' for situation A goes through the northeast of point μ^C and, at the same time, cc' for situation C also goes through the northeast of point μ^A, we have both $(A, X^A) \succ_{\mathrm{K}} (C, X^C)$ and $(C, X^C) \succ_{\mathrm{K}} (A, X^A)$ simultaneously — the Kaldor criterion makes a contradictory judgment and the Hicks criterion is silent about the comparison between situations A and C.

Relation to the fictitious social utility function: Let us consider two consumption allocations $X^A = \{x_h^A\}_{h \in H}$ and $X^B = \{x_h^B\}_{h \in H}$ and the corresponding aggregate consumption bundles $x^A \equiv \sum_{h \in H} x_h^A$ and $x^B = \sum_{h \in H} x_h^B$. For simplicity, we assume that X^k is Pareto-efficient relative to x^k for $k = A, B$. Define two situations $(\{x^A\}, X^A)$ and $(\{x^B\}, X^B)$ and call them as situation A and situation B, respectively.[13] Further, let $u_h^k = U_h(x_h^k)$ denote the utility level of household h in situation k; in vector form, $\mu^k \equiv \mu(X^k) \equiv (U_h(x_h^k))_{h \in H}$ for $k = A, B$. If the conditions in Proposition 4.1 are satisfied, there exists a fictitious social utility function $U^\sharp$.

By Lemma 4.1, we know that $U^\sharp(x^k) = \sum_{h \in H} u_h^k \geq \sum_{h \in H} U_h(x_h)$ for all consumption allocations $\{x_h\}_{h \in H} \in \mathscr{A}(x^k)$ for $k = A, B$.[14] Now suppose that $U^\sharp(x^A) > U^\sharp(x^B)$. We have $\sum_{h \in H} u_h^A = U^\sharp(x^A) > U^\sharp(x^B) = \sum_{h \in H} u_h^B \geq \sum_{h \in H} U_h(x_h)$ for all $\{x_h\}_{h \in H} \in \mathscr{A}(x^B)$. Then, we have $(\{x^A\}, X^A) \succ_{\mathrm{Sm}} (\{x^B\}, X^B)$. That is, we can say that situation A is socially preferable to situation B according to the Samuelson criterion.[15] Under the conditions in

---

[13]The expression $\{x^A\}$ in the definition of $(\{x^A\}, X^A)$ stands for a singleton set consisting of an aggregate consumption bundle x^A. The same is true for $(\{x^B\}, X^B)$.

[14]Actually, under the conditions in Proposition 4.1, we have $\sum_{h \in H} u_h^k = \sum_{h \in H} U_h(x_h^k)$ for all *Pareto-efficient* consumption allocations relative to x^k ($k = A, B$).

[15]Clearly, other criteria in the compensation principle also give the same judgment in favor of situation A.

Proposition 4.1, the judgment via the fictitious social utility function and the judgment via the compensation principle coincide with each other.

Relation to the revealed preference in the aggregate: Let $(\{x^A\}, X^A)$ and $(\{x^B\}, X^B)$ be situations A and B as defined in the previous paragraphs. Further, let p^A be the competitive price vector that prevails in situation A. Suppose that $p^A x^A \geq p^A x^B$ as in Eq. (4.2). That is, x^A is socially preferable to x^B in the sense of the revealed preference in the aggregate. Then, by Proposition 4.2, we know that there is no consumption allocation in situation B that Pareto-dominates X^A. Therefore, we have $(\{x^A\}, X^A) \succ_H (\{x^B\}, X^B)$. The judgment via the revealed preference in the aggregate implies the judgment via the Hicks criterion. In other words, the foundation of the value judgment behind the revealed preference in the aggregate is the Hicks criterion.

4.1.5 *Social Welfare Function*

The compensation principle faces some difficulties of the trade-off between the logical consistency and the applicability. One way to avoid those difficulties is to introduce the notion of *social welfare function*, which reflects the social value judgment in a society concerned. The domain and properties of a social welfare function may depend on various social considerations prevailed in a society such as ethics, morals, customs, traditions, ideologies, religious beliefs, and so forth. Let $\mathcal{W}$ denote the social welfare function. Here, we assume that the domain of $\mathcal{W}$ is the space of utility vectors:

$$\mathcal{W}(\mu) \equiv \mathcal{W}((u_h)_{h \in H}).$$

Further, we assume that $\mathcal{W}$ is monotonically increasing in its arguments; this follows from the Pareto criterion. Of course, the definition of $\mathcal{W}$ here reflects our consideration that the utilities of individuals (households) are the most important components of the social welfare and every individual should be respected.

Let $\mu(X')$ and $\mu(X'')$ be the utility vectors associated with two consumption allocations X' and X'', respectively. If $\mathcal{W}(\mu(X')) > \mathcal{W}(\mu(X''))$, then we can say that X' is socially preferable to X''; in addition, if $\mathcal{W}(\mu(X')) = \mathcal{W}(\mu(X''))$, we say that X' and X'' are *socially indifferent* to each other. In this way, we can define a binary relation $\succcurlyeq_{\mathcal{W}}$ over the set of all consumption allocations such that $X' \succcurlyeq_{\mathcal{W}} X''$ if and only if $\mathcal{W}(\mu(X')) \geq \mathcal{W}(\mu(X''))$. The binary relation $\succcurlyeq_{\mathcal{W}}$ represents the welfare judgment induced from the social welfare function $\mathcal{W}$. Obviously, $\succcurlyeq_{\mathcal{W}}$ is both *complete* and *transitive* as far as $\mathcal{W}$ is defined well. We shall write $X' \succ_{\mathcal{W}} X''$ if $X' \succcurlyeq_{\mathcal{W}} X''$ but not $X'' \succcurlyeq_{\mathcal{W}} X'$. Due to the monotonicity of $\mathcal{W}$, we have $X' \succ_{\mathcal{W}} X''$ if X' is Pareto-superior to X'' (i.e., if $X' \succ_P X''$); however, the converse is not necessarily true.

Figure 4.1 illustrates some examples. Points μ^A, μ^B, and μ^C corresponds to three consumption allocations X^A, X^B, and X^C, respectively: $\mu^k \equiv \mu(X^k)$ for $k = A, B, C$. The broken curves represent *iso-social-welfare curves*. Reflecting the monotonicity of the social welfare function, they are downward-sloping.[16] In the figure, we have $\mathcal{W}(\mu^B) > \mathcal{W}(\mu^C) > \mathcal{W}(\mu^A)$. Correspondingly, we have $X^B \succ_{\mathcal{W}} X^C$, $X^C \succ_{\mathcal{W}} X^A$, and $X^B \succ_{\mathcal{W}} X^A$.

Derived social utility function: Apparently, the notion of social welfare function by itself has nothing to do with the valuation of aggregate consumption bundles. However, we can derive a *social utility function* defined on the space of aggregate consumption bundles, which associates an aggregate consumption bundle x with the *maximum* social welfare that can be attained by reallocating x among the households:

$$U_{\mathcal{W}}(x) \equiv \max \{ \mathcal{W}(\mu(X)) \mid X \in \mathscr{A}(x) \}. \tag{4.3}$$

Let us denote the solution to the maximization problem appeared in the right-hand side of Eq. (4.3) by $X_{\mathcal{W}}(x)$. Following Chipman and Moore (1972), we call $X_{\mathcal{W}}(x)$ the $\mathcal{W}$-*optimal allocation* of an aggregate consumption bundle x among the households.[17] The welfare implication of the derived social utility function is straightforward: for two aggregate consumption bundles x' and x'', we have $U_{\mathcal{W}}(x') > U_{\mathcal{W}}(x'')$ if and only if x' can give rise to a higher level of social welfare (in terms of $\mathcal{W}$) than x'' by optimally allocating these bundles.

---

[16]Iso-social-welfare curves are not necessarily convex to the origin.
[17]For simplicity, we assume a unique solution for each x.

Concerning the properties of the derived social utility function, the following result is well known:

Proposition 4.3 (Negishi, 1963). *The social utility function $U_{\mathcal{W}}$ derived from the social welfare function $\mathcal{W}$ is monotonically increasing and quasi-concave in x if the following conditions are satisfied:*

   (i) *the social welfare function $\mathcal{W}(\mu)$ is monotonically increasing and quasi-concave in μ;*
   (ii) *for all $h \in H$, the utility function $U_h(x_h)$ is monotonically increasing and concave in x_h.*

Proof. For aggregate consumption bundles $x', x'' \in \mathbb{R}^n_+$, the corresponding $\mathcal{W}$-optimal allocations are denoted by $X' \equiv X_{\mathcal{W}}(x')$ and $X'' \equiv X_{\mathcal{W}}(x'')$, respectively. For an arbitrary λ with $0 \le \lambda \le 1$, let us define $x^\lambda \equiv \lambda x' + (1 - \lambda)x''$ and $X^\lambda \equiv \{x_h^\lambda\}_{h \in H} \equiv \lambda X' + (1 - \lambda)X''$. Clearly, we have $\sum_{h \in H} x_h^\lambda = x^\lambda$, that is, X^λ is feasible under x^λ. Note that X^λ may not be equal to $X_{\mathcal{W}}(x^\lambda)$. Then, we can show the following relations, which prove the quasi-concavity of $U_{\mathcal{W}}$:

$$U_{\mathcal{W}}(x^\lambda) \equiv \mathcal{W}(\mu(X_{\mathcal{W}}(x^\lambda))) \ge \mathcal{W}(\mu(X^\lambda)) \quad \text{(definition of } U_{\mathcal{W}})$$
$$\ge \mathcal{W}(\lambda\mu(X') + [1 - \lambda]\mu(X'')) \quad \text{(monotonicity and}$$
$$\text{concavity of } U_h)$$
$$\ge \min\{\mathcal{W}(\mu(X')), \mathcal{W}(\mu(X''))\} \quad \text{(quasi-concavity of } \mathcal{W})$$
$$= \min\{U_{\mathcal{W}}(x'), U_{\mathcal{W}}(x'')\}.$$

To show the monotonicity, suppose that $x' < x''$. Because the utility functions are monotonic, there exists a consumption allocation $X^\circ \equiv \{x_h^\circ\}_{h \in H}$ such that $\sum_{h \in H} x_h^\circ = x''$ and $\mu(X') < \mu(X^\circ)$. Then, we have

$$U_{\mathcal{W}}(x') \equiv \mathcal{W}(\mu(X')) < \mathcal{W}(\mu(X^\circ)) \le \mathcal{W}(\mu(X'')) \equiv U_{\mathcal{W}}(x'').$$

The first inequality follows from the monotonicity of $\mathcal{W}$ and the second from the definition of X''.   □

The social demand function: With the derived social utility function $U_{\mathcal{W}}$, we can define the social demand function, which depends on price vector p and the aggregate income I:[18]

$$D_{\mathcal{W}}(p, I) \equiv \arg\max_{x} \{U_{\mathcal{W}}(x) \mid px \leq I\}. \tag{4.4}$$

Let $D_h(p, I_h)$ be the individual demand function of household h, where I_h denotes the individual income level. A set of coefficients $\{\theta_h\}_{h \in H}$ satisfying $\theta_h \geq 0$ and $\sum_{h \in H} \theta_h = 1$ represents an income redistribution of the total income I which is redistributed among households such that $I_h = \theta_h I$ for all $h \in H$. The following result shows that the social demand function $D_{\mathcal{W}}$ can be obtained through the aggregation of individual demand functions accompanied by appropriate income redistribution policies.

Proposition 4.4 (Chipman and Moore, 1972). *For $D_{\mathcal{W}}(p, I)$, there exists an optimal income redistribution policy $\{\theta_h\}_{h \in H}$ such that*

$$X_{\mathcal{W}}(D_{\mathcal{W}}(p, I)) = \{D_h(p, \theta_h I)\}_{h \in H}. \tag{4.5}$$

That is, the $\mathcal{W}$-optimal allocation of $D_{\mathcal{W}}(p, I)$ can be realized by appropriately redistributing the total income among the households.

(Proof is omitted.) Of course, we have $D_{\mathcal{W}}(p, I) = \sum_{h \in H} D_h(p, \theta_h I)$ as far as the income redistribution policy $\{\theta_h\}_{h \in H}$ is chosen optimally.

Summary: We have considered several welfare criteria with paying particular attention to the relation to the existence and welfare implications of social utility functions. Figure 4.2 summarizes the results. The single-household assumption is equivalent to assuming the existence of a social utility function that has a clear welfare implications.

In the case of multiple households, there are two alternative routes that lead to the existence of a social utility function. One is to restrict the preferences or utility functions of households. If all the households share the same homothetic preference or possess utility functions that are quasi-linear in a common numéraire good, then there exists a fictitious social utility function $U^{\sharp}$ (Proposition 4.1). However, the fictitious social utility function $U^{\sharp}$ by itself does not carry any welfare implications; it is only a demand-generating device. By introducing the compensation principle,

---

[18]For a given pair of p and I, $D_{\mathcal{W}}(p, I)$ is not a singleton set in general.

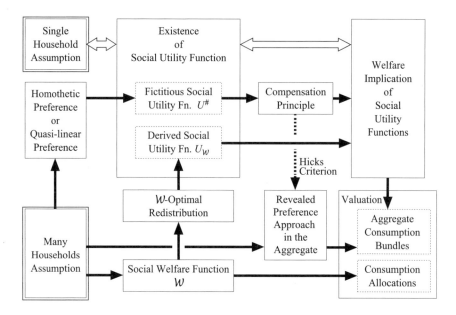

Fig. 4.2   Assumptions on Households, Social Utility Functions, and the Welfare Criteria

we can attach welfare implications to the fictitious social utility function. The other route is to introduce a social welfare function $\mathcal{W}$, from which we can derive a social utility function $U_{\mathcal{W}}$ that associates an aggregate consumption bundle x with the maximum social welfare attained by real-locating x among households optimally (in terms of $\mathcal{W}$).[19]

4.2   Gains from Trade and Income Redistribution

4.2.1   *Basic Proposition*

Once its meaning, implications, and limitations have been recognized well, we can safely make use of the notion of social utility function. Let U be the social utility function of a country. If $U(x') > U(x'')$ for two different consumption vectors x' and x'', we can say that the country is better-off

---

[19]Once a social welfare function has been introduced, we can judge the "welfare of a country" according to the social welfare function itself. We do not have to resort to the notion of social utility function.

at x' than at x''. In this case, we can easily establish the following *gains-from-trade proposition*:

Proposition 4.5 (Gains from Free Trade). *A country is better-off (not worse-off) under free trade than in autarky.*[20]

Proof. Let $\bar{x}$, $\bar{y}$, $\bar{p}$, $\bar{u}$ be the consumption, production, price vectors, and the utility level in autarky, respectively; also, let x, y, p, u be the corresponding variables under free trade. The expenditure function corresponding to U and the GDP function of this country are denoted by E and Y, respectively. Obviously, we have $\bar{u} = U(\bar{x})$ and $\bar{x} = \bar{y}$ in autarky, and $u = U(x)$ and $px = E(p,u) = Y(p) = py$ under free trade. Then, we obtain the following relation:

$$
\begin{aligned}
E(p,u) - E(p,\bar{u}) &= Y(p) - p\bar{y} + p\bar{x} - E(p,\bar{u}) + p\{\bar{y} - \bar{x}\} \\
&= [Y(p) - p\bar{y}] + [p\bar{x} - E(p,\bar{u})].
\end{aligned}
\tag{4.6}
$$

By the definitions of Y and E, we have $Y(p) - p\bar{y} \geq 0$ and $p\bar{x} - E(p,\bar{u}) \geq 0$. Hence, $E(p,u) - E(p,\bar{u}) \geq 0$. Since E is increasing in the utility index, we obtain $u \geq \bar{u}$. □

The first bracketed term in the right-hand side of Eq. (4.6) is called the *production gain* (or the *specialization gain*) and the second is called the *consumption gain* (or the *substitution gain*). The *trade gain* can be decomposed into these two non-negative effects. If the production possibility frontier has a sufficient curvature or if the indifference surface does so, one of the production gain and the consumption gain will become strictly positive. In this case, the trade gain will be strictly positive (i.e., $u > \bar{u}$).

Figure 4.3 illustrates the gains from trade and its decomposition into the production gain and the consumption gain. Curve ab represents the production possibility frontier (PPF) of a country. The autarkic equilibrium is attained at point e at which the PPF and an indifference curve $\bar{u}$ are tangent with each other. The slope of the common tangency line $\bar{\ell}$ represents the autarkic equilibrium price $\bar{p}$. Let us consider trade liberalization of the country. Suppose that the world market price p is higher than in autarky

[20]The first rigorous treatment of the gains-from-trade proposition was given by Samuelson (1938) and Samuelson (1939). Later, Kemp (1962) has extended Samuelson's arguments.

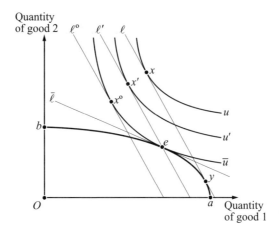

Fig. 4.3   Gains from Trade and Welfare Decomposition

as represented by the slope of line ℓ. The production point moves from point e to point y, where the marginal rate of transformation is equal to p. The budget line under free trade is represented by line ℓ; then the consumption point will be point x at which the budget line and an indifference curve u are tangent. Clearly, the household enjoys a higher utility level (i.e., $u > \bar{u}$) than at point e. This explains the gains from trade.

Now let us consider the welfare decomposition. Let u' be an utility index implicitly defined by $E(p, u') = p\bar{y}$ and let x° be the point that realizes $E(p, \bar{u})$, which is represented by line ℓ°. As illustrated in Fig. 4.3, x' is the utility maximizing point under the constraint of $px = p\bar{y}$ (i.e., line ℓ'). Then, the production gain can be represented by the gap between lines ℓ and ℓ', which corresponds to the difference in the utility indices $u - u' > 0$. Further, the consumption gain can be represented by the gap between lines ℓ' and ℓ°, which corresponds to the difference in the utility indices $u' - \bar{u} > 0$.

Although the consumption of a country in autarky has to be confined within the country's production possibility set, the consumption under free trade is no longer subject to this constraint. In other words, trade liberalization expands the "consumption possibility set" of a country — Roughly and intuitively speaking, this simple fact is the source of the gains from trade.

4.2.2 *Pareto-Improvement via Lump-sum Transfers*

Proposition 4.5, which relies on the existence of a social utility function, shows that the transition from autarky to free trade is *potentially beneficial* to a country with many households. This means that if trade liberalization is accompanied by some appropriate auxiliary policies, every household in a country can be made better-off (at least, cannot be made worse-off). In this and subsequent subsections, we consider two redistribution policies accompanying trade liberalization that can *realize* a Pareto-improvement.

Modification of the model: To simplify the exposition, we slightly modify the description of the model. In particular, we make no explicit distinction among consumption goods, intermediate goods, and primary factors of production.[21] We simply call those commodities as "goods". The space of production vectors is identified with $\mathbb{R}^n$. For a production vector $y = (y_1, y_2, \ldots, y_n)$, positive entries are interpreted as outputs, while negative entries as inputs. Therefore, given a price vector p, the profit obtained from y is represented by py.[22] The production technology (of a country) is described by the *production set* denoted by $\mathscr{Y}$. We assume that $\mathscr{Y}$ is a *closed convex cone*, which implies the constant-returns-to-scale (CRS) technology. On the other hand, the space of consumption vectors is identified with $\mathbb{R}_+^n$. Household h possesses a certain initial endowment of goods $\omega_h \in \mathbb{R}_+^n$. Then, given a price vector p, household h's budget constraint becomes $px_h \leq p\omega_h$. The aggregate initial endowment vector is denoted by $\omega \equiv \sum_{h \in H} \omega_h$. Given a production vector $y \in \mathscr{Y}$, the total supply of goods becomes $y + \omega$.

Grandmont–McFadden scheme: The first redistribution policy is based on lump-sum transfers among households. Under free trade, if a household can afford to buy the same consumption vector that the household actually consumed in autarky, then it can be made at least as well-off as in autarky. Let p be the price vector under free trade and $\bar{x}_h$ be the autarkic consumption vector of household h. If $p\bar{x}_h < p\omega_h$, household h can buy $\bar{x}_h$ under free trade without any financial support from the government. In this case,

---

[21] We are following the way of usual *general equilibrium analysis*.
[22] If good j is a production factor, then p_j represents the factor reward.

even if the government subtract a certain amount of money (i.e., $p\omega_h - p\bar{x}_h$) from household h, it can afford to buy $\bar{x}_h$. On the other hand, if $p\bar{x}_h > p\omega_h$, household h cannot buy $\bar{x}_h$ under free trade; household h needs to be compensated for the shortage of income (i.e., $p\bar{x}_h - p\omega_h$). The government can collect money by taxing the winners of trade liberalization and distribute it among the losers in a lump-sum fashion and, thereby, make everyone under free trade at least as well-off as in autarky.

Based on this idea, Grandmont and McFadden (1972) have proposed the following lump-sum transfer scheme, which we call the *Grandmont–McFadden (GM) scheme*:

$$T_h(p) \equiv [p\bar{x}_h - p\omega_h] + \theta_h \{Y(p) - p\bar{y}\}, \quad h \in H.$$

The bracketed term in the right-hand side above represents the shortage of household h's income that falls short of the amount necessary to buy the autarkic consumption vector. By the definition of the GDP function, we always have $Y(p) \geq p\bar{y}$, where $\bar{y}$ is the autarkic production vector.[23] The parameters θ_h ($h \in H$) are constants that satisfy $0 < \theta_h < 1$ and $\sum_{h \in H} \theta_h = 1$. Therefore, the second term, $\theta_h \{Y(p) - p\bar{y}\}$, represents a dividend of the production gain for household h.

If household h is given the transfer $T_h(p)$ after trade liberalization, then the disposable income becomes $p\omega_h + T_h(p)$. Accordingly, the budget constraint under the GM scheme becomes $px_h \leq p\omega_h + T_h(p) \equiv p\bar{x}_h + \theta_h \{Y(p) - p\bar{y}\}$. Because the dividend for household h is non-negative, household h can afford to buy the autarkic consumption vector $\bar{x}_h$ under free trade accompanying the GM scheme. If the production gain is strictly positive, household h can buy a consumption vector that is strictly better than $\bar{x}_h$; even if the production gain is zero, household h can do so as far as the indifference surface of the household has a sufficient curvature. Hence, we can say that trade liberalization accompanied by the GM scheme gives rise to a Pareto-improvement.

---

[23]The definition of the GDP function here is given by $Y(p) \equiv \max\{py|\, y \in \mathscr{Y}\}$. Because the production set $\mathscr{Y}$ does not depend on the endowment vector, so does Y as well. In addition, as far as $Y(p)$ is defined for p, we have $Y(p) = 0$ due to the CRS technology.

Fiscal feasibility: If $T_h(p) > 0$, household h receives a lump-sum subsidy. On the other hand, if $T_h(p) < 0$, household h pays a lump-sum tax. If the GM scheme generates a fiscal deficit, it cannot be feasible. Fortunately, because the total of the (net) payments to households is zero, the government can run a balanced budget under the GM scheme: for any p,

$$
\begin{aligned}
\sum_{h \in H} T_h(p) &\equiv \sum_{h \in H} [p\bar{x}_h - p\omega_h] + \sum_{h \in H} \theta_h [Y(p) - p\bar{y}] \\
&= p \sum_{h \in H} \bar{x}_h - p \sum_{h \in H} \omega_h + [Y(p) - p\bar{y}] \sum_{h \in H} \theta_h \\
&= p[\bar{x} - \bar{y} - \omega] + Y(p) = 0.
\end{aligned}
$$

To derive the last equality, we make use of the autarkic equilibrium condition $\bar{x} = \bar{y} + \omega$, where $\bar{x} \equiv \sum_{h \in H} \bar{x}_h$, and the fact that $Y(p) = 0$ due to the CRS technology.

4.2.3 *Pareto-Improvement via Consumption Tax/Subsidies*

In their celebrated textbook, Dixit and Norman (1980) have argued that a Pareto-improvement can be attained if trade liberalization is accompanied by some appropriate consumption tax-subsidy policies. Their argument goes as follows: (i) set the tax-subsidy vector t equal to the gap between the autarkic equilibrium price $\bar{p}$ and the free trade price p, i.e., $t = \bar{p} - p$; then (ii) under free trade, all households face the same price vector $p + t$ as in autarky and choose the same consumption vectors; (iii) with this tax-subsidy policy, the government's net revenue is non-negative; (iv) if the net revenue is strictly positive, the government can redistribute it among households by (slightly) lowering tax rates or raising subsidy rates; consequently, (v) every household will be made better-off than in autarky.

Unfortunately, the Dixit–Norman argument does not always hold true. By carefully examining the above argument, Kemp and Wan (1986) have pointed out that there are a set of economies in which a Pareto-improvement is possible only by lump-sum transfers and another set of economies in which a Pareto-improvement is possible only by non-lump-sum transfers; further, that neither set includes the other. In reply to the criticism by Kemp and Wan, Dixit and Norman (1986) have clarified conditions under which their argument for a Pareto-improvement via consumption tax-subsidy policy holds true. They have shown two critical conditions: one is the existence of *strict production gain* and the other is the *Weymark condition* (Weymark, 1979). The former condition is easy to explain. Let $\bar{p}$ and $\bar{y}$ be the autarkic price and production vectors, respectively. Then, we say that there exists a strict production gain if $Y(p) > p\bar{y}$ for $p \neq \bar{p}$.[24] The latter needs more detailed explanation.

Weymark condition: Let $E_h(p, u_h)$ and ω_h be the expenditure function and the initial endowment of household h, respectively. The budget constraint of household h becomes $E_h(p, u_h) = p\omega_h$. Then, changes in the utility indices of households induced by a (small) change in price vector can be written as follows: for $h \in H$,

$$\frac{\partial E_h}{\partial u_h} \mathrm{d}u_h + \left[\frac{\partial E_h}{\partial p} - \omega_h \right] \mathrm{d}p = 0.$$

Without loss of generality, we can normalize $\partial E_h / \partial u_h$ equal to unity for all $h \in H$.[25] By Shepard's lemma, we have $\partial E_h / \partial p = x_h$ for all $h \in H$. Then, we can summarize the above relations for all households in the following matrix form:

$$\mathbb{I}\mathrm{d}\mu + \mathbb{A}\mathrm{d}p = 0, \tag{4.7}$$

where $\mathbb{I}$ denotes the $|H| \times |H|$ identity matrix; $\mathbb{A}$ is a $|H| \times n$ matrix with its (h, j)-element being equal to $x_{hj} - \omega_{hj}$, which is the net consumption of good j by household h; in addition, we have $\mathrm{d}\mu \equiv (\mathrm{d}u_1, \ldots, \mathrm{d}u_{|H|})$ and $\mathrm{d}p = (\mathrm{d}p_1, \ldots, \mathrm{d}p_n)$.[26]

   If the linear equation system (4.7) has a solution such that $\mathrm{d}\mu > 0$ for some $\mathrm{d}p$, then we can say that such a price change $\mathrm{d}p$ induces a Pareto-improvement. According to Motzkin's Theorem of the Alternative, Eq. (4.7) has a solution $\mathrm{d}\mu > 0$ for some $\mathrm{d}p$ if and only if there is *no*

---

[24]The existence of strict production gain corresponds to the condition that the production surface has a sufficient curvature.

[25]We are concerned with small changes in prices and utilities in the neighborhood of the initial equilibrium.

[26]Here, $\mathrm{d}\mu$ and $\mathrm{d}p$ should be understood as "column" vectors.

$|H|$-vector $\lambda \equiv (\lambda_1, \ldots, \lambda_{|H|})$ that satisfies the following system[27]:

$$\lambda \mathbb{A} = 0 \quad \text{and} \quad \lambda > 0.$$

The jth equation in $\lambda \mathbb{A} = 0$ can be written as follows: for $j = 1, 2, \ldots, n$,

$$\sum_{h \in H} \lambda_h (x_{hj} - \omega_{hj}) = 0.$$

If, for some j, either $x_{hj} - \omega_{hj} > 0$ for all $h \in H$ or $x_{hj} - \omega_{hj} < 0$ for all $h \in H$, then we cannot choose $\lambda > 0$ so as to satisfy the above equation. The Weymark condition requires that there exists at least one good such that some households are (net) buyers of it and none are (net) sellers, or vice versa. If the Weymark condition is satisfied, there can be a Pareto-improving direction of price change dp; in other words, we can find a consumption allocation realized under the resulting price $p + dp$ that is Pareto-superior to the initial consumption allocation realized under price p.

Proposition 4.6 (Dixit–Norman Scheme: Dixit and Norman, 1986). *Suppose that the production technology exhibits constant-returns-to-scale and that the free trade price vector p is different from the autarkic price vector $\bar{p}$ (i.e., $p \neq \bar{p}$). If both (i) a strict production gain due to trade liberalization and (ii) the Weymark condition are satisfied, then there exists a consumption tax-subsidy policy with which the free trade equilibrium can be made Pareto-superior to the autarkic equilibrium.*

Proof. Let $\bar{p}$, $\bar{x} \equiv \sum_{h \in H} \bar{x}_h$, and $\bar{y}$ be the price, aggregate consumption, and production vectors in autarky; let p and y be the price and production vectors under free trade, respectively. The initial endowment vector of household h is denoted by ω_h; the aggregate initial endowment vector is denoted by $\omega \equiv \sum_{h \in H} \omega_h$. Due to the strict production gain, we have $py > p\bar{y}$. Substituting the autarkic equilibrium condition $\bar{y} = \bar{x} - \omega$ into this inequality, we obtain $py > p(\bar{x} - \omega)$. Then, we can choose a vector e such that $py = pe$ and $e \gg \bar{x} - \omega$.

By the Weymark condition, we can find a Pareto-improving direction of price change dp. Let $\tilde{p}$ be the resulting price vector, that is, $\tilde{p} = \bar{p} + dp$.

---

[27]For Motzkin's Theorem of the Alternative, see Mangasarian (1969).

Further, let $\tilde{x}_h$ be the consumption vector of household h that corresponds to $\tilde{p}$, that is, $\tilde{x}_h = D_h(\tilde{p}, \tilde{p}\omega_h)$ for $h \in H$; we have $\tilde{x} \equiv \sum_{h \in H} \tilde{x}_h$. If we choose a sufficiently small price change dp, then $\tilde{p}$ becomes sufficiently close to the autarkic price $\bar{p}$. Accordingly, due to the continuity of demand functions, we can set $\tilde{x}$ sufficiently close to $\bar{x}$ by choosing $\tilde{p}$ appropriately so that it satisfies $e \geq \tilde{x} - \omega$.

Now, let us define $g \equiv e - \tilde{x} + \omega$. By definition, g is a non-negative vector. Suppose that the government purchases g at the world market. The government's budget becomes as follows:

$$
\begin{aligned}
pg = p(e - \tilde{x} + \omega) &= py - p(\tilde{x} - \omega) \\
&= -p(\tilde{x} - \omega) \\
&= \tilde{p}(\tilde{x} - \omega) - p(\tilde{x} - \omega) \\
&= (\tilde{p} - p)(\tilde{x} - \omega).
\end{aligned}
$$

The first line follows from the definitions of g and e; the second line from the CRS technology (i.e., $py = 0$); the third line from the budget constraints of households (i.e., $\tilde{p}\tilde{x}_h = \tilde{p}\omega_h$ for all $h \in H$). Therefore, if we set the consumption tax-subsidy vector t equal to $\tilde{p} - p$, the government can purchase g under the balanced budget; the net tax revenue $t(\tilde{x} - \omega)$ just offsets the government's expenditure pg. Furthermore, because all households face the price vector $p + t$ $(= \tilde{p})$ under free trade with consumption tax-subsidy policy, they are made better-off than in autarky. (The government may redistribute the purchased goods to the households or just throw them away.)   □

4.3   Offer Curve and Free Trade Equilibrium

In this section, we introduce some analytical devices used to examine the trading equilibria and the welfare of countries. To do so, we now return to the usual description of the model: we assume that the preference of a country is described by a social utility function $U: \mathbb{R}_+^n \to \mathbb{R}$, which is monotonic and (strictly) quasi-concave and that the production sector is described by a production possibility set $\mathcal{Y} \subset \mathbb{R}_+^n$, which is convex and comprehensive.[28]

4.3.1   *Trade Utility Function*

When a country produces y and consumes x, the net import vector becomes $z \equiv x - y$. In other words, given z, the consumption vector x becomes $z + y$. The *trade utility function* W associates a given net import vector z with the maximum utility that can be attained by appropriately choosing a production vector y in $\mathcal{Y}$:

$$W(z) \equiv \max \{ U(z + y) \mid y \in \mathcal{Y} \}.$$

As is obvious from the definition, the trade utility function carries information about both the preference and the production possibility of a country; it provides us with an integrated way of describing international trade and the welfare of a country.

Properties of the trade utility function: The shape of the trade utility function W reflects the properties of the social utility function U and the production possibility set $\mathcal{Y}$. If U is monotonic, then W becomes monotonic, too. For z', z'' such that $z' < z''$,[29] there exist corresponding $y', y'' \in \mathcal{Y}$ such that $W(z') \equiv U(z' + y')$ and $W(z'') \equiv U(z'' + y'')$. Then, we have $W(z') \equiv U(z' + y') < U(z'' + y') \leq W(z'')$; this proves the monotonicity of W.

If U is quasi-concave and $\mathcal{Y}$ is convex, then W becomes quasi-concave. Let us take z' and z'' and let λ be an arbitrary real number with $0 \leq \lambda \leq 1$. Further, let us define $z^\lambda \equiv \lambda z' + [1 - \lambda]z''$. Then, there exist corresponding $y', y'' \in \mathcal{Y}$ such that $W(z') \equiv U(z' + y')$ and $W(z'') \equiv U(z'' + y'')$. We obtain

---

[28]Here, $\mathcal{Y}$ describes the subset of final good vectors that can be produced by using a given factor endowment vector. Unless necessary, we omit an explicit indication of the factor endowment vector from the notation of $\mathcal{Y}$.

[29]Strictly speaking, net import vectors cannot be chosen arbitrarily. A net import vector z is said to be *admissible* if there exists a production vector $y \in \mathcal{Y}$ such that $z + y$ is included in the consumption set $\mathbb{R}_+^n$. We are considering only admissible net import vectors.

the following relation:

$$\min\{W(z'),\ W(z'')\} = \min\{U(z'+y'),\ U(z''+y'')\}$$
$$\leq U\left(\lambda(z'+y') + [1-\lambda](z''+y'')\right)$$
$$= U\left(z^{\lambda} + \lambda y' + [1-\lambda]y''\right)$$
$$\leq W(z^{\lambda}).$$

The first line follows from the definitions of y' and y''; the second line from the quasi-concavity of U; the third from the definition of z^{λ}; the last inequality holds true because $\mathcal{Y}$ is a convex set. This proves the quasi-concavity of W.[30]

Trade Indifference Curve: The graph of a set of net import vectors that gives rise to a certain utility level is called a *trade indifference surface (curve)*. In Fig. 4.4, net import of good 1 is measured to the right, while net import of good 2 upward. Curves $\bar{u}$, u', u'', u''' are some examples of trade indifference curves. The more "northeast" a trade indifference curve is located, the higher the corresponding utility level is. Therefore, we have $u''' < \bar{u} < u' < u''$ in our example.[31] Due to the monotonicity

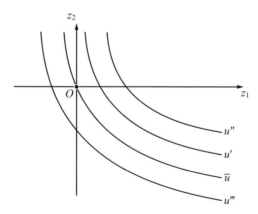

Fig. 4.4   Trade Indifference Curves

---

[30]The *strict quasi-concavity* of U and the convexity of $\mathcal{Y}$ do not necessarily guarantee the strict quasi-concavity of W. Readers may consider the case of a Ricardian model with a strictly quasi-concave social utility function.

[31]With a slight abuse of notation, we identify the labels of curves with their corresponding utility levels.

and quasi-concavity of the trade utility function, trade indifference curves are drawn downward-sloping and convex to the "southwest". It should be noted that a trade indifference curve can go through the strictly positive quadrant (i.e., the northeast of the origin) or through the strictly negative quadrant (i.e., the southwest of the origin). The origin O corresponds to the autarkic equilibrium of a country. Therefore, the trade indifference curve passing through the origin represents the autarkic utility level.

4.3.2 *Offer Curve*

Net import function: For a given price vector p, the production point y is determined so that it maximize the GDP subject to the production possibility set $\mathcal{Y}$. The maximized GDP, in turn, defines the budget constraint of the household. The household chooses the consumption point x so as to maximize the social utility subject to the budget constraint. Then, the net import $x - y$ is determined. In order to describe the behavior of net import vector by the procedure *without* the trade utility function, we have to solve the following *two-step* maximization:

$$\max_{x} U(x) \quad \text{subject to} \quad px \le Y(p) \equiv \max_{y} \{py|\, y \in \mathcal{Y}\}. \qquad (\clubsuit)$$

Let $\tilde{y}(p)$ be the solution to the (first-step) GDP maximization part and $\tilde{x}(p)$ the solution to the (second-step) utility maximization part. Then, the behavior of the net import of a country can be described by $\tilde{x}(p) - \tilde{y}(p)$. We may call $\tilde{x}(p) - \tilde{y}(p)$ the *net import function* of a country. Because both $\tilde{x}(p)$ and $\tilde{y}(p)$ are homogeneous of degree zero in p, so is the net import function.

The derivation of the net import function $\tilde{x}(p) - \tilde{y}(p)$ involves a two-step maximization procedure. By virtue of the trade utility function that embodies the integrated information of both the preference and the production possibility, we can compress the two-step maximization procedure into a single-step maximization of the trade utility function:

$$\max_{z} W(z) \quad \text{subject to} \quad pz \le 0. \qquad (\heartsuit)$$

Let $\tilde{z}(p)$ be the solution to the above maximization problem, which can be called the net import function of a country, too. Actually, we can show that $\tilde{z}(p) \equiv \tilde{x}(p) - \tilde{y}(p)$. In other words, the two-step maximization problem $(\clubsuit)$ is equivalent to the single-step maximization problem $(\heartsuit)$.

Equivalence of the two derivations: We first show that (♣) implies (♡). For a given p, let $\tilde{x}$ and $\tilde{y}$ be the solution to (♣). Let us define $z^* \equiv \tilde{x} - \tilde{y}$. We have to show z^* solves (♡). Suppose, in negation, that there exists another z' such that $pz' \leq 0$ and $W(z') > W(z^*)$. Correspondingly, there exist x' and $y' \in \mathscr{Y}$ such that $z' = x' - y'$. Because $pz' \leq 0$, we have $px' \leq py' \leq Y(p)$, while $U(x') = U(z' + y') = W(z') > W(z^*) \geq U(z^* + \tilde{y}) = U(\tilde{x})$. This contradicts the fact that $\tilde{x}$ is the solution to the utility maximization part of (♣).

Next, let us show that (♡) implies (♣). For a given p, let $\tilde{z}$ be the solution to (♡). We have $p\tilde{z} \leq 0$ and $W(\tilde{z}) \equiv U(\tilde{z} + y^*)$ for some $y^* \in \mathscr{Y}$. Define $x^* \equiv \tilde{z} + y^*$. Note that we have $p\tilde{z} = p(x^* - y^*) \leq 0$. First, we show y^* solves the GDP maximization part of (♣). Suppose, in negation, that there exists another production vector $y' \in \mathscr{Y}$ such that $py' > py^* \geq px^*$. Because we have $p(x^* - y') < 0$, we can choose z' such that $z' \gg x^* - y'$ and $pz' \leq 0$. By the monotonicity of U and the definition of W, we have $W(z') \geq U(z' + y') > U([x^* - y'] + y') = U(x^*) = W(\tilde{z})$. This contradicts the fact that $\tilde{z}$ is the solution to (♡). Hence, we have $Y(p) = py^*$. In turn, suppose x^* does not solve the utility maximization part of (♣). Then, there exists another consumption vector x' such that $px' \leq py^*$ and $U(x') > U(x^*)$. Define $z'' \equiv x' - y^*$. By definition, we have $pz'' \leq 0$ and $W(z'') \geq U(z'' + y^*) = U(x') > U(x^*) = W(\tilde{z})$ — a contradiction, again. Hence, problems (♣) and (♡) are logically equivalent.

Trade balance condition: As far as the monotonicity of the trade utility function is assumed, the solution to (♡) satisfies the weak-inequality constraint with equality: $pz = 0$. This means that the total value of the net import is zero, implying balanced trade.

In a two-good case, we can rewrite the trade balance condition as follows:

$$pz_1 + z_2 = 0 \quad \Leftrightarrow \quad z_2 = -pz_1,$$

where p is understood to be the relative price of good 1 in terms of good 2: $p \equiv p_1/p_2$. On the z_1–z_2 plane, the trade balance condition for a given p is represented by a negatively-sloped straight line passing through the origin with its slope being equal to "$-p$". We call this line a *trade balance line*.[32]

---

[32]In an n-goods case, the trade balance condition $pz = 0$ defines an $(n - 1)$-dimensional subspace normal to p (i.e., a hyper-plane containing the origin with the normal vector p).

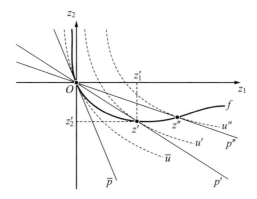

Fig. 4.5   Derivation of Offer Curve

Determination of the net import point: Figure 4.5 illustrates the determination of net import points of a country. Suppose that the relative price is given equal to the autarkic equilibrium price $\bar{p}$ of the country. By definition, the net import vector for $\bar{p}$ is zero. Accordingly, the maximum of the trade utility function must be attained at the origin — the trade indifference curve $\bar{u}$ (i.e, the autarkic trade indifference curve) must be tangent to the trade balance line for $\bar{p}$ (i.e., line $O\bar{p}$) at the origin. With this observation, we can say that the (absolute value of) slope of the autarkic trade indifference curve at the origin represents the autarkic equilibrium price of a country.[33]

Next, suppose that the relative price is p', which is lower than $\bar{p}$ as represented by the slope of the trade balance line Op' in the figure. The maximum of the trade utility is attained at point $z' = (z_1', z_2')$, at which a trade indifference curve is tangent to the trade balance line Op'. In this case, we have $z_1' > 0$ and $z_2' < 0$. The country imports z_1' units of good 1 and exports $|z_2'|$ units of good 2.

Further, let us consider another relative price p'', which is lower than p' as represented by the slope of the trade balance line Op''. The net import for p'' becomes point z'', at which a trade indifference curve is tangent to line Op''. In this way, as relative price changes from $\bar{p}$ to p', p'' and

---

[33] In an n-goods case, we can say that the gradient vector $\nabla W(z) \equiv (\partial W(z)/\partial z_1, \ldots, \partial W(z)/\partial z_n)$ of the trade utility function evaluated at the origin ($z = 0$) is proportional to the autarkic equilibrium price vector $\bar{p}$: that is, there exists a positive scalar $\lambda > 0$ such that $\nabla W(0) = \lambda \bar{p}$.

so forth, the net import changes correspondingly. The graph of a curve obtained by connecting the net import points that correspond to various relative prices is called the *offer curve* of this country (i.e., the bold curve $Oz'z''f$ in Fig. 4.5).

Properties of the offer curve: First, the offer curve necessarily go through the origin, which corresponds to the autarkic equilibrium. If the relative price is given higher than $\bar{p}$, then the net import $z = (z_1, z_2)$ becomes such that $z_1 < 0$ and $z_2 > 0$. Therefore, the offer curve can extend from the southeast area to the northwest area. However, the offer curve never goes through either the strictly positive or strictly negative quadrants (i.e., the northeast and southwest areas). That is, a country cannot be an importer or exporter of *all* goods. (Remember that we assumed away international income transfers.)

Furthermore, the offer curve is located "above" the autarkic trade indifference curve $\bar{u}$. In other words, the utility level at any point (other than the origin) on the offer curve is higher than the autarkic utility. Clearly, this reflects the gains-from-trade proposition. Furthermore, this implies that the offer curve is tangent to the autarkic trade indifference curve at the origin. Therefore, the absolute value of the slope of the offer curve at the origin, which is equal to the slope of the autarkic trade indifference curve, represents the autarkic equilibrium price of a country.

4.3.3   *Free Trade Equilibrium*

General description: Let us first consider a general case with n-goods and many countries. Let M be the (finite) set of trading countries and $\tilde{z}^s : \mathbb{R}^n_+ \to \mathbb{R}^n$ be the net import function of country $s \in M$. An array of net import vectors $\{z^s\}_{s \in M}$ is called a *trade allocation*. A trade allocation $\{z^s\}_{s \in M}$ is said to be *feasible* if $\sum_{s \in M} z^s \leq 0$. The free trade equilibrium is attained if $\sum_{s \in M} \tilde{z}^s_j(p) = 0$ for all $j = 1, 2, \ldots, n$. However, as is well-known, these n equations are not independent. Summing the trade balance conditions of all the countries, we obtain the following relation:

$$\sum_{s \in M} p z^s = \sum_{j=1}^{n} p_j \left[\sum_{s \in M} z^s_j \right] = 0.$$

Therefore, if the world markets for arbitrary $n - 1$ goods are in equilibrium, the only remaining market will also be in equilibrium. This is known as the *Walras law*. We can drop one of the market clearing conditions (say, the good-n market) from the free trade equilibrium conditions. Then, assuming good n is not a free good in equilibrium and taking account of the zero-degree homogeneity of the net import functions, we can rewrite the free trade equilibrium conditions as follows: for $j = 1, 2, \ldots, n - 1$,

$$\sum_{s \in M} \tilde{z}_j^s \left(\frac{p_1}{p_n}, \frac{p_2}{p_n}, \ldots, \frac{p_{n-1}}{p_n}, 1 \right) = 0.$$

The above system of $n - 1$ equations determines $n - 1$ relative prices p_j/p_n for $j = 1, 2, \ldots, n-1$. As in Chapter 1, we set $p_n = 1$ and regard p_j itself as the relative price of good j. When we refer to a price vector p, it should be read $p = (p_1, p_2, \ldots, p_{n-1}, 1)$. Let p_j^* be the free trade equilibrium price of good j. Correspondingly, $p^* = (p_1^*, p_2^*, \ldots, p_{n-1}^*, 1)$ denotes the free trade equilibrium price vector. The array $\{z^{s*}\}_{s \in M}$ where $z^{s*} \equiv \tilde{z}^s(p^*)$ for all $s \in M$ is called the *free trade equilibrium allocation*.

Two-by-two illustration: Let us consider a simpler case with two goods (1 and 2) and two countries (A and B). In this case, the offer curves provide us with a very convenient way of describing and analyzing free trade equilibria. We write the relative price of good 1 in terms of good 2 as p, which is a scalar rather than a vector. A trade allocation is a pair of net import vectors $\{z^A, z^B\}$.

In Fig. 4.6, country A's net import of good 1 is measured to the right, while country B's net import of good 1 is measured to the left; similarly, country A's net import of good 2 is measured upward, while country B's net import of good 2 is measured downward. Since, for a given relative price p, the trade balance conditions of countries A and B take the same form $z_2^s = -pz_1^s$ ($s = A, B$), they can be illustrated by a single straight line passing through the origin. Bold curves Of^A and Of^B represent the offer curves of countries A and B, respectively. At the origin O, the offer curve of country A is steeper than that of country B. This implies that country A's autarkic price $\bar{p}^A$ is higher than country B's autarkic price $\bar{p}^B$. That is, country B has a comparative advantage in good 1 over country A.

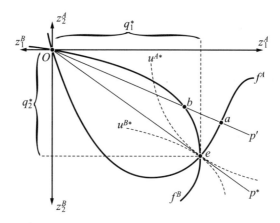

Fig. 4.6   Free Trade Equilibrium

Let us consider a case where the relative price is given arbitrarily, say p', which is in the middle of $\bar{p}^A$ and $\bar{p}^B$, as represented by the slope of the trade balance line Op' in the figure. The net import point of country A for p' is point a, while the net import point of country B is point b. Let $z^{A\prime} \equiv (z_1^{A\prime}, z_2^{A\prime})$ and $z^{B\prime} \equiv (z_1^{B\prime}, z_2^{B\prime})$ be the net import vectors that correspond to points a and b, respectively. As can be seen from the figure, we have $z_1^{A\prime} > 0$, $z_1^{B\prime} < 0$, and $z_1^{A\prime} > |z_1^{B\prime}|$. Since we have $z_1^{A\prime} + z_1^{B\prime} > 0$ (i.e., the world market for good 1 is in excess demand), the relative price p' cannot be a free trade equilibrium price.[34]

An intersection of the offer curves (other than the origin) represents a free trade equilibrium allocation. In Fig. 4.6, there is a unique intersection (i.e., point e) of the offer curves Of^A and Of^B. Now, let us consider the relative price p^* represented by the slope of the trade balance line that connects the origin O and point e. Let $z^{A*} \equiv (z_1^{A*}, z_2^{A*})$ and $z^{B*} \equiv (z_1^{B*}, z_2^{B*})$ be the net import vectors of countries A and B that correspond to point e. As can be seen from the figure, we have $z_1^{A*} > 0$, $z_1^{B*} < 0$, and $q_1^* = z_1^{A*} = |z_1^{B*}|$. Therefore, $z_1^{A*} + z_1^{B*} = 0$. By the Walras law, we also obtain $z_2^{A*} + z_2^{B*} = 0$. We can conclude that p^* is a free trade equilibrium price. In the free trade

---

[34] At the same time, the world market for good 2 is in excess supply: $z_2^{A\prime} + z_2^{B\prime} < 0$.

equilibrium under p^*, country A imports q_1^* units of good 1 and exports q_2^* units of good 2, while country B vice versa.

Note on the uniqueness: In our example of Fig. 4.6, point e is the only intersection of the offer curves other than the origin and, therefore, the free trade equilibrium is determined uniquely. However, it is easy to draw other examples that have several intersections without violating basic properties of the offer curves. In those cases with many intersections, each one of the intersections represents a free trade equilibrium allocation. There can be multiple free trade equilibria.[35]

Pareto-efficiency of the free trade equilibrium: Given the free trade equilibrium price p^*, the net import point of country A is point e in Fig. 4.6. By the definition of the offer curve, a trade indifference curve of country A, say u^{A*}, must be tangent to the trade balance line Op^* at point e. By the same token, a trade indifference curve of country B, say u^{B*}, must be tangent to Op^* at point e from the opposite direction. Consequently, these trade indifference curves u^{A*} and u^{B*} turn out to be tangent with each other back to back at point e. This implies the free trade equilibrium allocation (i.e., point e) is Pareto-efficient from a point of view of the world as a whole. In fact, if we were to move from point e to another point on the plane, at least one of the countries inevitably becomes worse-off. From point e, Pareto-improvement is not possible — the free trade equilibrium is Pareto-efficient. This observation can be generalized to a many-good many-country case.

Proposition 4.7 (Pareto-efficiency of free trade). *Consider a many-good many-country case. Let $p^* > 0$ and $\{z^{s*}\}_{s \in M}$ be a free trade equilibrium price vector and the corresponding free trade equilibrium allocation. Then, $\{z^{s*}\}_{s \in M}$ is Pareto-efficient from the world point of view.*

Proof. Suppose $\{z^{s*}\}_{s \in M}$ is not Pareto-efficient. Then, there exists another feasible trade allocation $\{z^{s\prime}\}_{s \in M}$ such that $W^s(z^{s\prime}) \geq W^s(z^{s*})$ for all $s \in M$ with strict inequalities for some $s \in M$. Then, we have $p^* z^{s\prime} \geq p^* z^{s*}$

---

[35]Readers may try to draw those examples.

for all $s \in M$ with strict inequalities for some $s \in M$. Summing these inequalities over the countries, we obtain $p^* \left[\sum_{s \in M} z^{s\prime} \right] > p^* z^* = 0$, where the last equality follows from the trade balance conditions. However, $p^* > 0$ and $\sum_{s \in M} z^{s\prime} \leq 0$ (i.e., the feasibility of $\{z^{s\prime}\}_{s \in M}$) together imply $p^* \left[\sum_{s \in M} z^{s\prime} \right] \leq 0$, which leads to a contradiction.   □

The above theorem is exactly the same as what is known as the *first fundamental theorem of welfare economics*, which asserts the Pareto-efficiency of a competitive general equilibrium.

4.4   Remarks and Further Topics

Besides perfect competition, the gains-from-trade proposition relies on one important (but implicit) assumption that the markets for *all* the relevant goods and services should be ready to serve — the *completeness* of the markets. This becomes particularly important when we consider a circumstance with *uncertainty*, for which the insurance markets that cover all the risks in an economy have to be taken account of. In reality, however, some of those insurance markets may fail to exist because of the possibilities of moral hazard, adverse selection, and/or other obstacles pertaining to uncertainty. By using a simple partial equilibrium model with uncertainty, Newbery and Stiglitz (1984) have shown that if the economy lacks the risk market, the opening of trade can make everyone worse-off than in autarky. Here, we briefly review the Newbery-Stiglitz model of *Pareto-inferior trade*.[36]

Setup: In a country, there are a continuum of identical producers of a unit mass and, also, a continuum of identical consumers of a unit mass. Both producers and consumers are assumed to be *risk averse*. Each producer has one unit of labor, which can be used to produce a *risky* good and a *safe* good. The labor productivity of the risky good is denoted by θ, which is a stochastic variable with its mean being equal to unity. In contrast, the labor productivity of the safe good is non-stochastic and normalized to unity. If a

---

[36]Shy (1988) has extended the partial equilibrium model by Newbery and Stiglitz (1984) to a general equilibrium framework and examined the conditions for Pareto-inferior trade.

producer devotes $q \in [0, 1]$ of its labor to the production of the risky good and the rest of labor to the safe good, it can produce $y_1 = \theta q$ units of the risky good and $y_2 = 1 - q$ units of the safe good, respectively. Then, the producer can earn the income

$$\pi \equiv p_1 y_1 + p_2 y_2 = \theta p_1 q + p_2 (1 - q),$$

where p_1 and p_2 denote the prices of the risky good and the safe good, respectively. The utility of a producer is represented by a von Neumann–Morgenstern utility function $U(\pi)$, which satisfies $U'(\cdot) > 0$ and $U''(\cdot) < 0$. Before knowing the realization of θ, each producer has to choose q in order to maximize the expected utility $E[U(\pi)]$.[37] If a producer were to produce *both* goods in equilibrium, the following equality has to be satisfied:

$$E[U'(\pi) \cdot (\theta p_1 - p_2)] = 0. \tag{4.8}$$

In turn, each consumer's behavior is represented by the following indirect utility function: for $\rho \neq 1$,[38]

$$V(p_1, p_2, I) \equiv \frac{\left(p_1^{-a} p_2^{-b} I\right)^{1-\rho}}{1 - \rho}, \tag{4.9}$$

where I denotes the income of a consumer, ρ is the coefficient of relative risk aversion, and a and b are positive constants. For simplicity, we assume I is given exogenously and equal to unity. By applying Roy's identity to Eq. (4.9), we can derive the demand for the risky good and that for the safe good:

$$x_1 = \frac{a}{p_1} \quad \text{and} \quad x_2 = \frac{b}{p_2}.$$

Autarky: We focus on the *competitive rational-expectation equilibrium* in the sense that producers do not have controls over prices but know the relation between the equilibrium prices, the producer's decision q, and the stochastic productivity parameter θ. Given q and θ, the market clearing

---

[37] $E[\cdot]$ represents the expectation operator.
[38] For $\rho = 1$, we have $V(p_1, p_2, I) \equiv \ln[I] - a \ln[p_1] - b \ln[p_2]$.

conditions (i.e., $y_1 = x_1$ and $y_2 = x_2$) can be solved for the prices of goods:

$$p_1 = \frac{a}{\theta q} \quad \text{and} \quad p_2 = \frac{b}{1 - q}. \tag{4.10}$$

With these results, we (as well as the producers) know that each producer earns an income

$$\bar{\pi} \equiv p_1 y_1 + p_2 y_2 = a + b,$$

which is independent of q and θ. Then, Eq. (4.8) reduces to $E[\theta p_1 - p_2] = 0$ or, equivalently,

$$\frac{a}{q} = \frac{b}{1 - q}. \tag{4.11}$$

From Eqs. (4.10)–(4.11), we obtain the equilibrium allocation of labor to the risky good, denoted by $\bar{q}$, and the equilibrium prices of the goods:

$$\bar{q} = \frac{a}{a + b}, \quad \bar{p}_1 = \frac{a}{\theta \bar{q}} = \frac{a + b}{\theta}, \quad \bar{p}_2 = \frac{b}{1 - \bar{q}} = a + b.$$

Every producer can secure the definite income $\bar{\pi}$ in spite of the productivity uncertainty, because the risk is transferred to the consumers through the changes in the autarkic price $\bar{p}_1$ of the risky good. In other words, the price fluctuation works as the income insurance for the producers.

By making use of the above results, we can write the expected utility of a consumer in autarky as a function of $\bar{q}$:

$$E\left[V(\bar{p}_1, \bar{p}_2, I)\right] = \gamma \left\{(\bar{q})^a (1 - \bar{q})^b\right\}^{1-\rho} E\left[\theta^{a(1-\rho)}\right],$$

where $\gamma \equiv (a^{-a} b^{-b})^{1-\rho}/(1 - \rho)$ is a positive constant.

Free trade: Suppose now that there are two countries, A and B, which are identical except for the productivity parameters θ^A and θ^B. We assume that θ^A and θ^B are completely negatively correlated so that $\theta^A + \theta^B = 2$. For simplicity, we write $\theta^A \equiv \theta$ and $\theta^B \equiv 2 - \theta$. Then, the supplies of the goods become $y_1^A = \theta q$, $y_1^B = (2 - \theta)q$, and $y_2^A = y_2^B = 1 - q$. The demands for the goods of both countries are identical to the case of autarky in a single country. Given q and θ, the market clearing conditions (i.e., $y_1^A + y_1^B = x_1^A + x_2^B$ and $y_2^A + y_2^B = x_2^A + x_2^B$) yield

$$p_1 = \frac{a}{q} \quad \text{and} \quad p_2 = \frac{b}{1-q},$$

which are independent of the stochastic fluctuation of the productivity of the risky goods. Because a productivity shock in one country is completely offset by an opposite productivity shock in the other country, the prices are stabilized under free trade. Hence, the price fluctuation can no longer work as an income insurance for the producers. In this case, we have $\pi = a\theta + b$, meaning that each producer faces the risk of stochastic income fluctuation. Then, Eq. (4.8) becomes

$$E\left[U'(a\theta + b) \cdot \left(\frac{a\theta}{q} - \frac{b}{1-q}\right)\right] = 0. \qquad (4.12)$$

The equilibrium allocation of labor to the risky good under free trade, denoted by q^*, is the solution to Eq. (4.12). Because the producers are risk averse, q^* is smaller than $\bar{q}$; further, the more risk averse are the producers the lower is q^*.[39]

Let $p_1^* \equiv a/q^*$ and $p_2^* \equiv b/(1 - q^*)$ be the equilibrium prices of the goods under free trade. Then, the expected utility of a consumer can be written as follows:

$$E\left[V(p_1^*, p_2^*, I)\right] = V(p_1^*, p_2^*, I) = \gamma\left\{(q^*)^a(1 - q^*)^b\right\}^{1-\rho}.$$

Comparison of the welfare: The expected utility of a producer in autarky is $E[U(a + b)]$ and that under free trade is $E[U(a\theta + b)]$. Because the producers are risk averse, we have $E[U(a + b)] < E[U(a\theta + b)]$. That is, trade liberalization surely worsens the welfare of the producers.

In turn, the expected utility of a consumer in autarky is $E[V(\bar{p}_1, \bar{p}_2, I)]$ and that under free trade is $E[V(p_1^*, p_2^*, I)]$. Hence, Pareto-inferior trade becomes possible if we have $E[V(p_1^*, p_2^*, I)] < E[V(\bar{p}_1, \bar{p}_2, I)]$, which

---

[39]For the proofs of these statements, see Newbery and Stiglitz (1984, Propositions 1 and 2).

is equivalent to

$$\frac{(q^*)^a(1-q^*)^b}{(\bar{q})^a(1-\bar{q})^b} < E[\theta^{a(1-\rho)}]^{\frac{1}{1-\rho}}. \qquad (4.13)$$

Let us define a function $f(q) \equiv (q)^a(1-q)^b$. The function f attains its maximum at $q = a/(a+b)$, which is equivalent to the autarkic labor allocation to the risky good $\bar{q}$. Therefore, the left-hand side of Eq. (4.13) gets smaller as q^* gets smaller. In contrast, the right-hand side of Eq. (4.13) is decreasing in the relative risk aversion ρ of consumer. Accordingly, we can conclude that the inequality in Eq. (4.13) tends to be satisfied or, equivalently, Pareto-inferior trade becomes more likely if the producers are more risk averse and the consumers are less risk averse.[40]

---

[40]By incorporating certain transfer schemes into the model, Kemp and Wong (1995) have explored the possibility of rehabilitating the gains-from-trade proposition (in the sense of a potential Pareto-improvement) when markets are incomplete.

Chapter 5

Oligopoly

Although the notion of comparative advantage plays crucial roles in determining trade patterns and gains from trade, in particular in the perfectly competitive circumstance, it is not the only cause of international trade. Other factors such as strategic interaction among agents, product differentiation and economies of scale come into play when the situation is *not* perfectly competitive. The first contributions to oligopolistic trade theory appeared in the early 1980s. By using a simple Cournot duopoly model, Brander (1981) has clearly shown that the strategic interaction among firms is a new independent cause of international trade and it explains "cross-hauling" or "intra-industry" trade in a homogeneous good. Built on Brander (1981)'s model, Brander and Krugman (1983) have shown that the strategic interaction among firms brings about "dumping" in the foreign market and this dumping is mutual. Following these contributions, a vast number of articles concerning the oligopolistic trade models has appeared and the literature is still growing.[1] In this chapter, by using a simple unified model of international oligopoly, we focus on the relation between the strategic interaction among firms and international trade and examine trade patterns and gains from trade.[2]

---

[1] We do not attempt here a comprehensive survey on oligopolistic trade theories. For a recent survey on this issue, see Leahy and Neary (2011) for example.

[2] We will deal with the roles of product differentiation and economies of scale in the next chapter within the framework of monopolistically competitive models.

5.1   Market Structures

5.1.1   *Classification of Imperfect Competition*

Unlike perfect competition, of which precise definition and characterization can be given, the notion of *imperfect competition* is not a single solid concept, but it consists of a wide range of situations/regimes that vary according to numerous combinations of certain aspects that characterize imperfect competition; (the only) one feature common to all imperfectly competitive situations is that some of agents in an economy have abilities to control prices of goods and services to some extent. How and why agents come to have controls over prices are different from situation to situation. Therefore, we would not (cannot) expect *the* general theory of international trade under imperfect competition. Rather, we have to take a one-by-one approach: in the first place, we specify one particular situation/regime by choosing a certain set of characterizing aspects; next, we examine the model specified by the chosen set of aspects; then, we proceed to examine another model based on a different set of characterizing aspects and so forth. Here, we list some of those characterizing aspects.

Technology and the cost structure: The cost of producing a good is represented by a function C of factor prices w and quantity y, that is, $C(w, y)$. The total cost function C is increasing in y. If $C(w, 0) > 0$, it means a positive *fixed cost*. Technology is said to exhibit (i) decreasing-returns-to-scale (DRS), (ii) constant-returns-to-scale (CRS), and (iii) increasing-returns-to-scale (IRS), if the average cost $AC(w, y) \equiv C(w, y)/y$ is (i) increasing in y, (ii) constant over y, and (iii) decreasing in y, respectively. Although both DRS and CRS are compatible with perfect competition, IRS is not. If we assume IRS, the situation must be imperfectly competitive.[3] The response of the marginal cost $MC(w, y) \equiv \partial C(w, y)/\partial y$ to changes in y also plays important roles. If CRS is assumed, MC becomes constant over y; but, the converse is not necessarily true. If, for example, MC is constant over y and the fixed cost is positive, then IRS holds. In the cases of IRS and DRS, MC can be either increasing or decreasing in y.

---

[3]Of course, DRS and/or CRS are possible in imperfectly competitive circumstances. In the case of the "Marshallian external economy", IRS can be compatible with the assumption of perfect competition.

Preference structure: When we examine international trade under imperfect competition, we often need to rely on a concrete parameterized model so that we can derive explicit solutions for endogenous variables by algebraic calculation. To do so, it is necessary to specify functional forms of various functions, in particular, those of utility and demand functions. For utility functions, Cobb–Douglas form, CES form, quadratic form, and their hybrids are frequently used. In addition, in order to avoid complicated "income effects", quasi-linear utility functions are sometimes assumed. The qualitative results obtained from parameterized models are dependent on the algebraic structure of functions and, inevitably, *less* general, but they can be *more* definite as far as we can obtain the closed-form solutions of endogenous variables.

Product differentiation: To attract consumers' demand, a firm may try to make its own product distinguishable from the other firms' products by emphasizing such *non-price* aspects as qualities, colors, logos, trademarks, brand names or after-sales services and so forth — this kind of firm's strategy is called *product differentiation*. Suppose that a firm is supplying a certain good and that there is a (potential) rival firm contemplating the entry to the market. On one hand, the rival firm can enter the market and engage in direct competition against the incumbent firm by supplying *the same* good as the existing one; on the other hand, if possible, the rival firm may decide to develop a new differentiated product, which is a close substitute for the existing one, and to compete against the incumbent firm in a somewhat indirect way so that it can avoid harsher competition and miserable outcomes. Anyway, the possibility of product differentiation considerably changes the economic environment in which the firms make their strategic decisions.

Market segmentation: Suppose that there are two countries, each of which has one oligopolistic good industry. In autarky, each country has its own market for the oligopolistic good and the autarkic prices of the oligopolistic good are different from country to country. If transportation costs or other impediments to trade are assumed away, trade liberalization between the countries realizes a *single equilibrium price* for the oligopolistic good produced in both countries — the markets for the oligopolistic good in both countries are said to be *integrated*. In contrast, if transportation costs are so high that *arbitrage* between the markets cannot be profitable, the equilibrium prices in these markets can be different even under free trade. In this case, the markets are said to be *segmented*. Firms can take different actions market-by-market when the markets are segmented. Strictly speaking, the market segmentation is an endogenous phenomenon that should be determined in the model, but, quite frequently, it is assumed *a priori*.

Strategic variables: In imperfectly competitive trade models, agents (in almost all cases, "firms") can manipulate, to some extent, the prices of goods and services that they sell or buy. The choice of strategic variables with which firms use to control prices has significant implications on the final outcomes. On one hand, firms can control the prices of their products directly and set them at certain levels; the firms sell the products as much as possible at those prices. On the other hand, firms can indirectly control the prices by adjusting the quantities supplied to the markets; the prices are determined so that the markets are cleared. The former situation is called the *Bertrand competition* and the latter is called the *Cournot competition*.[4]

Free entry and the number of firms: In order to make an appropriate decision in a strategic situation, each agent has to take full account of how the other agents behave. Therefore, it is important for each agent to know *who* are (potentially) involved or, at least, *how many* rival agents are involved in the situation. When the market for a good is dominated by a single supplier firm, the situation is called *monopoly*. The situation with plural (but finite) supplier firms is called *oligopoly*. In particular, the situation with two firms is called *duopoly*. The number of firms may not be fixed. We distinguish two cases: one where the number of firms is given and fixed at the outset and the other where the number of firms is determined endogenously in the model. When a firm can enter and exit the market

---

[4]Cournot (Antoine Augustin, 1801–1877) was a french mathematician/economist. His book *Recherches sur les principes mathématiques de la théorie des richesses* was one of the earliest contributions to mathematical analysis of economics and a pioneering work of Game Theory. Bertrand (Joseph Louis François, 1822–1900) was also a French mathematician, who criticized the assumption of quantity-setting competition by Cournot and proposed an alternative model of price-setting competition.

without incurring any additional cost, we say that *free entry–exit* prevails. If a potential firm finds it profitable to enter the market, it will do so. In contrast, if an incumbent firm suffers from a negative profit, it will exit the market. In this way, the number of firms changes and the profits of firms will vanish in the long run. By the term "long run" here, we mean a situation where the entry–exit by firms ceases and the number of firms is determined.

5.1.2 The Base Model

Consider a world economy consisting of two symmetric countries A and B, each of which can produce both an oligopolistic good and a homogeneous good. The homogeneous good is taken as the numèraire. In country $s (= A, B)$, there is a single firm that produces the oligopolistic good, which is called "firm s" for simplicity. Without international trade, firm s is a monopoly in country s. The oligopolistic markets in both countries are segmented.

Technology: Both countries have the Ricardian technology: goods are produced by using only labor as inputs; the labor input coefficient for the oligopolistic good production is $c^s > 0$ in country s and that for the homogeneous good is one in both countries. We assume away fixed costs. In addition, we introduce *unit transportation cost* for the oligopolistic good: it is necessary to employ $t \geq 0$ units of labor in order to deliver one unit of the oligopolistic good to the importing country from the exporting country. In effect, the labor input coefficient for export from country s becomes $c^s + t$. The homogeneous good sector is assumed to be perfectly competitive. Therefore, as far as the homogeneous good is produced in each country, the real wage rate is normalized to unity. This implies that c^s represents the (real) marginal cost of producing the oligopolistic good.

Utility function: We assume that there is a single household in each country and that the households in both countries share the same utility function. Let x, y, and z be the consumption of the domestic oligopolistic good, the imported oligopolistic good, and the homogeneous good, respectively. We assume the following quasi-linear quadratic utility function:

$$U(x, y, z) \equiv \alpha(x + y) - \frac{\beta - \gamma}{2}(x^2 + y^2) - \frac{\gamma}{2}(x + y)^2 + z, \qquad (5.1)$$

where $\alpha > 0$ and $\beta > \gamma \geq 0$. Given α and β, the parameter γ represents the degree of *substitutability* between the domestic and imported oligopolistic goods: (i) if $\gamma = 0$, x and y are *independent* with each other and (ii) if $\gamma \to \beta$, x and y become *perfect substitutes*.

Demand functions: Let p_x and p_y be the (consumer) prices of domestic and imported oligopolistic goods, respectively. In addition, let I be the income of a household. Then, the budget constraint becomes $p_x x + p_y y + z = I$. The first-order conditions for the constrained utility maximization yield the inverse demand functions for x and y:

$$p_x = P_x(x, y) \equiv \alpha - \beta x - \gamma y, \qquad (5.2)$$

$$p_y = P_y(x, y) \equiv \alpha - \gamma x - \beta y. \qquad (5.3)$$

Further, by solving Eqs. (5.2)–(5.3) for x and y, we obtain the ordinary demand functions:

$$x = D_x(p_x, p_y) \equiv \frac{1}{\Delta}[\alpha(\beta - \gamma) - \beta p_x + \gamma p_y], \qquad (5.4)$$

$$y = D_y(p_x, p_y) \equiv \frac{1}{\Delta}[\alpha(\beta - \gamma) + \gamma p_x - \beta p_y], \qquad (5.5)$$

where $\Delta \equiv \beta^2 - \gamma^2 > 0$. Obviously, an increase in the price of the local oligopolistic good (i.e., p_x) leads to a decrease in x and an increase in y. Symmetrically, an increase in the price of the imported oligopolistic good (i.e., p_y) leads to an increase in x and a decrease in y.

5.2 Quantity-Setting Duopoly

Let us consider the Cournot competition where the oligopolistic firms use *quantities* as their strategic variables. If international trade is allowed, each firm begins to export its product to the other country's market in addition to the local market. Because the markets are segmented, the firms compete with each other in each of the markets.

Profits of firms: Let x^s and y^s be the local supply and the export supply by firm s and let p_x^s and p_y^s be the consumer price of the local oligopolistic good and that of the imported oligopolistic good in country s, respectively. For the moment, let us focus on the behavior of firm A under free trade. Firm A supplies x^A to country A's local market and also exports y^A to country B. Symmetrically, firm B supplies x^B to country B's local market and exports y^B to country A. From the inverse demand functions (5.2)–(5.3), the price of firm A's product in country A is given by $p_x^A = P_x(x^A, y^B)$ and that in country B is given by $p_y^B = P_y(x^B, y^A)$. Then, we can write the total profit of firm A as a function of x^A, y^A, x^B, and y^B:

$$\Pi^A(x^A, y^A; x^B, y^B) \equiv p_x^A x^A + p_y^B y^A - \{c^A x^A + (c^A + t)y^A\}$$
$$= \underbrace{P_x(x^A, y^B)x^A - c^A x^A}_{\text{local supply}} + \underbrace{P_y(x^B, y^A)y^A - (c^A + t)y^A}_{\text{export supply}}.$$

Due to the assumption of constant marginal cost, the total profit of firm A can be divided *additively* into two parts: one is the profit from local supply, which depends on x^A but not on y^A, and the other is the profit from export supply, which depends on y^A but not on x^A. To maximize the total profit, firm A can choose x^A independently of y^A and vice versa. The same argument applies to firm B as well.

In light of the above argument, we can concentrate our attention on the behavior of firms in only one of the markets. Let us focus on the market in country A, where firm A is a local supplier and firm B is an exporter. Hereafter, x and y should be regarded as firm A's local supply and firm B's export supply (i.e., $x = x^A$ and $y = y^B$), respectively. Then, the profit of firm A obtained in the local (country A's) market can be written as

$$\pi^A(x, y) \equiv P_x(x, y)x - c^A x = \{\alpha - \beta x - \gamma y\}x - c^A x. \tag{5.6}$$

Similarly, the profit of firm B obtained in country A's market becomes

$$\pi^B(x, y) \equiv P_y(x, y)y - (c^B + t)y = \{\alpha - \gamma x - \beta y\}y - (c^B + t)y. \tag{5.7}$$

Note that, although an explicit indication is omitted, the profit function of firm B depends on the unit transportation cost t.

5.2.1   The Cournot Duopoly Game

Strategic form game: Firm A's profit depends not only on its local supply x, which can be controlled directly by firm A, but also on firm B's export supply y, which *cannot* be controlled by firm A; a similar argument also applies to firm B. Knowing such interdependence of gains and losses, each firm has to decide the quantity of supply in order to maximize its own profit. The analysis of such a situation fits into the framework of *game theory*. Let $M \equiv \{A, B\}$ be the set of firms (i.e., *players*) and $X^s \equiv \mathbb{R}_+$ be the set of possible quantities supplied by firm s (i.e., *strategies*); further, let us think of the profit function $\pi^s \colon X^A \times X^B \to \mathbb{R}$ as the *payoff function* of firm s. The triple $(M, \{X^s\}_{s \in M}, \{\pi^s\}_{s \in M})$ defines a strategic form game called the *Cournot duopoly game*, which describes the conflicting situation between the firms in country A's market.

Reaction functions and the Nash equilibrium: The most fundamental solution concept for strategic form games is the *Nash equilibrium*. In our context here, the Nash equilibrium is a pair of strategies, denoted by (x^*, y^*), that satisfies the following conditions: for all $x \in X^A$ and for all $y \in X^B$,

$$\pi^A(x^*, y^*) \geq \pi^A(x, y^*) \quad \text{and} \quad \pi^B(x^*, y^*) \geq \pi^B(x^*, y).$$

That is, given the other firm's Nash equilibrium strategy, each firm maximizes its payoff by taking its own Nash equilibrium strategy.

To find the Nash equilibrium of the Cournot duopoly game, we introduce an analytical device called the *reaction function*. Let us consider the profit maximization problem of firm A with respect to x. The first-order condition gives an equation of x and y. By solving it for x, we obtain

$$\frac{\partial \pi^A(x, y)}{\partial x} = 0 \quad \Leftrightarrow \quad x = \psi^A(y) \equiv \frac{\alpha - c^A}{2\beta} - \frac{\gamma}{2\beta} y. \tag{5.8}$$

The right-hand-side of the above expression defines the (quantity-) reaction function of firm A: $\psi^A \colon X^B \to X^A$, which associates each export supply y by firm B with the profit-maximizing local supply by firm A.[5] For each

---

[5]We are assuming here the interior solution to the maximization of π^A with respect to x. If y is sufficiently large, then the maximization obtains the boundary solution: $\psi^A(y) = 0$ if $y \geq (\alpha - c)/\gamma$.

$y \in X^B$, $\psi^A(y)$ represents the *best response* of firm A to y.[6] In our case here, the reaction function ψ^A is decreasing in y. When the best response of a player decreases against an increase in the strategy of the rival player, the strategy of the former player is said to be a *strategic substitute* for the rival's strategy.

Similarly, we can define the reaction function $\psi^B : X^A \to X^B$ of firm B:

$$y = \psi^B(x) \equiv \frac{\alpha - c^B - t}{2\beta} - \frac{\gamma}{2\beta} x. \tag{5.9}$$

By symmetry, the functional form of firm B's reaction function is almost identical to firm A's. Unlike firm A's reaction function, however, ψ^B depends *negatively* on the unit transportation cost t.

The reaction functions of the firms naturally define a mapping ψ from $X^A \times X^B$ to itself such that $\psi : (x, y) \to (\psi^A(y), \psi^B(x))$. Then, it is easy to verify that a pair of strategies (x^*, y^*) is a Nash equilibrium of the Cournot duopoly game if and only if it is a *fixed point* of the mapping ψ. In other words, (x^*, y^*) is a Nash equilibrium of the Cournot duopoly game if and only if $\psi(x^*, y^*) = (x^*, y^*)$.

5.2.2 *Free Trade Equilibrium*

The Nash equilibrium of the Cournot duopoly game, which is sometimes referred to as the "Cournot–Nash equilibrium" for short, describes the outcome in country A's market under free trade. Figure 5.1 illustrates the Cournot–Nash equilibrium. Curve aa' is the graph of the reaction function (i.e., *reaction curve*) of firm A and curve bb' is the reaction curve of firm B.[7] The intersection of the reaction curves (i.e., point e) represents the Cournot–Nash equilibrium.

By solving the fixed point condition $\psi(x^*, y^*) = (x^*, y^*)$, we obtain the equilibrium values of the local supply by firm A and the export

---

[6] Sometimes the reaction function is called the *best-reply mapping*.

[7] As noted before, we have $\psi^A(y) = 0$ if $y \geq (\alpha - c)/\gamma$. Therefore, if firm B's quantity exceeds a' in the figure, the reaction curve of firm A coincides with the vertical axis. Similar argument also applies to the reaction curve of firm B.

supply by firm B:

$$x^* = \frac{\alpha(2\beta - \gamma) - 2\beta c^A + \gamma(c^B + t)}{\Delta^*} = \frac{(2\beta - \gamma)(\alpha - c)}{\Delta^*} + \frac{\gamma}{\Delta^*}t, \qquad (5.10)$$

$$y^* = \frac{\alpha(2\beta - \gamma) + \gamma c^A - 2\beta(c^B + t)}{\Delta^*} = \frac{(2\beta - \gamma)(\alpha - c)}{\Delta^*} - \frac{2\beta}{\Delta^*}t, \qquad (5.11)$$

where $\Delta^* \equiv 4\beta^2 - \gamma^2 > 0$. To derive the right-most expressions for x^* and y^* in the above results, we assumed $c^A = c^B = c$; we shall maintain this symmetry assumption hereafter. Further, by substituting the above results into Eqs. (5.2)–(5.3), we obtain the equilibrium prices of x and y:

$$p_x^* \equiv \frac{(2\beta - \gamma)\{\beta(\alpha + c) + \gamma c\}}{\Delta^*} + \frac{\beta\gamma}{\Delta^*}t, \qquad (5.12)$$

$$p_y^* \equiv \frac{(2\beta - \gamma)\{\beta(\alpha + c) + \gamma c\}}{\Delta^*} + \frac{2\beta^2 - \gamma^2}{\Delta^*}t. \qquad (5.13)$$

The equilibrium quantities and prices depend on the unit transportation cost. If necessary, we shall write them as functions of t: $x^*(t)$, $y^*(t)$, $p_x^*(t)$, and $p_y^*(t)$, respectively.

It is easy to check that if $t = 0$, we have $x^* = y^*$ and $p_x^* = p_y^*$. Next, suppose that the initial equilibrium is point e as illustrated in Fig. 5.1. If the unit transportation cost increases, the effective marginal cost (i.e., $c + t$) of firm B increases. Because of this cost disadvantage, the export supply

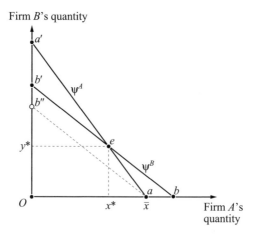

Fig. 5.1   The Reaction Curves and the Cournot–Nash Equilibrium

by firm B decreases, which brings about an increase in its price p_y. In turn, since the local and foreign products are substitutes, an increase in p_y leads to an increase in the demand for the local product. Then, firm A can increase both its local supply x and price p_x simultaneously. Due to an increase in the unit transportation cost, the reaction curve of firm B shifts inward, while that of firm A remains at the initial position. Then, the equilibrium point moves to the "southeast" of point e (not illustrated) along the reaction curve of firm A. Consequently, x^* increases, while y^* decreases. As for the prices, both p_x^* and p_y^* increase simultaneously.

Positive trade and the prohibitive transportation cost: Equation (5.11) shows that positive international trade in the oligopolistic good can occur if the transportation cost is sufficiently low. Actually, we have $y^*(t) > 0$ if and only if $t < \bar{t} \equiv (2\beta - \gamma)(\alpha - c)/(2\beta)$, where $\bar{t}$ is the prohibitive unit transportation cost.[8] Because the countries are completely identical, the notion of comparative advantage plays no role in determining the trade pattern in the oligopolistic goods in our model.[9] Instead, the *strategic interaction* between firms comes into play as a new driving force of international trade.[10]

If the transportation cost reaches the prohibitive level (i.e., $\bar{t}$), the reaction curve of firm B becomes curve ab'' in Fig. 5.1. The Cournot–Nash equilibrium is point a, where the local supply is equal to the autarkic (monopoly) quantity $x^*(\bar{t}) = \bar{x} \equiv (\alpha - c)/(2\beta)$ and the export supply by firm B is $y^*(\bar{t}) = 0$. The equilibrium price of x is equal to the autarkic (monopoly) price $p_x^*(\bar{t}) = \bar{p}_x \equiv (\alpha + c)/2$. That is, the free trade equilibrium under the prohibitive transportation cost replicates the autarkic (monopoly) equilibrium.

Reciprocal dumping: Due to the symmetry assumption, the equilibrium price of "firm A's export to country B" is equal to the equilibrium price of "firm B's export to country A", that is, p_y^*. In other words, firm A's product

---

[8]Of course, $\bar{t}$ is the solution to $y^*(t) = 0$.

[9]Because the autarkic equilibrium prices of the oligopolistic good are the same in both countries, there is no room for international arbitrage.

[10]The importance of firms' strategic interaction as a source of international trade in oligopolistic goods has been pointed out first by Brander (1981).

is sold at price p_x^* in country A, while at price p_y^* in country B.[11] The FOB price of firm A's export is $p_y^* - t$.[12] If $p_x^* < p_y^* - t$, an arbitrageur can make positive profits by purchasing firm A's product in country A and exporting it to country B. In our model, however, this cannot be the case. From Eqs. (5.12)–(5.13), simple calculation yields

$$p_x^* - (p_y^* - t) = \frac{\beta(2\beta + \gamma)}{\Delta^*}t > 0 \quad \text{if } t > 0. \tag{5.14}$$

The FOB price of firm A's export is lower than the local price of firm A's product — "dumping" occurs. Because the same is true for firm B's product, dumping in the oligopolistic good is mutual. Brander and Krugman (1983) termed this as *reciprocal dumping*.

In contrast, if $p_x^* > p_y^* + t$, an arbitrageur can also make positive profits by reimporting firm A's product from country B back to country A; this cannot be the case, either. From Eqs. (5.12)–(5.13), we have

$$p_x^* - (p_y^* + t) = \frac{-(2\beta + \gamma)(3\beta - 2\gamma)}{\Delta^*}t < 0 \quad \text{if } t > 0.$$

The difference in the local and foreign prices cannot exceed the unit transportation cost: $\left| p_x^* - p_y^* \right| \le t$ with equality only when $t = 0$. That is, no profitable arbitrage is possible in our model.

5.2.3 *Welfare Under the Cournot Duopoly*

The equilibrium profit: By substituting Eqs. (5.10)–(5.13) into Eqs. (5.6)–(5.7) and by taking account of the symmetry assumption, we can write the equilibrium profits that a firm can obtain from the domestic supply and the export supply as functions of t:

$$\pi_D(t) \equiv \pi^A(x^*(t), y^*(t)) \equiv \beta[x^*(t)]^2 \quad \text{and}$$
$$\pi_{EX}(t) \equiv \pi^B(x^*(t), y^*(t)) \equiv \beta[y^*(t)]^2.$$

By symmetry, π_D and π_{EX} do not depend on the identities of firms. Firm A earns $\pi_D(t)$ in its domestic (country A) market and $\pi_{EX}(t)$ in the foreign

---

[11] Symmetrically, firm B's product is sold at price p_x^* in country B, while at price p_y^* in country A.
[12] FOB stands for "Free On Board".

(country B) market. Similarly, firm B earns $\pi_D(t)$ in its domestic (country B) market and $\pi_{EX}(t)$ in the foreign (country A) market. It is easy to see that π_D is increasing but π_{EX} is decreasing in t, respectively. The total profit of a firm becomes

$$\Pi^*(t) \equiv \pi_D(t) + \pi_{EX}(t) \equiv \beta[x^*(t)]^2 + \beta[y^*(t)]^2.$$

Because the equilibrium quantities are linear in t as shown in Eqs. (5.10)–(5.11), the equilibrium total profit Π^* becomes quadratic in t.

Let us examine the properties of Π^* with respect to t. First, we consider the case where the unit transportation cost is prohibitive: $t = \bar{t}$. We have $x^*(\bar{t}) = \bar{x}$ and $y^*(\bar{t}) = 0$ and $\Pi^*(\bar{t}) = \overline{\Pi} \equiv \beta[(\alpha - c)/(2\beta)]^2$. Further, we have

$$\frac{d\Pi^*(\bar{t})}{dt} = 2\beta x^*(\bar{t}) \frac{dx^*(\bar{t})}{dt} > 0.$$

The equilibrium total profit Π^* is increasing in t if t is sufficiently close to the prohibitive level. Next, let us consider the case where the unit transportation cost is zero: $t = 0$. We have $x^*(0) = y^*(0)$ and $\Pi^*(0) = 2\beta[(2\beta - \gamma)(\alpha - c)/\Delta^*]^2$. Further, we have

$$\frac{d\Pi^*(0)}{dt} = 2\beta x^*(0) \left[\frac{dx^*(0)}{dt} + \frac{dy^*(0)}{dt} \right] = \frac{-2\beta(2\beta - \gamma)x^*(0)}{\Delta^*} < 0.$$

The equilibrium total profit Π^* is decreasing in t sufficiently close to zero.

As t moves from zero to the prohibitive level, the equilibrium total profit Π^* first decreases from $\Pi^*(0)$; reaches the minimum somewhere in between zero and $\bar{t}$; then begins to increase; finally, reaches the autarkic level $\overline{\Pi}$. Whether $\Pi^*(0)$ is higher than the autarkic level $\overline{\Pi}$ depends on the substitutability (i.e., γ) between the local and foreign oligopolistic goods. Actually, we have

$$\overline{\Pi} \gtreqless \Pi^*(0) \quad \Leftrightarrow \quad f(\gamma) \equiv \gamma^2 + 4\beta\gamma - 4\beta^2 \gtreqless 0.$$

The function f of γ is defined on the half-open interval $[0, \beta)$; it is monotonically increasing and satisfies $f(0) = -4\beta^2 < 0$ and $\lim_{\gamma \to \beta} f(\gamma) = \beta^2 > 0$. Hence, there exists a threshold value of γ, say $\hat{\gamma}$, such that $\overline{\Pi} \geq \Pi^*(0)$ if and only if $\gamma \geq \hat{\gamma}$. We distinguish two cases: one is the high-substitutability

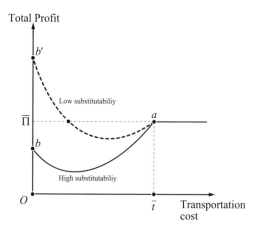

Fig. 5.2   The Equilibrium Total Profit and the Transportation Cost

case where $\gamma > \hat{\gamma}$ and the other is the low-substitutability case where $\gamma < \hat{\gamma}$.

Figure 5.2 summarizes the above results. Curves ab and ab' represent the graphs of Π^* in the high-substitutability case and in the low-substitutability case, respectively. Both curves are U-shaped; downward-sloping at the intercepts on the vertical axis; upward-sloping at point a corresponding to the prohibitive transportation cost.[13] In the high-substitutability case, the graph of Π^* is located entirely below $\overline{\Pi}$. This means that, for any non-prohibitive transportation cost, trade liberalization surely makes each firm worse-off. In contrast, in the low-substitutability case, the graph of Π^* is located above $\overline{\Pi}$ if t is sufficiently low, while it is located below $\overline{\Pi}$ if t is sufficiently high (close to $\bar{t}$). In the low-substitutability case, trade liberalization makes oligopolistic firms better-off if the transportation cost is low, while worse-off if the transportation cost is high.

Trade liberalization affects the profit of a firm through two different channels. On one hand, due to trade liberalization, each local firm comes to face harsher competition in the local market with the foreign rival than in autarky. This *pro-competitive effect* tends to reduce the profit. On the other hand, trade liberalization enables each firm to access the foreign market

---

[13]The height of point a represents the autarkic total profit $\overline{\Pi}$.

in addition to the local market. This *market-expansion effect* opens a new opportunity to earn additional profits and, therefore, tends to increase the profit. The more substitutable the local and foreign oligopolistic goods are, the severer the competition between the local and foreign firms under free trade is. When the substitutability parameter γ is sufficiently low, the pro-competitive effect becomes weaker and the market-expansion effect tends to outweigh it as far as the transportation cost is low.

The equilibrium consumer surplus: Let us consider the consumer side. Similar to the equilibrium total profit, the equilibrium consumer surplus can be written as a function of t:

$$\mathrm{CS}^*(t) = 2\alpha\chi^* - (\beta + \gamma)(\chi^*)^2 - \frac{(\alpha\beta + \beta c + \gamma c)}{(2\beta + \gamma)^2}t - \frac{\beta(4\beta^2 - 3\gamma^2)}{2(\Delta^*)^2}t^2,$$
(5.15)

where $\chi^* \equiv x^*(0) = y^*(0) = (\alpha - c)/(2\beta + \gamma)$. CS^* is quadratic in t and monotonically decreasing on the closed interval $[0, \bar{t}]$. Therefore, we have $\mathrm{CS}^*(t) > \mathrm{CS}^*(\bar{t})$ for all $t \in [0, \bar{t}]$ with $t \neq \bar{t}$. This implies that, for any non-prohibitive transportation cost, trade liberalization makes the consumer better-off.

Gains or losses from trade: If the unit transportation cost reaches the prohibitive level $\bar{t}$, the export supply by firm B reaches zero — the situation becomes equivalent to country A's autarky. Let $\bar{x}$ and $\bar{p}_x$ be the autarkic equilibrium quantity and price, respectively: $\bar{x} = x^*(\bar{t}) = \psi^A(0) = (\alpha - c)/(2\beta)$ and $\bar{p}_x = P_x(\bar{x}, 0) = (\alpha + c)/2$. In autarky, firm A earns its profit only from the local market and the consumer in country A only consumes the local oligopolistic good as well as the numéraire. The profit and consumer surplus in autarky are $\bar{\Pi} = (\bar{p}_x - c)\bar{x} = (\alpha - c)^2/(4\beta)$ and $\overline{\mathrm{CS}} = 3(\alpha - c)^2/(8\beta)$. The autarkic total welfare is, therefore, $\overline{W} = 5(\alpha - c)^2/(8\beta)$. The welfare of a country, denoted by W^*, is measured by the sum of the total profit and the consumer surplus:

$$W^*(t) \equiv \Pi^*(t) + \mathrm{CS}^*(t).$$

Because both Π^* and CS^* are quadratic in t, so is W^*, too. Note that we have $\Pi^*(\bar{t}) = \bar{\Pi}$, $\mathrm{CS}^*(\bar{t}) = \overline{\mathrm{CS}}$, and $W^*(\bar{t}) = \overline{W}$.

Change in the equilibrium welfare with respect to t is represented by

$$\frac{dW^*(t)}{dt} = \frac{dCS^*(t)}{dt} + \frac{d\Pi^*(t)}{dt}$$

$$= [p_x^*(t) - c]\frac{dx^*(t)}{dt} + [p_y^*(t) - c - t]\frac{dy^*(t)}{dt} - y^*(t).$$

We can show that

$$\frac{dW^*(0)}{dt} < 0 \quad \text{and} \quad \frac{dW^*(\bar{t})}{dt} = \frac{(\alpha - c)\gamma}{2\Delta^*} > 0.$$

The former inequality follows from the fact that both CS^* and Π^* are decreasing in t at zero. The latter inequality can be derived by simple calculation. Furthermore, after tedious calculation, we can show that

$$W^*(0) - \overline{W}$$

$$= \frac{\alpha - c}{8\beta(2\beta + \gamma)^2}[\alpha(28\beta^2 - 4\beta\gamma - 3\gamma^2) + c(4\beta^2 + 20\beta\gamma + 3\gamma^2)] > 0.$$

The last inequality follows from the fact that $28\beta^2 - 4\beta\gamma - 2\gamma^2$ is positive for any γ with $0 \leq \gamma < \beta$.

Figure 5.3 illustrates the graph of W^*, which is U-shaped; downward-sloping at the intercept on the vertical axis; and upward-sloping at point a corresponding to the prohibitive transportation cost. As is easily seen from the figure, there exists a threshold value of the transportation cost, denoted

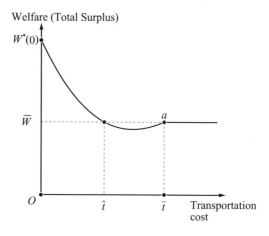

Fig. 5.3   The Equilibrium Total Surplus and the Transportation Cost

by $\hat{t}$, such that $W^*(t) > \overline{W}$ if $t < \hat{t}$ and that $W^*(t) < \overline{W}$ if $\hat{t} < t < \bar{t}$. With this observation, we can establish the following *gains-from-trade proposition* in the case of the Cournot duopoly:

Proposition 5.1. *Under the Cournot duopoly, there exist gains from trade if the transportation cost is sufficiently low. However, if the transportation cost is sufficiently high, countries may lose from trade.*[14]

5.3 Price-Setting Duopoly

Let us turn to consider the Bertrand competition where the oligopolistic firms use *prices* as their strategic variables.[15]

5.3.1 The Bertrand Duopoly Game

With the ordinary demand functions (5.4)–(5.5), the profits of firm A and firm B obtained in country A can be written as functions of prices:

$$\widetilde{\pi}^A(p_x, p_y) \equiv \frac{1}{\Delta}\left[p_x - c\right]\left[\gamma p_y - \beta p_x + \alpha(\beta - \gamma)\right],$$

$$\widetilde{\pi}^B(p_x, p_y) \equiv \frac{1}{\Delta}\left[p_y - c - t\right]\left[\gamma p_x - \beta p_y + \alpha(\beta - \gamma)\right].$$

Then, we can define a strategic-form game $(M, \{\widetilde{X}^s\}_{s \in M}, \{\widetilde{\pi}^s\}_{s \in M})$, which is called the *Bertrand duopoly game*, where $\widetilde{X}^s \equiv \mathbb{R}_+$ is the set of all possible prices of firm s. The Nash equilibrium of the Bertrand duopoly game is a pair of prices, denoted by (p_x°, p_y°), that satisfies the following conditions: for all $p_x \in \widetilde{X}^A$ and for all $p_y \in \widetilde{X}^B$,

$$\widetilde{\pi}^A(p_x^\circ, p_y^\circ) \geq \widetilde{\pi}^A(p_x, p_y^\circ) \quad \text{and} \quad \widetilde{\pi}^B(p_x^\circ, p_y^\circ) \geq \widetilde{\pi}^B(p_x^\circ, p_y).$$

The Nash equilibrium of the Bertrand duopoly game is sometimes called the "Bertrand–Nash equilibrium" for short.

---

[14]Kemp and Shiomomura (2001) have examined the gains from trade in a more general setting of a Cournot oligopoly.

[15]The exposition in this section heavily relies on Clarke and Collie (2003). We shall make some modifications and simplifications.

The range of positive demand: In order to define the best response of firm A to firm B's price strategy p_y appropriately, we have to take explicit account of the non-negative constraint of the export by firm B, because it may be the case that $y = D_y(p_x, p_y) = 0$ for some combinations of strictly positive prices. Equation (5.5) implies that $y = D_y(p_x, p_y) > 0$ if and only if $\alpha(\beta - \gamma) + \gamma p_x > \beta p_y$. Based on this observation, we define two subsets of the strategy space $\widetilde{X}^A \times \widetilde{X}^B$ as follows:

$$H_0 \equiv \left\{ (p_x, p_y) \,\middle|\, \alpha(\beta - \gamma) + \gamma p_x \leq \beta p_y \right\},$$
$$H_+ \equiv \left\{ (p_x, p_y) \,\middle|\, \alpha(\beta - \gamma) + \gamma p_x > \beta p_y \right\}.$$

By definition, we have $D_y(p_x, p_y) = 0$ for all $(p_x, p_y) \in H_0$ and $D_y(p_x, p_y) > 0$ for all $(p_x, p_y) \in H_+$. The boundary between H_0 and H_+ is represented by an upward-sloping line ff' in Fig. 5.4. Let μ be the function that represents the boundary: $p_x = \mu(p_y) \equiv (\beta/\gamma)p_y - \alpha(\beta - \gamma)/\gamma$ for $p_y \geq \alpha(\beta - \gamma)/\beta$.[16]

Firm A's best response: Ignoring the non-negative constraint of y for the moment, the first-order condition for the maximization of $\widetilde{\pi}^A$ with respect to p_x yields the following relation between p_x and p_y:

$$\frac{\partial \widetilde{\pi}^A(p_x, p_y)}{\partial p_x} = 0 \quad \Leftrightarrow \quad p_x = \lambda^A(p_y) \equiv \frac{\gamma p_y + \alpha(\beta - \gamma) + \beta c}{2\beta}.$$

Line aa' in Fig. 5.4 represents the above relation. Note that line aa' is steeper than line ff' and that they intersect at point g. Let $\hat{p}_y$ be firm B's price that corresponds to point g. If $y = 0$ is assured (irrespective of price pairs) as in autarky, then firm A's best policy is to set the monopoly price $\bar{p}_x$. Let us define $\check{p}_y$ such that $\bar{p}_x = \mu(\check{p}_y)$, which corresponds to the intersection of line ff' and the vertical line at $\bar{p}_x$ (i.e., point h) in Fig. 5.4. It is easy to check that $\check{p}_y > \hat{p}_y$. With these threshold values of p_y, $\widetilde{X}^B$ is divided into three sub-intervals: $\widetilde{X}^B_1 \equiv [0, \hat{p}_y]$, $\widetilde{X}^B_2 \equiv (\hat{p}_y, \check{p}_y)$, and $\widetilde{X}^B_3 \equiv [\check{p}_y, +\infty)$.

We consider three cases in turn. First, if $p_y \in \widetilde{X}^B_1$, we have $(\lambda^A(p_y), p_y) \in H_+$; therefore, $\lambda^A(p_y)$ is actually the best response to $p_y \in \widetilde{X}^B_1$. Next, if

---

[16]To be complete, we have to take account of the possibility that $x = D_x(p_x, p_y) = 0$ for some combinations of strictly positive prices, too. But, since the situation is symmetric for both firms, we omit here the consideration of this possibility in order to avoid unnecessary complication.

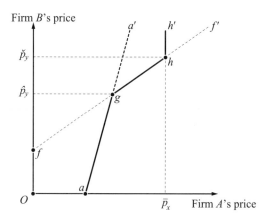

Fig. 5.4 The Price Reaction Curve of Firm A

$p_y \in \widetilde{X}_2^B$, we have $(\lambda^A(p_y), p_y) \in H_0$, implying that $\lambda^A(p_y)$ is not the best response to p_y. Because we have $\lambda^A(p_y) < \mu(p_y) < \bar{p}_x$, firm A can increase its profit by unilaterally increasing p_x until the price pair reaches the boundary ff'. Once the price pair has reached the boundary, a further increase in p_x will lower the profit of firm A. Therefore, $\mu(p_y)$ is the best response to $p_y \in \widetilde{X}_2^B$. Lastly, if $p_y \in \widetilde{X}_3^B$, we have $(\bar{p}_x, p_y) \in H_0$, implying that $\bar{p}_x$ is the best response to $p_y \in \widetilde{X}_3^B$. With these observations, we can define the (price-) reaction function of firm A, denoted by φ^A, as follows:

$$\varphi^A(p_y) \equiv \begin{cases} \lambda^A(p_y) & \text{if} \quad 0 \leq p_y \leq \hat{p}_y, \\ \mu(p_y) & \text{if} \quad \hat{p}_y < p_y < \check{p}_y, \\ \bar{p}_x & \text{if} \quad \check{p}_y \leq p_y. \end{cases}$$

In Fig. 5.4, the graph of φ^A is represented by the kinked line $aghh'$.

Firm B's best response: Let us turn to the (price-) reaction function of firm B. Ignoring the non-negative constraint of y for the moment, the first-order condition for the maximization of $\widetilde{\pi}^B$ with respect to p_y yields the following relation:

$$\frac{\partial \widetilde{\pi}^B(p_x, p_y)}{\partial p_y} = 0 \Leftrightarrow p_y = \lambda^B(p_x) \equiv \frac{\gamma p_x + \alpha(\beta - \gamma) + \beta(c + t)}{2\beta}.$$

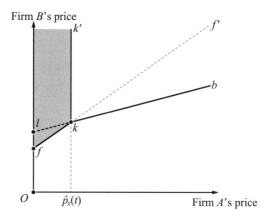

Fig. 5.5   The Price Reaction Curve of Firm *B*

Note that λ^B is positively dependent on the unit transportation cost t. Line *bkl* in Fig. 5.5 represents the graph of λ^B for a mildly high t. The graph of λ^B intersects with the boundary ff'. Let $\hat{p}_x(t)$ be firm *A*'s price that corresponds to the intersection. Because line *bkl* is flatter than line ff' and it shifts up when t increases, $\hat{p}_x(t)$ is increasing in t. With this threshold value, $\widetilde{X}^A$ is divided into two sub-intervals: $\widetilde{X}_1^A(t) \equiv [0, \hat{p}_x(t)]$ and $\widetilde{X}_2^A(t) \equiv (\hat{p}_x(t), +\infty)$.

Let us consider two cases in turn. First, suppose $p_x \in \widetilde{X}_1^A(t)$ and take an arbitrary $p_y \in \widetilde{X}^B$ such that $0 \le p_y < \mu^{-1}(p_x)$; we have $(p_x, p_y) \in H_+$ in this case. From (p_x, p_y), firm *B* can increase its profit by unilaterally increasing p_y until it reaches $\mu^{-1}(p_x)$. Therefore, p_y with $0 \le p_y < \mu^{-1}(p_x)$ cannot be the best response to $p_x \in \widetilde{X}_1^A(t)$. Once price pair (p_x, p_y) has reached H_0, a further increase in p_y will not increase nor decrease the profit of firm *B*. Actually, the profit becomes zero for all p_y with $p_y \ge \mu^{-1}(p_x)$, because the sales of export is zero for all $(p_x, p_y) \in H_0$. Therefore, any p_y with $p_y \ge \mu^{-1}(p_x)$ is the best response to $p_x \in \widetilde{X}_1^A(t)$. The best response is not determined uniquely, rather it is the half-open interval $[\mu^{-1}(p_x), +\infty)$.[17] Next, suppose $p_x \in \widetilde{X}_2^A(t)$. Then, we have $(p_x, \lambda^B(p_x)) \in H_+$, implying that

---

[17]Although Clarke and Collie (2003) have argued that no firm imposes the price less than the effective marginal cost (i.e., $c + t$) and the best response is $c + t$ in this case, it is not true when the sales is expected to be zero.

$\lambda^B(p_x)$ is the best response to p_x. Summarizing these results, we can define the (price-) reaction function of firm B[18]:

$$\varphi^B(p_x) \equiv \begin{cases} [\mu^{-1}(p_x), +\infty) & \text{if } 0 \leq p_x \leq \hat{p}_x(t), \\ \lambda^B(p_x) & \text{if } p_x > \hat{p}_x(t). \end{cases}$$

In Fig. 5.5, the graph of φ^B is represented by the kinked line bkf together with the shaded area.

Similar to the Cournot duopoly case, the reaction functions naturally defines a mapping φ from $\widetilde{X}^A \times \widetilde{X}^B$ to itself such that $\varphi: (p_x, p_y) \rightarrow (\varphi^A(p_y), \varphi^B(p_x))$. The Bertrand–Nash equilibrium, denoted by (p_x°, p_y°), is nothing but a fixed point of φ.

5.3.2 *Free Trade Equilibrium with Positive Trade*

Suppose that the unit transportation cost is reasonably low such that the reaction curve of firm B is represented by the kinked line bkf in Fig. 5.6. The reaction curve of firm A is the kinked line $aghh'$. The intersection (i.e., point e) of these reaction curves represents the Bertrand–Nash equilibrium. Because point e is in H_+, positive export by firm B occurs in equilibrium. By solving the fixed point condition, we obtain the equilibrium prices:

$$p_x^\circ = \frac{(2\beta + \gamma)\{\alpha(\beta - \gamma) + \beta c\}}{\Delta^*} + \frac{\beta\gamma}{\Delta^*}t, \tag{5.16}$$

$$p_y^\circ = \frac{(2\beta + \gamma)\{\alpha(\beta - \gamma) + \beta c\}}{\Delta^*} + \frac{2\beta^2}{\Delta^*}t. \tag{5.17}$$

Further, by substituting Eqs. (5.16)–(5.17) into the demand functions (5.4)–(5.5), we obtain the equilibrium quantities:

$$x^\circ = \frac{\beta(\beta - \gamma)(2\beta + \gamma)(\alpha - c)}{\Delta\Delta^*} + \frac{\beta^2\gamma}{\Delta\Delta^*}t, \tag{5.18}$$

$$y^\circ = \frac{\beta(\beta - \gamma)(2\beta + \gamma)(\alpha - c)}{\Delta\Delta^*} - \frac{\beta(2\beta^2 - \gamma^2)}{\Delta\Delta^*}t. \tag{5.19}$$

---

[18]Mathematically, φ^B is not a function but a *correspondence* that associates each $p_x \in \widetilde{X}^A$ with a certain subset of $\widetilde{X}^B$.

The equilibrium prices and quantities depend on the unit transportation cost; if necessary, we shall write them as $p_x^*(t)$, $p_y^*(t)$, $x^\circ(t)$, and $y^\circ(t)$. As is obvious from Eqs. (5.16)–(5.19), both the equilibrium prices are increasing in t; the equilibrium local supply is also increasing in t; while the equilibrium export supply is decreasing in t. The responses of the equilibrium prices and quantities against an increase in the transportation cost are qualitatively the same as in the Cournot duopoly case.

Comparisons with the Cournot case: Let t° be the (minimum) prohibitive transportation cost that solves $y^\circ(t) = 0$, that is, $t^\circ \equiv (\beta - \gamma)(2\beta + \gamma)$ $(\alpha - c)/(2\beta^2 - \gamma^2)$. It is easy to verify that the prohibitive transportation cost $\bar{t}$ in the Cournot case is higher than t° in the Bertrand case.

$$\bar{t} - t^\circ = \frac{(\alpha - c)\gamma^3}{2\beta(2\beta^2 - \gamma^2)} > 0.$$

To make meaningful comparisons between the Cournot and Bertrand cases with positive international trade, we assume $0 \le t \le t^\circ$ for the moment.

Both the equilibrium prices of local supply and export supply in the Cournot case are higher than those in the Bertrand case, respectively:

$$p_x^*(t) - p_x^\circ(t) = \frac{(\alpha - c)\gamma^2}{\Delta^*} > 0,$$

$$p_y^*(t) - p_y^\circ(t) = \frac{(\alpha - c - t)\gamma^2}{\Delta^*} > 0.$$

Intuitively, the competition between firms when they are using prices as the strategic variables is harsher than when they are using quantities. Accordingly, the equilibrium prices tend to be lower in the Bertrand case.

The equilibrium local supply in the Cournot case is smaller than that in the Bertrand case:

$$x^*(t) - x^\circ(t) = \frac{-(\alpha - c)(\beta - \gamma)\gamma^2}{\Delta\Delta^*} - \frac{\gamma^3}{\Delta\Delta^*}t < 0.$$

The difference in the equilibrium quantities of export supply in two cases is not monotonic, but dependent on the transportation cost.

$$y^*(t) - y^\circ(t) = \frac{-(\alpha - c)(\beta - \gamma)\gamma^2}{\Delta\Delta^*} + \frac{\beta\gamma^2}{\Delta\Delta^*}t.$$

If t is sufficiently close to zero, we have $y^*(t) < y^\circ(t)$. In contrast, if t is sufficiently close to t° (but, less than $\bar{t}$), we have $y^*(t) > y^\circ(t) \approx 0$.

Reciprocal dumping revisited: In the Bertrand case, we can confirm the reciprocal dumping, too. As in the Cournot case, the price of export by firm B in country A is equivalent to the price of export by firm A in country B. Therefore, the FOB price of firm A's export to country B is $p_y^\circ - t$. The *dumping margin* — the difference between the local price and the FOB price — is calculated as follows:

$$p_x^\circ - (p_y^\circ - t) = \frac{(\beta\gamma + 2\beta^2 - \gamma^2)t}{\Delta^*} > 0. \tag{5.20}$$

By comparing Eqs. (5.14) and (5.20), we recognize that the dumping margin in the Bertrand case is smaller than that in the Cournot case: $p_x^\circ - (p_y^\circ - t) < p_x^* - (p_y^* - t)$. The parallel-export is not profitable; the reverse-import is not profitable, either.

$$p_x^\circ - (p_y^\circ + t) = \frac{-(2\beta - \gamma)(3\beta + \gamma)t}{\Delta^*} < 0.$$

Therefore, we have $|p_x^\circ - p_y^\circ| \leq t$ with equality only if $t = 0$. No profitable arbitrage is possible in the Bertrand case as in the Cournot case.

The equilibrium profit: By substituting Eqs. (5.16)–(5.17) into the definition of the profit and taking account of the symmetry assumption, we can write the profit of a firm obtained from the domestic market and from the foreign market, respectively, as functions of t: for $t \in [0, t^\circ]$,

$$\widetilde{\pi}_D(t) \equiv \widetilde{\pi}^A(p_x^\circ(t), p_y^\circ(t)) \equiv \frac{\Delta}{\beta}[x^\circ(t)]^2,$$

$$\widetilde{\pi}_{EX}(t) \equiv \widetilde{\pi}^B(p_x^\circ(t), p_y^\circ(t)) \equiv \frac{\Delta}{\beta}[y^\circ(t)]^2.$$

The equilibrium total profit of a firm is

$$\Pi^\circ(t) \equiv \widetilde{\pi}_D(t) + \widetilde{\pi}_{EX}(t) = \frac{\Delta}{\beta}[x^\circ(t)]^2 + \frac{\Delta}{\beta}[y^\circ(t)]^2.$$

Because the equilibrium quantities are linear in t, the equilibrium total profit becomes quadratic in t. Simple calculation yields

$$\frac{d\Pi^\circ(0)}{dt} = \frac{-2(\beta - \gamma)(2\beta + \gamma)\chi^\circ}{\Delta^*} < 0,$$

$$\frac{d\Pi^\circ(t^\circ)}{dt} = \frac{2\beta\gamma(4\beta\gamma + 2\beta^2 - \gamma^2)\chi^\circ}{(2\beta^2 - \gamma^2)\Delta^*} > 0,$$

where $\chi^\circ \equiv x^\circ(0) = y^\circ(0) > 0$. Similar to the Cournot case, the equilibrium total profit has a U-shaped graph on the interval $[0, t^\circ]$.

The equilibrium consumer surplus: The consumer surplus can be written as a function of t: for $t \in [0, t^\circ]$,

$$\begin{aligned} CS^\circ(t) = &\frac{\beta(2\beta + \gamma)(\alpha - c)\chi^\circ}{\Delta^*} - \frac{\beta(\beta - \gamma)(2\beta + \gamma)(\alpha - \rho)}{\Delta\Delta^*}t \\ &+ \frac{\beta^3(4\beta^2 - 3\gamma^2)}{2\Delta(\Delta^*)^2}t^2, \end{aligned} \tag{5.21}$$

where $\rho \equiv p_x^\circ(0) = p_y^\circ(0)$. Simple calculation yields

$$\frac{dCS^\circ(0)}{dt} = \frac{-\beta(\beta - \gamma)(2\beta + \gamma)(\alpha - \rho)}{\Delta\Delta^*} < 0,$$

$$\frac{dCS^\circ(t^\circ)}{dt} = \frac{-\beta\gamma(\beta - \gamma)(2\beta + \gamma)^2(\alpha - c)\{(4\beta^2 - 3\gamma^2)\beta + \gamma^3\}}{(2\beta^2 - \gamma^2)(\Delta^*)^2} < 0.$$

Therefore, CS° is monotonically decreasing in $t \in [0, t^\circ]$.

The equilibrium welfare: The welfare of a country is measured by the equilibrium total surplus:

$$W^\circ(t) \equiv \Pi^\circ(t) + CS^\circ(t).$$

Simple calculation yields

$$\frac{dW^\circ(0)}{dt} < 0 \quad \text{and} \quad \frac{dW^\circ(t^\circ)}{dt} = \frac{\beta\gamma x^\circ(t^\circ)}{\Delta^*} > 0.$$

The first inequality follows from the fact that both Π° and CS° are decreasing in t at zero. Despite that CS° is decreasing in t at the prohibitive transportation cost, the second inequality holds, reflecting the fact that Π° is increasing in t there. Similar to the Cournot case, the equilibrium total surplus W° has a U-shaped graph on the interval $[0, t^\circ]$.

5.3.3 Free Trade Equilibrium with No Trade

When the unit transportation cost reaches the (minimum) prohibitive level t°, the export by firm B vanishes. But, this does not replicate the autarkic situation in country A. To see this, let us consider the case where the unit transportation cost t is slightly higher than the (minimum) prohibitive level t° but lower than the prohibitive level $\bar{t}$ in the Cournot case. In this case, the reaction curve of country B is represented by the kinked curve $fe'b'$ in Fig. 5.6, while that of country A is represented by the kinked curve $aghh'$.[19]

Multiple equilibria: The graphs of the reaction functions of both firms overlap on the line segment ge' in Fig. 5.6, which represents the set of the Bertrand–Nash equilibria. There exists a continuum of equilibria when $t > t^\circ$. As t increases, the reflecting point of firm B's reaction curve (such as point e') moves up along the boundary ff'. Consequently, the *maximum* equilibrium prices of both local supply and export supply increase. Hereafter, to simplify the exposition, we concentrate on the relation between the unit transportation cost and the endogenous variables determined under the *maximum* equilibrium prices.

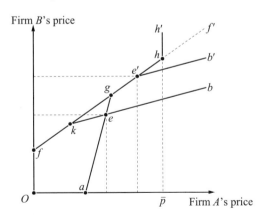

Fig. 5.6   The Bertrand–Nash Equilibria

---

[19]We can safely ignore the shaded part of the graph of firm B's reaction function.

The *maximum* equilibrium price of local supply is

$$p_x^\circ(t) = \alpha - \frac{\beta\{\alpha - (c + t)\}}{\gamma}$$

and the *maximum* equilibrium price of export supply is $p_y^\circ(t) = c + t$. Because the equilibrium points are on the boundary between H_0 and H_+, the equilibrium export supply is zero: $y^\circ(t) = 0$ for all $t \geq t^\circ$. In contrast, the equilibrium quantity of local supply that corresponds to the maximum equilibrium prices is

$$x^\circ(t) = \frac{\alpha - c - t}{\gamma}.$$

It is easy to verify that if $t^\circ \leq t < \bar{t}$, we have both $p^\circ(t) < \bar{p}_x$ and $x^\circ(t) > \bar{x}$. Despite the fact that actual entry of firm B does not occur and, therefore, firm A is the *de facto* monopoly in its local market when $t \geq t^\circ$, firm A still sets its price lower than the monopoly price and supplies the good more than in autarky. Facing the *threat of potential entry* by firm B under free trade, firm A refrains from imposing the monopoly price.

Trade gains without actual trade: Although trade liberalization (when t is high) does not induce positive international trade, it has substantial effects on the welfare of country A. Comparing to the autarkic situation, firm A reduces its price, increases the local supply, and suffers from a lower profit. In contrast, the consumer in country A can enjoy a higher surplus and the total welfare is also higher than in autarky. Formally, we can easily calculate the equilibrium profit, consumers surplus, and the total welfare: for $t \in [t^\circ, \bar{t})$,

$$\Pi^\circ(t) = \frac{-\beta t^2 + (2\beta - \gamma)(\alpha - c)t - (\beta - \gamma)(\alpha - c)^2}{\gamma^2},$$

$$CS^\circ(t) = \frac{3\beta(\alpha - c - t)^2}{2\gamma^2},$$

$$W^\circ(t) = \frac{\beta t^2 - 2(\beta + \gamma)(\alpha - c)t + (\beta + 2\gamma)(\alpha - c)^2}{2\gamma^2}.$$

The equilibrium profit Π° is quadratic in t and attains its maximum at $\bar{t}$. Therefore, Π° is monotonically increasing in $t \in [t^\circ, \bar{t})$. The equilibrium consumer surplus CS° is also quadratic and monotonically decreasing in t.

The equilibrium total welfare $W°$ is quadratic and attains its minimum at $t = (\beta+\gamma)(\alpha-c)/\beta$, which is greater than $\bar{t}$. Therefore, $W°$ is monotonically decreasing in $t \in [t°, \bar{t})$.

5.3.4 Welfare Under the Bertrand Duopoly

Figure 5.7 summarizes the welfare consequences of trade liberalization under the Bertrand duopoly. The range of the transportation cost is divided into three sub-intervals: $[0, t°)$, $[t°, \bar{t})$ and $[\bar{t}, +\infty)$. If the transportation cost t is in the first sub-interval, positive trade between countries occurs and the total welfare becomes a U-shaped function of t. If the transportation cost becomes higher and goes into the second sub-interval, no actual trade occurs. However, the country can obtain a higher welfare than in autarky; the total welfare is monotonically decreasing in t. If t reaches $\bar{t}$, the situation becomes identical to autarky and, therefore, the total welfare becomes $\overline{W}$. Here, we obtain the following theorem:

Proposition 5.2 (Clarke and Collie, 2003). *Under the Bertrand duopoly, there always exist gains from free trade.*[20]

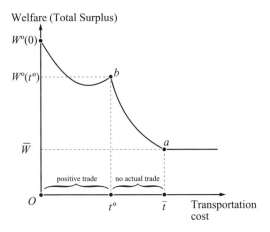

Fig. 5.7   The Equilibrium Welfare under the Bertrand Duopoly

---

[20]Strictly speaking, we have to show that the bottom of the U-shaped part of the graph of $W°$ is higher than $\overline{W}$. For the proof, see Clarke and Collie (2003).

5.4   Remarks and Further Topics

In this section, we take up two topics: one is the general oligopolistic equilibrium model developed by Neary (2003) and the other is the theoretical difficulty in endogenizing the mode of oligopolistic competition.

5.4.1   *The General Oligopolistic Equilibrium Approach*

As only one oligopolistic sector is assumed, the model used in the previous sections takes on an aspect of the *partial equilibrium* analysis. Partly because of this, trade pattern of the oligopolistic goods is not derived from fundamental parameters of the model, rather, it is assumed *a priori*. By introducing *multiple* oligopolistic sectors, Neary (2003) has developed a model that can deal with, among others, the endogenous determination of trade pattern of the oligopolistic goods in a *general equilibrium* setting. To avoid some technical/conceptual difficulties pertaining to firms' strategic decision making in a general equilibrium setting, a continuum of oligopolistic sectors is assumed. With this assumption, we can concentrate our attention only on the strategic interactions between firms *within* each one of oligopolistic sectors and safely ignore the strategic interactions *across* different oligopolistic sectors. We briefly review a simplified version of Neary (2003)'s model.

Basic setting: There are two countries A and B. The oligopolistic sectors are indexed by the real numbers in the unit interval $[0, 1]$. For $i \in [0, 1]$, we call the good produced in the ith oligopolistic sector as "good i". The markets for good i in two countries are segmented. In each country, there is a single firm who can produce good i. Therefore, in autarky, the market for good i in a country is dominated by a monopoly. In contrast, under free trade, the market becomes duopoly à la Cournot in which firms of both countries use quantities as the strategic variables. Goods are produced by using only labor as inputs. The labor input coefficient of good i in country s is denoted by $c^s(i)$. We *do not* assume the symmetric technology between firms. Similar to the continuum Ricardian model, we assume that the oligopolistic goods are numbered so that the ratio of the labor input coefficients, $c^A(i)/c^B(i)$, is increasing in $i \in [0, 1]$. Actually, we adopt a stronger assumption that $c^A(i)$ is increasing but $c^B(i)$ is decreasing in i. This implies that country A tends to have comparative advantages in terms of the labor input coefficients over country B in those oligopolistic goods with lower indices. To simplify the exposition, we assume away transportation costs.

Utility and demand functions: Let Q_i be the consumption of good i and z be that of the numéraire. We assume the following utility function:

$$U = \int_0^1 \left[\alpha Q_i - \frac{\beta}{2}(Q_i)^2 \right] di + z, \qquad (5.22)$$

which is a multisector extension of the utility function (5.1) with the assumption $\gamma \to \beta$.[21] We assume that α and β are independent of the identities of goods and countries. In this sense, the demand structures are symmetric between countries and across the oligopolistic sectors. From the utility function (5.22), we can derive the inverse demand function: for $i \in [0, 1]$,

$$p_i = \alpha - \beta Q_i,$$

where p_i is the price of good i.

Equilibrium in one sector: Let us concentrate on the situation in one typical oligopolistic sector in country A. We write the labor input coefficients of the countries simply as c^A and c^B without explicit indication of the identity of the oligopolistic good. Let x and y be the domestic supply by firm A and the export supply by firm B, respectively. Then, we have $Q = x + y$. The reaction function of firm A is $\psi^A(y) \equiv (\alpha - c^A)/(2\beta) - y/2$, which can be derived from Eq. (5.8) by setting $\gamma \to \beta$. Note that the domestic supply x by firm A can vanish if c^A is sufficiently high. That is, if $c^A \geq \alpha$, then $\psi^A(y) = 0$ for all $y \geq 0$. Similarly, the reaction function $\psi^B(x)$ of firm B can be derived from Eq. (5.9).

---

[21]In order to examine the general-equilibrium interaction between the factor market and the good market, which is realized through the income effects (more specifically, through the changes in the marginal utility of income), Neary (2003) has assumed away the numéraire. In this subsection, to make the model as simple as possible, we introduce the numéraire and, thereby, omit the income effects on the oligopolistic goods.

By solving the fixed point condition $(\psi^A(y^*), \psi^B(x^*)) = (x^*, y^*)$, we obtain the equilibrium values of the local supply by firm A and the export supply by firm B:

$$x^* = \frac{\alpha - 2c^A + c^B}{3\beta} \quad \text{and} \quad y^* = \frac{\alpha + c^A - 2c^B}{3\beta},$$

which can be derived from Eqs. (5.10)–(5.11) by setting $\gamma \to \beta$. The equilibrium values depend on the labor input coefficients (i.e., the marginal costs) of the firms. We have that $x^* \geq 0$ if $2c^A \leq c^B + \alpha$ and that $y^* \geq 0$ if $2c^B \leq c^A + \alpha$. Therefore, if the combinations of the labor input coefficients (c^A, c^B) violate one of these inequality conditions, it is possible to have $x^* = 0$ or $y^* = 0$.

Figure 5.8, in which c^A is measured horizontally and c^B vertically, illustrates the relation between the combinations of the labor input coefficients and the production/specialization patterns. The $c^A - c^B$ plane is divided into four subregions by the conditions of $\psi^A(y) = 0$, $x^* = 0$, $\psi^B(x) = 0$, and $y^* = 0$. Segment km represents the boundary of $x^* = 0$ and segment lm represents the boundary of $y^* = 0$. Then, we have (i) if the combination of the labor input coefficients (c^A, c^B) for a certain oligopolistic good is in the subregion labeled "Both", then both firm A and firm B supply positive amounts of the oligopolistic good to country A's market; (ii) if (c^A, c^B) is

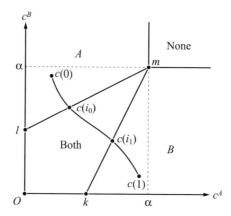

Fig. 5.8   Combinations of the Labor Input Coefficients and the Oligopolistic General Equilibrium

Source: Neary (2003) with appropriate modifications.

in the subregion labeled "None", no firm supplies the oligopolistic good; (iii) if (c^A, c^B) is in the subregion A, only firm A supplies a positive amount to country A's market — the domestic monopoly prevails; (iv) if (c^A, c^B) is in the subregion B, only firm B supplies a positive amount to country A's market — the foreign monopoly prevails.[22]

Specialization/trade patterns: Define a mapping $c\colon [0, 1] \rightarrow \mathbb{R}_+^2$ such that $c(i) \equiv (c^A(i), c^B(i))$. Curve $c(0) - c(1)$ in Fig. 5.8 represents the image of c. As we assumed that $c^A(i)$ is increasing but $c^B(i)$ is decreasing in i, the curve becomes downward-sloping. The curve has an intersection $c(i_0)$ with segment km and another intersection $c(i_1)$ with segment lm.[23] With this observation, we can divide the range of the oligopolistic goods into three subintervals: $[0, 1] = [0, i_0] \cup (i_0, i_1) \cup [i_1, 1]$. The first subinterval $[0, i_0]$ is the set of the oligopolistic goods that only firms in country A can produce positive amounts of goods and export them to country B. The second subinterval (i_0, i_1) is the set of the oligopolistic goods that firms in both countries produce positive amounts. Accordingly, intra-industry trade of these oligopolistic goods occurs. The last subinterval $[i_1, 1]$ is the set of the oligopolistic goods that only firms in country B can produce positive amounts of goods and export them to country A. Similar to the continuum Ricardian model, each country tends to export those goods that the country has comparative advantages (in terms of the ratio of the labor input coefficients) over the other country. This associates the differences in technologies of producing the oligopolistic goods with trade patterns.

5.4.2 Difficulty in Endogenizing the Mode of Competition

In the main part of this chapter, we dealt with two different modes of oligopolistic competition separately: the Cournot competition, in which firms use "quantity" as the strategic variable, and the Bertrand competition, in which firms use "price" as the strategic variable. Although there sometimes arises an attempt to construct a unified model endogenizing the mode

---

[22]For each given (c^A, c^B), because we assumed the symmetric demand structures in both countries, the same production pattern arises in country B as well.

[23]The image of c may fail to have intersections with the boundaries of $x^* = 0$ and $y^* = 0$. To assure the existence of the intersections, we need some additional assumptions on the properties of $c^s(i)$.

of competition, it will be confronted with some theoretical difficulties. The mode of competition depends on what firms know about the demand structure and also on how each firm thinks of (or believes) the rival's behavior. The mode of competition cannot be regarded as a result of the firms' deliberate choice.

Choice of price–quantity combinations: To see the point, let us consider a situation where each firm can have control over pairs of price and quantity of its own product. Suppose that firms' knowledge and beliefs are the same as in the case of the Cournot competition. Specifically, let us assume that [K_C]: each firm knows the inverse demand function for its own product and that [B_C]: each firm believes that the rival firm uses "quantity" as the strategic variable.[24] Take firm A for example. That firm A knows the inverse demand function P_x means that firm A knows the relation between price p_x, its own quantity x, and firm B's quantity y depicted by $p_x = P_x(x, y)$. Then, the price–quantity combinations available to firm A are restricted to the set $X^A_{\text{cournot}} \equiv \{(p_x, x) \mid p_x = P_x(x, y)\}$. Similarly we can define $X^B_{\text{cournot}} \equiv \{(p_y, y) \mid y = P_y(x, y)\}$ for firm B.

   Taking the rival's quantity as given, firm s chooses the profit-maximizing price–quantity combination from X^s_{cournot} — this reflects the definition of the reaction function. It should be noted that each firm cannot choose both price and quantity separately; the degree of freedom to choose an appropriate price–quantity combination is *one*. Each firm can use either "price" or "quantity" (but, not both) as the independent strategic variable. Whichever each firm opts to use as the independent strategic variable, the result (i.e., the Cournot–Nash equilibrium) will not be altered.[25]

Assumptions for endogenizing the mode of competition: In order to construct a model in which the mode of competition is endogenously determined through firms' deliberate choice, it is necessary to assume that [K_E]: each firm knows *both* the inverse and ordinary demand functions for its

---

[24]Here, K_C and B_C stand for "Knowledge" (about the demand structure) and "Belief" (about the rival's behavior) in the "Cournot" case, respectively.

[25]Similar argument also applies to the Bertrand competition case, in which the sets of available price–quantity combinations are defined follows: $X^A_{\text{bertrand}} \equiv \{(p_x, x) \mid x = D_x(p_x, p_y)\}$ and $X^B_{\text{bertrand}} \equiv \{(p_y, y) \mid y = D_y(p_x, p_y)\}$.

own product and that [B$_E$]: each firm believes that the rival firm uses *both* price and quantity as the strategic variables.[26] Assumption [K$_E$] is required in order for each firm to be able to make a meaningful comparison between the results of the Cournot and Bertrand cases. It should be noted that Assumption [K$_E$] is equivalent to an alternative assumption that each firm knows *the system of demand*, which is represented by either Eqs. (5.2)–(5.3) or Eqs. (5.4)–(5.5). Assumption [B$_E$] is required because we are considering firms' deliberate choice of the strategic variables. In this case, the sets of price–quantity combinations available to firms are defined as follows: $X^A \equiv \{(p_x, x)| \ p_x = P_x(x, y), \ x = D_x(p_x, p_y)\}$ for firm A and $X^B \equiv \{(p_y, y)| \ p_y = P_y(x, y), \ y = D_y(p_x, p_y)\}$ for firm B.

Indeterminacy of equilibria: To be specific, let us consider firm A. Under the assumptions of [K$_E$] and [B$_E$], firm A can solve the system of equations $p_x = P_x(x, y)$ and $x = D_x(p_x, p_y)$ for (p_x, x). In other words, for a given pair of firm B's price and quantity, the set X^A becomes a singleton. In this case, firm A's profit maximization problem becomes degenerate, because the degree of freedom to choose (p_x, x) from X^A is *zero*. The same argument applies to firm B as well. Accordingly, whatever the games between firms are, the equilibria of those games will be indeterminate in the sense that *every* possible tuple of prices and quantities that satisfies the "system of demand" can constitute an equilibrium. This is the difficulty we are confronted with when we try to endogenize the mode of competition in an oligopolistic situation. It is important to note that the indeterminacy argument here only depends upon the assumptions on the knowledge and belief of each single firm (Assumptions [K$_E$] and [B$_E$]), but not on the structure of the "Common Knowledge" of the firms.

---

[26] Subscript E to K$_E$ and B$_E$ stands for "Endogenous" (determination of the mode of competition).

Chapter 6

Monopolistic Competition

We develop models incorporating monopolistic competition, which are characterized by the increasing-returns-to-scale technology and product differentiation. The monopolistically competitive models have been first introduced to international trade theory in order to explain so-called *intra-industry trade* — the phenomenon that goods or services *within the same category* of a certain classification are exchanged internationally. Since then, they have been applied to various topics that are difficult (sometimes, impossible) to explain within the framework of classical theories of comparative advantage based on perfect competition.

Earlier models of monopolistic competition heavily rely on the assumption of technological symmetry among firms.[1] Stimulated by the recent empirical findings that firms even within the same industry have different characteristics and diversified productivities, the monopolistically competitive models have been modified so as to suitably incorporate such *firm heterogeneity*. Moreover, the development of monopolistically competitive models has brought about a renewal or a revival of a branch of economics that examines geographic characteristics of an economy such as locational decisions and distribution of economic agents (firms and/or workers), regional concentration of industries, formation of cities, and others. This is now known as the *New Economic Geography* (NEG) or *Spatial Economics*.

---

[1]In the course of the development of monopolistically competitive trade models, P. R. Krugman has played a central role and made a great deal of contributions. For his earlier contributions, see Krugman (1979, 1980, 1981).

6.1   Product Differentiation

Suppose that there are two goods of which basic functions are the same. When consumers can distinguish one good from the other by such *non-price aspects* as qualities, colors, trademarks, logos, brand names, packaging, after-sales services, and so forth, we say that these goods are *differentiated*. When goods are distinguished by their qualities (from low to high), this is called *vertical differentiation*; other cases are called *horizontal differentiation*. In this chapter, we focus on the horizontal differentiation.

Product differentiation is a firm's strategy that makes its own product distinguishable from those produced by the other firms. If a firm somehow succeeds in product differentiation, it can exercise market power to control the price of its own product to some extent. On the other hand, if a rival firm succeeds in developing a new differentiated good, which is recognized as a close substitute for the existing ones, and enters the market, the new entrant and the incumbent firms will have to compete for the market with each other. In this way, product differentiation makes it possible to incorporate the aspects of "monopoly" and "competition" simultaneously into a formal model.

6.1.1   *Demand for Varieties*

To construct a formal model of product differentiation, we follow the *love-of-variety approach* proposed by Dixit and Stiglitz (1977). In this approach, one category of goods is assumed to be composed of a number of *varieties* and each consumer obtains utility from consuming a number of different varieties simultaneously.[2]

Let us consider the behavior of a single household, who consumes two kinds of goods: one is a differentiated good consisting of many varieties and the other is a homogeneous good. Let Ω be the set of all varieties of the differentiated good. As we assume a continuum of varieties, the set Ω

---

[2]Another well-known approach to product differentiation is Lancaster's *ideal characteristics approach* (Lancaster, 1966). In this approach, one physical unit of a good is considered to be composed of various *characteristics* or *attributes*; goods can embody those characteristics or attributes in different proportions and, thereby, they are differentiated. Each consumer has a preference over the set of possible combinations of those characteristics and obtain utilities from consuming different combinations of characteristics embodied in physical units of goods.

can be identified with a certain closed interval on the reals; the (Lebesgue) measure of Ω can be identified with the "number" of varieties available to the household.

Specification of the utility function: The preference of a household is represented by the following utility function U, which is a composite of a Cobb–Douglas function and a Constant-Elasticity-of-Substitution (CES) function:

$$U(\{x_k\}_{k\in\Omega}, x_n) \equiv \beta \ln[D] + (1-\beta) \ln[x_n],$$

where

$$D \equiv \left[\int_{k\in\Omega} (x_k)^{\frac{\sigma-1}{\sigma}} \, dk\right]^{\frac{\sigma}{\sigma-1}} \tag{6.1}$$

with $\sigma > 1$ and $1 > \beta > 0$, where x_k denotes the consumption of the kth variety of the differentiated good and x_n denotes the consumption of the homogeneous good. The CES part (i.e., D) can be seen as the *aggregate quantity index* of the differentiated good and it captures the household's attitude of "love-of-variety". To see this, let us consider a hypothetical case where the total amount of the differentiated good is fixed at X, but divided equally into m varieties. The consumption of each variety becomes $x_k = X/m$ for all $k \in \Omega$. Then, we have

$$D = \left[\int_{k\in\Omega} (X/m)^{\frac{\sigma-1}{\sigma}} \, dk\right]^{\frac{\sigma}{\sigma-1}} = m^{\frac{1}{\sigma-1}} X.$$

Because $\sigma - 1 > 0$, the quantity index D is increasing in m. That is, the household can enjoy a higher utility by consuming a larger number of varieties with smaller quantities.

Utility maximization: We take the homogeneous good as a *numéraire* and set its price equal to unity. Then, the budget constraint of a household becomes

$$I = x_n + \int_{k\in\Omega} p_k x_k \, dk, \tag{6.2}$$

where $I > 0$ is the household's income and p_k is the consumer price of variety k ($k \in \Omega$). The household's utility maximization subject to Eq. (6.2) yields the demand functions for each variety and the homogeneous good:

$$x_i = \frac{p_i^{-\sigma}\beta I}{P^{1-\sigma}}, \quad i \in \Omega,$$

$$x_n = (1-\beta)I,$$

(6.3)

where P is the *aggregate price index* of the differentiated good:

$$P \equiv \left[\int_{k\in\Omega}(p_k)^{1-\sigma}\,dk\right]^{\frac{1}{1-\sigma}}.$$

Unlike the case of discrete varieties, the price index P is not affected by changes in the price of any single variety. Therefore, Eq. (6.3) shows that the demand for variety i is decreasing in its own price p_i and that the own price elasticity of demand for variety i is constant and equal to σ for all $i \in \Omega$.

From Eqs. (6.1) and (6.3), we can verify the relation between the quantity and price indices:

$$D = \left[\int_{k\in\Omega}(p_k)^{1-\sigma}dk\right]^{\frac{\sigma}{\sigma-1}}\frac{\beta I}{P^{1-\sigma}} = \frac{\beta I}{P}.$$

That is, we have $PD = \beta I$. The aggregate price index P can be seen as the unit cost of the aggregate quantity index D. The parameter β stands for the expenditure share of the differentiated good.

6.1.2 *Production of the Differentiated Good*

Each variety of the differentiated good is produced by a single firm. In this sense, each firm is a monopoly for its own product. A firm that produces variety i is called "firm i".

Symmetric technology: Each variety can be produced by using only labor as inputs. Before starting the production of a variety, each firm has to hire a fixed amount of labor, $f > 0$, regardless of how much quantities it will produce. The fixed labor input f can be interpreted in several different ways: for example, it represents the workers for the research and development activities necessary to create a new variety of the differentiated good;

or the workers for advertisement that promotes consumers' recognition of the variety; or, the managers in the headquarter of a firm. To produce one additional unit of a variety, $a > 0$ units of labor is required. We assume that f and a are identical across all varieties. In this sense, technologies of firms producing varieties of the differentiated good are *symmetric*.

Let y_i be the quantity of production of variety i. Then, the total labor input ℓ_i required for producing y_i units of variety i becomes $\ell_i = ay_i + f$. Let w be the wage rate for labor, then the cost of producing y_i units of variety i becomes

$$C(y_i) \equiv w\ell_i = way_i + wf.$$

Obviously, the marginal cost $\mathrm{MC}(y_i) \equiv \partial C(y_i)/\partial y_i = wa$ is independent of y_i, while the average cost $\mathrm{AC}(y_i) \equiv C(y_i)/y_i = wa + wf/y_i$ is decreasing in y_i. That is, the cost function C exhibits "increasing-returns-to-scale".

6.2   Trading World and Free Entry–Exit

Now let us consider a trading world. We assume there are two countries, Home and Foreign, that have identical production technologies. The homogeneous good is produced by using only labor under the Ricardian technology with its labor input coefficient being equal to unity. Each variety of the differentiated good is produced under the technology described in the previous section. The set Ω of all varieties of the differentiated good available to the household sector is divided into two subsets: one is the set M of varieties produced in Home and the other is the set M^* of varieties produced in Foreign.[3] Let m and m^* be the measures of M and M^*, which represent the numbers of varieties produced in Home and in Foreign, respectively.

Income of a household: Home and Foreign are endowed with identical households. Let L and L^* be the numbers of households in Home and in Foreign, respectively. The preference of each household is represented by

---

[3] In general, "Foreign" variables are denoted by attaching an asterisk ($*$) to the corresponding "Home" variables.

the utility function (6.1). Every household possesses one unit of labor and supplies it inelastically only to the domestic labor market. Further, every household in one country holds equal share of the profits of the domestic firms. Let Π be the total profit of firms in Home, then the dividend income of a household in Home becomes Π/L. The total income I of a household in Home becomes $I = w \times 1 + \Pi/L$. Similarly, that of a household in Foreign becomes $I^* = w^* \times 1 + \Pi^*/L^*$.

Transportation costs and market segmentation: International trade of the differentiated good is subject to transportation costs, but domestic transactions do not incur any transportation cost. We assume *iceberg-type costs*. That is, in order to deliver one unit of the differentiated good to the importing country, $\tau > 1$ units of the differentiated good has to be shipped out from the exporting country.

Due to transportation costs, the markets in Home and Foreign are segmented. Therefore, we have to distinguish the consumer and producer prices of a variety of the differentiated good in Home and Foreign. Let p_k and $\tilde{p}_k$ be the producer price and the consumer price of variety k in Home. The producer price p_k is also called the *mill price* or the *FOB price*.[4] Correspondingly, we write p_k^* and $\tilde{p}_k^*$ for the producer and consumer prices in Foreign. If variety k is produced in Home (i.e., $k \in M$), we have $p_k = \tilde{p}_k$ and $\tilde{p}_k^* = \tau p_k$. Similarly, if variety k is produced in Foreign (i.e., $k \in M^*$), we have $p_k^* = \tilde{p}_k^*$ and $\tilde{p}_k = \tau p_k^*$.

6.2.1   *Profit Maximization of a Firm*

We concentrate on the behavior of a firm producing variety i in Home. The demand for variety i from Home is $x_i L$ and that from Foreign is $x_i^* L^*$. It should be noted that, in order to deliver $x_i^* L^*$ units to Foreign, the firm has to produce and dispatch $\tau x_i^* L^*$ units. Let y_i be the quantity of production of variety i. Taking account of Eq. (6.3), we have

$$y_i = x_i L + \tau x_i^* L^* = p_i^{-\sigma} \beta \left[\frac{Y}{P^{1-\sigma}} + \frac{\tau^{1-\sigma} Y^*}{(P^*)^{1-\sigma}} \right], \qquad (6.4)$$

---

[4]FOB stands for "Free On Board".

where $Y \equiv IL$ and $Y^* \equiv I^*L^*$ denote the total income of Home and that of Foreign, respectively. The price indices are modified as follows:

$$P = \left[\int_{k \in M} (p_k)^{1-\sigma}\, dk + \int_{k \in M^*} (\tau p_k^*)^{1-\sigma}\, dk \right]^{\frac{1}{1-\sigma}},$$

$$P^* = \left[\int_{k \in M} (\tau p_k)^{1-\sigma}\, dk + \int_{k \in M^*} (p_k^*)^{1-\sigma}\, dk \right]^{\frac{1}{1-\sigma}}.$$

It is easy to verify that the own price elasticity of y_i with respect to p_i is constant and equal to σ.

We can write the profit π_i of firm i in Home as follows:

$$\begin{aligned}
\pi_i &= \tilde{p}_i x_i L + \tilde{p}_i^* x_i^* L^* - wa\left(x_i L + \tau x_i^* L^*\right) - wf \\
&= p_i x_i L + \tau p_i x_i^* L^* - wa\left(x_i L + \tau x_i^* L^*\right) - wf \qquad (6.5) \\
&= p_i y_i - wa y_i - wf.
\end{aligned}$$

The first-order condition for profit maximization determines the *equilibrium mill price* p_i of variety i:

$$\frac{\partial \pi_i}{\partial p_i} = y_i + p_i \frac{\partial y_i}{\partial p_i} - wa \frac{\partial y_i}{\partial p_i} = 0 \Leftrightarrow p_i = \frac{wa\sigma}{\sigma - 1}. \qquad (6.6)$$

The equilibrium mill price is equal to the marginal cost wa multiplied by a constant mark-up $\sigma/(\sigma - 1)$. The *Lerner index* $(p_i - wc)/p_i$ measures the market power of a firm. With the above result, we can show that the Lerner index is equal to $1/\sigma$. This means that the lower the elasticity of substitution is, the stronger the market power of a firm is.

The maximized profit of a firm: With Eq. (6.6), the maximized profit of firm i can be written as follows: for $i \in M$,

$$\pi_i = Rw^{1-\sigma} a^{1-\sigma} - wf, \qquad (6.7)$$

where

$$R \equiv \sigma^{-\sigma}(\sigma - 1)^{\sigma-1} \beta \left[\frac{Y}{P^{1-\sigma}} + \frac{\tau^{1-\sigma} Y^*}{(P^*)^{1-\sigma}} \right].$$

Note that R comprises the total income of both countries (and other exogenous parameters). Then, R can be seen as an indicator of the market size. The labor input coefficient a can be seen as an indicator of "technology level": a lower a (i.e., higher $a^{1-\sigma}$) implies a more advanced technology.

Equation (6.7) means that the maximized profit of a firm can be decomposed into four distinctive elements: the market size R, technology $a^{1-\sigma}$, unit variable cost $w^{1-\sigma}$, and the fixed cost wf. A larger market size or a higher technology implies a higher profit, while a higher wage rate or a larger fixed input implies a lower profit.

6.2.2 The Long-run Equilibrium

Because the right-hand side of Eq. (6.6) does not depend on the identities of varieties, the equilibrium prices of all varieties produced in Home will be the same: $p_i = p \equiv wa\sigma/(\sigma - 1)$ for all $i \in M$. Similarly, we have $p_i^* = p^* \equiv w^* a\sigma/(\sigma - 1)$ for all $i \in M^*$. With these symmetry results, we can show that all Home firms share the same profit and so do all Foreign firms: $\pi_i = \pi$ for all $i \in M$ and $\pi_i^* = \pi^*$ for all $i \in M^*$. In addition, as far as the homogeneous good is produced in both countries, the wage rates are equalized to unity: $w = w^* = 1$. Then, we can rewrite the price indices and the profits of firms as follows:

$$P = \frac{a\sigma}{\sigma - 1} \left[m + \phi m^* \right]^{\frac{1}{1-\sigma}}, \tag{6.8}$$

$$P^* = \frac{a\sigma}{\sigma - 1} \left[\phi m + m^* \right]^{\frac{1}{1-\sigma}}, \tag{6.9}$$

$$\pi = \frac{\beta}{\sigma} \left[\frac{Y}{m + \phi m^*} + \frac{\phi Y^*}{\phi m + m^*} \right] - f,$$

$$\pi^* = \frac{\beta}{\sigma} \left[\frac{\phi Y}{m + \phi m^*} + \frac{Y^*}{\phi m + m^*} \right] - f,$$

where $\phi \equiv \tau^{1-\sigma}$. The parameter ϕ is called the *freeness of trade*, which is inversely related to τ. As we assume $\tau > 1$ and $\sigma > 1$, we have $0 < \phi < 1$; if $\tau \to +\infty$, then $\phi \to 0$; if $\tau \to 1$, then $\phi \to 1$. As the name of ϕ properly indicates, a higher transportation cost implies a lower freeness of trade ϕ.

Entry and exit: If $\pi > 0$, potential firms have incentives to develop new varieties and enter the market. In this case, the number of varieties produced in Home, m, increases. In contrast, if $\pi < 0$, some incumbent firms exit from the market and m decreases. Similar conditions hold true for Foreign. The *long-run equilibrium* is defined as the situation where entry and exit by firms cease and the numbers of varieties produced in both countries become definite. In other words, the long-run equilibrium is attained if and only if the following conditions are satisfied:

$$\begin{cases} \pi = 0, \\ \pi^* = 0. \end{cases} \Leftrightarrow \begin{cases} \dfrac{Y}{m + \phi m^*} + \dfrac{\phi Y^*}{\phi m + m^*} = \dfrac{f\sigma}{\beta}, \\ \dfrac{\phi Y}{m + \phi m^*} + \dfrac{Y^*}{\phi m + m^*} = \dfrac{f\sigma}{\beta}. \end{cases} \tag{6.10}$$

Because the profits of all firms vanish in the long run, the total income of every household becomes equal to the wage income, which in turn equal to unity, implying $I = I^* = 1$ and, therefore, $Y = L$ and $Y^* = L^*$. With these results, we can solve Eq. (6.10) for m and m^*:

$$m = \frac{\beta(L - \phi L^*)}{(1 - \phi)f\sigma}, \qquad m^* = \frac{\beta(L^* - \phi L)}{(1 - \phi)f\sigma}. \tag{6.11}$$

For a given ϕ, we have both $m \geq 0$ and $m^* \geq 0$ if and only if

$$\phi \leq \frac{L}{L^*} \leq \frac{1}{\phi}. \tag{6.12}$$

The total number of varieties produced in the world depends positively on the total number of households (laborers), but independent of the freeness of trade ϕ:

$$m + m^* = \frac{\beta(L + L^*)}{f\sigma}.$$

The total number of varieties becomes larger if (i) the expenditure share on the differentiated good is larger; (ii) the total number of households is larger; (iii) the fixed cost f is smaller; and (iv) the market power of each firm is larger (equivalently, σ is smaller).

Grubel–Lloyd index: Several statistical indices that measure the degree of intra-industry trade have been proposed. Among them, the Grubel–Lloyd index (Grubel and Lloyd, 1975) is the most well known and widely used one in empirical studies. Let EX and IM be the amounts of exports and imports of the differentiated good in Home, respectively. Then, the Grubel–Lloyd index, denoted by GL, is defined as follows:

$$GL \equiv 1 - \frac{|EX - IM|}{EX + IM}. \tag{6.13}$$

By definition, we have $0 \leq GL \leq 1$. If either $EX = 0$ or $IM = 0$, in other words, if Home does not engage in intra-industry trade at all, then we have

GL = 0. On the other hand, if EX = IM, that is, if Home exports and imports the differentiated good simultaneously in equal amounts, then we have GL = 1. The greater the Grubel–Lloyd index, the more active the intra-industry trade is.

In our model, we can obtain a theoretical expression of the Grubel–Lloyd index. First, let us calculate Home's import IM and export EX, the former is equal to Home's expenditure on the Foreign-produced varieties and the latter is equal to Foreign's expenditure on the Home-produced varieties. Then, we have

$$\text{IM} = \int_{k \in M^*} \tilde{p}_k x_k L \, dk = \frac{\beta \phi (L^* - \phi L)}{1 - \phi^2}.$$

$$\text{EX} = \int_{k \in M} \tilde{p}_k^* x_k^* L^* \, dk = \frac{\beta \phi (L - \phi L^*)}{1 - \phi^2}.$$

Then, the trade surplus in the differentiated good becomes

$$\text{EX} - \text{IM} = \frac{\phi \beta}{1 - \phi}(L - L^*).$$

If Home is larger than Foreign (i.e., $L > L^*$), then Home experiences trade surplus in the differentiated good. A larger country becomes a *net exporter* of the differentiated good; a smaller country a *net importer*.

Suppose $L \geqq L^*$ for brevity, then the Grubel–Lloyd index reduces to

$$\text{GL} = 1 - \frac{1 + \phi}{1 - \phi} \cdot \frac{L - L^*}{L + L^*}. \tag{6.14}$$

The right-hand side of the above expression is decreasing in ϕ and $L - L^*$. Therefore, if the difference in the country size expands or if the freeness of trade ϕ increases, intra-industry trade in the differentiated good becomes less active.[5]

Home market effect: The numbers of varieties produced in both countries depend on the relative size of the countries, which is measured by the

---

[5]It should be noted that our derivation of Eq. (6.14) depends upon the assumption of Eq. (6.12). That is, ϕ, L, and L^* are not totally independent of each other; when $\phi \rightarrow 1$, we must have $L = L^*$ by Eq. (6.12).

ratio of the numbers of households in both countries. From Eq. (6.11), we can calculate the ratio of the numbers of varieties:

$$\frac{m}{m^*} = \frac{L}{L^*} \cdot \frac{1 - \phi(L^*/L)}{1 - \phi(L/L^*)}.$$

If $L/L^* > 1$, we have $[1 - \phi(L^*/L)]/[1 - \phi(L/L^*)] > 1$, implying that $m/m^* > L/L^*$. This means that the number of varieties produced in the larger country is more-than-proportionally greater than that in the smaller country. Because the total number of varieties is independent of the distribution of households among countries, we can say that the larger country attracts a more-than-proportionally greater number of firms than the smaller country. This is known as the *home market effect*. It is well recognized that the home market effect is quite sensitive to the assumptions on transportation costs. Davis (1998) has shown that if both the differentiated good sector and the homogeneous good sector have to incur transportation costs, then the home market effect may disappear.

6.2.3 *Gains from Trade*

In Home, per capita consumption of each variety in the long run is

$$x_i = \begin{cases} \beta(\sigma - 1)(m + \phi m^*)^{-1}/(a\sigma) & \text{if } i \in M, \\ \tau^{-\sigma}\beta(\sigma - 1)(m + \phi m^*)^{-1}/(a\sigma) & \text{if } i \in M^*. \end{cases}$$

Then, the aggregate quantity index D of the differentiated good becomes

$$D = \left[\int_{k \in M} \left\{ \frac{\beta(\sigma - 1)}{a\sigma(m + \phi m^*)} \right\}^{\frac{\sigma-1}{\sigma}} dk + \int_{k \in M^*} \left\{ \frac{\tau^{-\sigma}\beta(\sigma - 1)}{a\sigma(m + \phi m^*)} \right\}^{\frac{\sigma-1}{\sigma}} dk \right]^{\frac{\sigma}{\sigma-1}}$$

$$= \frac{\beta(\sigma - 1)}{a\sigma} [m + \phi m^*]^{\frac{1}{\sigma-1}}.$$

Further, we can easily show that

$$m + \phi m^* = \frac{(1 + \phi)\beta L}{f\sigma}.$$

By substituting the above result together with $x_n = (1 - \beta)I$ and $I = 1$ into the utility function (6.1), we can write the utility level of a household in

Home as a function of the freeness of trade ϕ:

$$u(\phi) \equiv \frac{\beta}{\sigma - 1} \ln\left[\frac{(1 + \phi)\beta L}{f\sigma}\right] + \underbrace{\beta \ln\left[\frac{\beta(\sigma - 1)}{\sigma a}\right] + (1 - \beta)\ln[1 - \beta]}_{\text{constant}},$$

which is monotonically increasing in ϕ. The utility level in autarky is represented by $\bar{u} \equiv \lim_{\phi \to 0} u(\phi)$. Therefore, for any $0 < \phi < 1$, we have $\bar{u} < u(\phi)$. This establishes the *gains-from-trade proposition* in a monopolistically competitive circumstance: every household will be made better-off by opening international trade. Further, we can say that the smaller the transportation cost is, the bigger the gains from trade is. It should be noted that the trade gain arises only from the consumption side — after trade liberalization, households can consume a greater number of varieties of the differentiated good than in autarky, while firms can receive only zero profits in both situations. (As far as we assume the technological symmetry, firms do not gain nor lose from trade liberalization.)

6.3 Firm Heterogeneity

The recent development of empirical studies based on firm-level microdata has revealed some intriguing characteristics of the structure of exporting industries.[6] Roughly summarizing, those studies have shown that (i) only a small portion of firms in a so-called "exporting industry" actually export to foreign countries, but others in the same industry are operating as "domestic" firms and do not engage in international transactions; (ii) active exporting firms are larger in size and have higher productivities; (iii) the exposure to trade induces the most productive larger firms to expand their production and export, while the least productive smaller firms to shrink their activities or even to exit from the market; (iv) due to trade liberalization, the (average) productivity of an exporting industry as a whole improves. Those observations suggest that firms are *heterogeneous* in their

---

[6]See, for example, Head and Ries (1999), Pavcnik (2002), Bernard *et al.* (2003), Bernard and Jensen (2004), and Bernard *et al.* (2006).

productivities and other characteristics even within the same exporting industry.

Since the monopolistically competitive trade model (à la Krugman) introduced in the previous sections assumed the symmetry among firms at the very outset, it cannot deal with firm heterogeneity. However, Melitz (2003) has shown that the Krugman model can be modified so as to deal with firm heterogeneity appropriately. In this subsection, we explain the outline of the Melitz model. Although the original Melitz model is built on an infinite-horizon dynamic model of entry–exit, we can rely on the static Krugman model for the most part as far as we are concerned with the steady-state equilibrium of the dynamic model.

The point of departure is to introduce "uncertainty" concerning the productivity of firms into the model.[7] Firms do not know their productivities *a priori*. Productivity is a *stochastic variable* that is determined (realized) after firms' entry into the market. Events occur in the following sequence:

(i) There is a large pool of potential firms, which are assumed to be identical — Firms are symmetric or homogeneous *ex ante*.

(ii) In advance of entry to the market, each firm has to pay a fixed entry cost $f_E > 0$, which is considered as an investment cost and assumed to be *sunk*.

(iii) Upon entry, an entrant firm draws its initial productivity parameter θ from a common distribution over $(0, \infty)$ represented by a cumulative distribution function $G(\theta)$, which has a continuous density function $g(\theta)$.

(iv) Given the realized productivity, an entrant firm comes to know its own cost function $C(y) \equiv wy/\theta + wf$, where f is a fixed labor input, and it can calculate the profit $\pi(\theta)$ — Firms become heterogeneous *ex post*.

(v) If $\pi(\theta) < 0$, the firm with θ immediately exits from the market.

---

[7]Instead of introducing uncertainty in the productivity, Yeaple (2005) has considered a model in which (*ex-ante*) homogeneous firms choose technologies and employ workers with heterogenous skills and showed that the interaction between the characteristics of chosen technologies and employed workers gives rise to firm heterogeneity.

(vi) If $\pi(\theta) > 0$, on the other hand, the firm with θ will receive $\pi(\theta)$ in each period of time forever after; however, it has to be subject to an exogenous probability δ ($0 < \delta < 1$) in every period of a bad shock that forces the firm to exit. (In each period, an operating firm can survive to the next period with probability $1 - \delta$.)

6.3.1   *Zero-Cutoff-Profit and Free-Entry Conditions*

Each firm has to make its decision in two stages. In the first stage, a firm decides whether to enter or stay out of the market *without* knowing its own productivity. (We assume that the distribution of productivity, g and G, is a common knowledge to all firms.) In the second stage, after productivity is revealed, each firm decides whether to stay in or exit the market.

Value of a firm: Let us first consider the second stage. We assume here that there is a single market (Home) for the differentiated good. Recall Eq. (6.7) and let us define the productivity parameter $\theta \equiv a^{-1}$, which represents the marginal productivity of labor (i.e., the inverse of labor input coefficient). Then, the firm's profit per period can be rewritten as a function of productivity θ:

$$\pi(\theta) = Rw^{1-\sigma}\theta^{\sigma-1} - wf, \qquad (6.15)$$

where $R \equiv \sigma^{-\sigma}(\sigma - 1)^{\sigma-1}\beta Y/P^{1-\sigma}$ in this case. Accordingly, the *present value of a firm* with productivity θ (i.e., the sum of profit flows discounted by the survival probability $1-\delta$) is denoted by $v(\theta)$ and defined as follows:[8]

$$v(\theta) \equiv \max\left\{0, \ \sum_{t=0}^{+\infty}(1 - \delta)^t\pi(\theta)\right\} = \max\left\{0, \ \frac{\pi(\theta)}{\delta}\right\}.$$

As is obvious from Eq. (6.15), $\pi(\theta)$ is monotonically increasing in θ and $\pi(0) < 0$, in addition, $\pi(\theta) > 0$ for sufficiently large θ. Therefore, we have $v(\theta) \geq 0$ for all θ. Let us define $\theta^* \equiv \inf\{\theta \mid v(\theta) > 0\}$, which is called the *cutoff level*. Practically, θ^* is the solution to $\pi(\theta) = 0$ and, therefore, we

---

[8]For simplicity, we omit the time discounting.

have $\theta^* > 0$. Firms with productivity $\theta \geqq \theta^*$ will stay in the market, while those with productivity $\theta < \theta^*$ immediately exit the market.

The equilibrium productivity distribution: The cutoff level θ^* determines the range of operating firms' productivities and, therefore, the equilibrium productivity distribution μ:

$$\mu(\theta) \equiv \begin{cases} \dfrac{g(\theta)}{1 - G(\theta^*)} & \text{if } \theta \geqq \theta^*, \\ 0 & \text{if } \theta < \theta^*. \end{cases}$$

With μ, we can calculate the aggregate (weighted average) productivity level, denoted by $\tilde{\theta}$:

$$\tilde{\theta} \equiv \left[\int_0^{+\infty} \theta^{\sigma-1} \mu(\theta) \mathrm{d}\theta \right]^{\frac{1}{\sigma-1}} = \left[\frac{1}{1 - G(\theta^*)} \int_{\theta^*}^{+\infty} \theta^{\sigma-1} g(\theta) \mathrm{d}\theta \right]^{\frac{1}{\sigma-1}}.$$

By substituting $\tilde{\theta}$ into $\pi(\theta)$, we obtain the average profit $\bar{\pi} = \pi(\tilde{\theta})$.[9] Further, taking account of the definition of θ^*, we can show the relation between the average profit and the cutoff level:

$$\bar{\pi} = wf \left[\left(\frac{\tilde{\theta}}{\theta^*} \right) - 1 \right] \tag{6.16}$$

This is called the *zero-cutoff-profit condition* (ZCP), which associates the cutoff level with the average profit. (Note that $\tilde{\theta}$ depends on the cutoff level θ^*.)

Entry decision: Next, let us consider the first stage of firms' entry decision. Let $\bar{v}$ be the average value of a firm conditional on successful entry. The *ex-ante* probability of successful entry is given by $1 - G(\theta^*)$. Taking account of the entry cost f_E, the net value of entry v_E can be written as follows: $v_E \equiv [1 - G(\theta^*)]\bar{v} - f_E$. If v_E is negative, then no firm enters the market. If actual entry by some firms were to occur in equilibrium, v_E must be non-negative. Furthermore, as far as entry by firms is unrestricted and

---

[9]Of course, we have $\bar{\pi} \equiv \int_0^\infty \pi(\theta)\mu(\theta)\mathrm{d}\theta = \pi(\tilde{\theta})$.

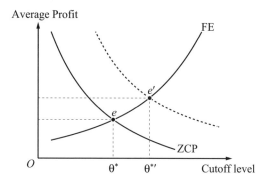

Fig. 6.1   Zero-Cutoff Profit Condition and Free-Entry Condition

the mass of prospective firms is unbounded, v_E cannot be strictly positive. Hence, we obtain the following condition:

$$v_E \equiv [1 - G(\theta^*)]\,\bar{v} - f_E = 0 \Leftrightarrow \bar{\pi} = \frac{\delta f_E}{1 - G(\theta^*)}, \qquad (6.17)$$

where $\bar{\pi} \equiv \delta\bar{v}$ denotes the amortized value of $\bar{v}$. This is called the *free-entry condition* (FE), which also associates the cutoff level with the average profit.

The equilibrium cutoff: Combining the zero-cutoff-profit condition (6.16) and the free-entry condition (6.17), we can determine the equilibrium cutoff level. Figure 6.1 illustrates the two conditions. The upward-sloping curve FE represents the free-entry condition, while the downward-sloping curve ZCP represents the zero-cutoff-profit condition.[10] The intersection, point e, of these curves determines the equilibrium cutoff level and the corresponding average profit.

6.3.2   *Export and Trade Liberalization*

Export expands the opportunity for firms to obtain additional profits by serving foreign markets on one hand, it imposes some additional costs on

---

[10]Because G is monotonically increasing, Eq. (6.17) implies that the FE curve is always upward-sloping. On the other hand, the ZCP curve is not necessarily downward-sloping. The slope of the ZCP curve depends on the shape of the cumulative distribution function G. However, the ZCP curve always cuts the FE curve from above; see Melitz (2003).

the other. We assume that a firm has to pay a fixed cost f_{EX} (once and for all) in order to participate in international transactions and that international trade requires transportation costs of iceberg-type (i.e., $\tau > 1$ as in the previous sections). The fixed cost f_{EX} may include those costs of, for example, advertising its own product to foreign markets, establishing subsidiaries, finding foreign business partners, adapting its product to foreign standards and rules, and so forth. By f_X, we denote the amortized per-period portion of f_{EX} (i.e., $f_X = \delta f_{EX}$).

Export cutoff: Suppose that there are two countries: Home and Foreign. We concentrate on firms in Home. If a firm with productivity θ operates in the Home market, it can earn the following profit from the Home (domestic) operation:

$$\pi_D(\theta) = Rw^{1-\sigma}\theta^{\sigma-1} - wf,$$

which is identical to Eq. (6.15). On the other hand, if this firm engages in export, it can obtain the following *additional* profit from export:

$$\pi_X(\theta) = R^*(\tau w)^{1-\sigma}\theta^{\sigma-1} - wf_X,$$

where $R^* = \sigma^{-\sigma}(\sigma - 1)^{\sigma-1}Y^*/(P^*)^{1-\sigma}$. If Home and Foreign are identical, we can set $R^* = R$. Note that, because of the transportation cost, the cost of delivering one unit of the differentiated good to the Foreign market is higher than that to the Home market (i.e., $\tau w > w$). This makes export less profitable than domestic operation.

Similar to Eq. (6.15), $\pi_X(\theta)$ is increasing in θ, $\pi_X(0) < 0$, and $\pi_X(\theta) > 0$ for sufficiently large θ. Depending on the sign of $\pi_X(\theta)$, a firm with productivity θ will decide whether to engage in export or not: if $\pi_X(\theta) > 0$, it engages in export; if $\pi_X(\theta) < 0$, it does not. There is another cutoff level θ_X^*, which solves $\pi_X(\theta) = 0$ and is called the *export cutoff*.

Cutoff under free trade: Now let us consider trade liberalization. Let $\pi^a(\theta)$ be the profit of a firm with productivity θ in autarky, which is identical to Eq. (6.15) or to $\pi_D(\theta)$. Let $\pi(\theta)$ be the profit under free trade, which is now defined as $\pi(\theta) \equiv \pi_D(\theta) + \max\{0, \pi_X(\theta)\}$. In addition, let $\bar{\pi}^a \equiv \int \pi^a(\theta)\mu(\theta)d\theta$ and $\bar{\pi} \equiv \int \pi(\theta)\mu(\theta)d\theta$ be the average profit in autarky and that under free trade, respectively. Because some additional export profits accrue to firms with sufficiently high productivities under free trade, we have $\bar{\pi}^a < \bar{\pi}$.

In autarky, the equilibrium cutoff level is determined as before. The intersection of the ZCP curve and the FE curve (i.e., point e) in Fig. 6.1 represents the equilibrium. Under free trade, $\bar{\pi}^a < \bar{\pi}$ implies that the ZCP curve shifts up as illustrated by the downward-sloping broken line in the figure. The FE curve is not affected by the introduction of export activities. Therefore, the equilibrium point moves to point e'. The equilibrium cutoff level increases from θ^* to $\theta^{*\prime}$. If the fixed export cost f_X is sufficiently large, we can show that $0 < \theta^{*\prime} < \theta_X^*$.

Productivity and the mode of operation: Let us consider a case where $0 < \theta^* < \theta^{*\prime} < \theta_X$. In autarky, firms with productivities less than θ^* do not enter the market in the first place and firms with higher productivities enter and serve the domestic market. By trade liberalization, the equilibrium cut-off increases to $\theta^{*\prime}$. Then, firms with productivities in-between θ^* and $\theta^{*\prime}$ are now forced to exit the market. Firms with productivity in-between $\theta^{*\prime}$ and θ_X^* serve the domestic market, but do not engage in export. Lastly, firms with productivity higher than θ_X^* supply the differentiated good both to the Home and Foreign markets. In sum, trade liberalization induces the least productive firms to exit, the middle productive firms to stay in the domestic market, the most productive firms to serve both domestic and foreign markets. Furthermore, as the least productive firms exit the market, the average productivity of the industry as a whole increases.

The classical trade models such as the Ricardo model and the HOS model show that trade liberalization induces *inter-industry* reallocation of resources. In contrast, the Melitz model emphasizes the importance of *intra-industry* reallocation of resources induced by trade liberalization.

6.4   New Economic Geography

The fruit of economic development is unevenly distributed over different regions. Within a single country, for example, economic activities tend to concentrate only on a limited number of metropolitan cities or industrialized areas. These regions can enjoy higher levels of development, while other regions fail to attract firms, workers and other economic resources and, consequently, suffer from stagnation. In the international scene, we know that there is a stark contrast between the developed countries and the less-developed countries. The well-developed regions are called the *core* of an economy, while other less-developed regions are called the *periphery*. By making intensive use of the monopolistically competitive models, the so-called *New Economic Geography* (or *Spatial Economics*) tries to identify such economic factors that endogenously determine the geographical structure of an economy. Those factors that facilitate the concentration of economic activities to a certain region are called the *agglomeration force* or the *centripetal force*, while those that restrain resources and activities from concentration are called the *dispersion force* or the *centrifugal force*. In this section, we briefly review some of basic ideas of the New Economic Geography.[11]

6.4.1 *Modification of the Model*

We return to the model with symmetric firms introduced in Sections 6.1 and 6.2 and, following Forslid and Ottaviano (2003), we slightly modify it.

Skilled and unskilled workers: Labor is now divided into two categories: skilled labor and unskilled labor. Skilled labor is used only in the research and development activities. Specifically, we assume that $f > 0$ units of skilled workers are required to develop a new variety of the differentiated good. On the other hand, unskilled labor is used to manufacture both the differentiated good and the homogeneous good. We assume that the input coefficient of unskilled labor for each variety of the differentiated good is equal to $a > 0$ and the input coefficient of unskilled labor for the homogeneous good is equal to unity.

Further, we assume that skilled workers can move freely between the countries, while unskilled workers cannot. Workers (either skilled or unskilled) spend their income and purchase consumption goods in the

---

[11] For the New Economic Geography and Spatial Economics, see Krugman (1991) and Fujita *et al.* (1999). Most of technical terms introduced in this section are taken from these works. For more recent textbooks on this subject, see, for example, Combes *et al.* (2008) and Fujita and Thisse (2013).

country of their residence.[12] Therefore, the movement or migration of skilled workers from one country to the other implies both an increase in the supply of skilled labor and an increase in the demand for goods (or, in the number of consumers) in the destination country.

Demand for the differentiated good: Both skilled and unskilled workers share the same utility function in Eq. (6.1). Let w and r be the wage rate for unskilled labor and that for skilled labor in Home, respectively. There are L unskilled workers and K skilled workers who work and live in Home. For the moment, we assume that K is given and fixed. Then, the total income spent in Home, denoted by Y, becomes $Y = wL + rK$. Similarly, the total income spent in Foreign becomes $Y^* = w^*L^* + r^*K^*$, where Foreign variables are denoted by attaching an asterisk to the corresponding Home variables. Then, the total demand for variety i of the differentiated good produced in Home can be represented by Eq. (6.4).

Profit maximization: The profit of a firm that produces variety i in Home can be rewritten as $\pi_i \equiv p_i y_i - w a y_i - rf$. The only difference between this definition and Eq. (6.5) appears in the "fixed cost" paid to the skilled workers. Therefore, the marginal conditions for profit maximization are not affected by this modification. This implies that the equilibrium *mill price* of each variety is determined by Eq. (6.6): $p_i = p \equiv wa\sigma/(\sigma - 1)$ for all varieties produced in Home. Therefore, the maximized profit of firm i in Home can be written similar to Eq. (6.7), where the fixed cost wf is now replaced by rf. Similar results hold for firms in Foreign.

6.4.2   *Equilibrium without Migration*

To simplify the exposition, we assume that the numbers of unskilled workers in Home and Foreign are the same: $L = L^*$. (Hereafter, we only use L.) The world endowment of skilled workers is $K + K^*$. Let λ denote the share of the skilled workers working and living in Home: $\lambda \equiv K/(K + K^*)$.

---

[12]Because "Home" and "Foreign" in our model can be regarded either as two different countries or as two regions within a single country, we use the terms "country" and "region" interchangeably.

Accordingly, the share of the skilled workers in Foreign is $1 - \lambda$. By appropriately choosing the unit of skilled labor, we can set the world endowment of skilled workers equal to unity: $1 = K + K^*$. Then, we can identify K and K^* with λ and $1 - \lambda$, respectively. It should be noted that, in the long run, K and K^* (hence, λ) will be determined endogenously through the migration of skilled workers.

The number of varieties: In the basic model, the numbers of varieties produced in both countries were determined through the zero-profit conditions for the long-run equilibrium. In this modified model, however, the numbers of varieties are determined through a different mechanism. Because $f > 0$ units of skilled workers are required to develop a new variety of the differentiated good, the number of varieties that can be produced in a country is restricted by the amount of skilled labor available in the country. Therefore, we must have

$$m = \frac{K}{f} = \frac{\lambda}{f} \quad \text{and} \quad m^* = \frac{K^*}{f} = \frac{1 - \lambda}{f}. \tag{6.18}$$

Price indices: If the homogeneous good is produced in both countries in equilibrium, the unskilled wage rates in both countries will be equal to unity: $w = w^* = 1$. Then, substituting Eq. (6.18) into Eqs. (6.8) and (6.9), we can write the price indices in Home and Foreign as functions of λ and ϕ:

$$P = \frac{a\sigma}{\sigma - 1} \cdot f^{\frac{1}{\sigma-1}} \cdot [\lambda + \phi(1 - \lambda)]^{\frac{1}{1-\sigma}}, \tag{6.19}$$

$$P^* = \frac{a\sigma}{\sigma - 1} \cdot f^{\frac{1}{\sigma-1}} \cdot [\phi\lambda + (1 - \lambda)]^{\frac{1}{1-\sigma}}. \tag{6.20}$$

If Home and Foreign are symmetric (i.e., $\lambda = 1/2$), we have $P = P^*$. The relative price index becomes as follows:

$$\frac{P}{P^*} \equiv \left[\frac{\lambda + \phi(1 - \lambda)}{\phi\lambda + (1 - \lambda)} \right]^{\frac{1}{1-\sigma}} = \left[\frac{(1 - \phi)\lambda + \phi}{1 - (1 - \phi)\lambda} \right]^{\frac{1}{1-\sigma}}.$$

By inspection, we can confirm that the relative price index of Home is decreasing in λ as far as $0 < \phi < 1$. By Eq. (6.18), an increase in λ implies that the number of firms producing the differentiated good in Home increases. Due to the home market effect, a harsher competition among a larger number of firms leads to a lower price index P in Home. Accordingly, the *cost of living* in a larger country becomes lower than that in a smaller country.

The skilled wage rates: Instead of determining the equilibrium numbers of the differentiated good produced in both countries, the zero-profit conditions determine the equilibrium skilled wage rates there. The total income spent in Home and that in Foreign become $Y = wL + rK = L + r\lambda$ and $Y^* = L + r^*(1 - \lambda)$, respectively. By substituting these results into the zero-profit conditions, we obtain the following system of linear equations for the skilled wage rates in Home and Foreign:

$$r = \frac{\beta}{\sigma} \left[\frac{L + r\lambda}{\lambda + \phi(1 - \lambda)} + \frac{\phi\{L + r^*(1 - \lambda)\}}{\phi\lambda + (1 - \lambda)} \right],$$

$$r^* = \frac{\beta}{\sigma} \left[\frac{\phi\{L + r\lambda\}}{\lambda + \phi(1 - \lambda)} + \frac{L + r^*(1 - \lambda)}{\phi\lambda + (1 - \lambda)} \right].$$

By solving the above system, we obtain the equilibrium skilled wage rates, which can be seen as functions of λ and ϕ:

$$r = \frac{L(\beta/\sigma)}{1 - (\beta/\sigma)} \cdot \frac{2\phi\lambda + B(1 - \lambda)}{\phi\{\lambda^2 + (1 - \lambda)^2\} + B\lambda(1 - \lambda)}, \qquad (6.21)$$

$$r^* = \frac{L(\beta/\sigma)}{1 - (\beta/\sigma)} \cdot \frac{2\phi(1 - \lambda) + B\lambda}{\phi\{\lambda^2 + (1 - \lambda)^2\} + B\lambda(1 - \lambda)}, \qquad (6.22)$$

where $B \equiv \{1 - (\beta/\sigma)\} + \{1 + (\beta/\sigma)\}\phi^2 > 0$.[13] The relative skilled wage rate (i.e., the ratio of r and r^*) becomes as follows:

$$\frac{r}{r^*} = \frac{2\phi\lambda + B(1 - \lambda)}{2\phi(1 - \lambda) + B\lambda}. \qquad (6.23)$$

Obviously, we have $r/r^* = 1$ if Home and Foreign are completely symmetric (i.e., if $\lambda = 1/2$). By simply calculating, we obtain

$$\frac{\partial(r/r^*)}{\partial\lambda} \gtreqqless 0 \Leftrightarrow (2\phi - B)(2\phi + B) \gtreqqless 0,$$

$$\Leftrightarrow 2\phi \gtreqqless \{1 - (\beta/\sigma)\} + \{1 + (\beta/\sigma)\}\phi^2.$$

$$(6.24)$$

---

[13] Since $0 < \beta < 1$ and $\sigma > 1$, we have $1 - (\beta/\sigma) > 0$.

The second line follows from $2\phi + B > 0$. The last inequality is equivalent to

$$(\phi - 1)(\phi - \phi_R) \lessgtr 0,$$

where $\phi_R \equiv \{1 - (\beta/\sigma)\}/\{1 + (\beta/\sigma)\}$. By definition, we have $0 < \phi_R < 1$. Therefore, Eq. (6.24) holds if and only if $\phi_R \leq \phi \leq 1$.[14] That is, if the freeness of trade ϕ is sufficiently high (i.e., higher than the threshold value ϕ_R), the relative skilled wage rate of Home becomes higher as Home gets larger — this is also a reflection of the "home market effect".

6.4.3 *Spatial Equilibrium*

For a given pair of λ and ϕ, endogenous variables in the short-run equilibrium such as the skilled wage rates and the price indices in Home and Foreign are determined. Observing these variables, skilled workers decide where to live in. If some skilled workers migrate from one country to the other, then λ changes. When no skilled worker has an incentive to move between countries, a *spatial equilibrium* — a geographical structure of the economy in the long run — is established.

Migration decision: Skilled workers seek a higher standard of living. The standard of living that a skilled worker can enjoy when he settles in a particular country is represented by the indirect utility function V, which is derived from the utility function (6.1):

$$V(I, P) \equiv \ln[I] - \beta \ln[P] + \underbrace{\ln[\beta^\beta (1 - \beta)^{1-\beta}]}_{\text{constant}},$$

where I and P denote the income level and the price index that the skilled worker faces in the country of residence.

Let V_H and V_F be the utility levels that a skilled worker enjoys when he resides in Home and in Foreign, respectively: $V_H \equiv V(r, P)$ and $V_F \equiv V(r^*, P^*)$, where r, r^*, P and P^* are given by Eqs. (6.19) through (6.22). If $V_H > V_F$, skilled workers in Foreign want to live in Home; on the other hand, if $V_H < V_F$, skilled workers in Home want to live in Foreign. Of course, if $V_H = V_F$, no skilled worker has an incentive to migrate from one

---

[14]The sign of $\partial(r/r^*)/\partial\lambda$ does not depend on λ, but its absolute value does.

country to the other. The difference between V_H and V_F can be written as follows:

$$\Delta V \equiv V_H - V_F = \ln[r] - \beta \ln[P] - \ln[r^*] + \beta \ln[P^*]$$

$$= \ln\left[\frac{r}{P^\beta}\right] - \ln\left[\frac{r^*}{(P^*)^\beta}\right].$$

The arguments of the logarithm in the above expression, r/P^β and $r^*/(P^*)^\beta$, represent the *real wage rate* in Home and that in Foreign, respectively. Therefore, we have $\Delta V \gtreqqless 0$ if and only if $r/P^\beta \gtreqqless r^*/(P^*)^\beta$. Clearly, this means that a skilled worker can enjoy a higher standard of living in Home if and only if the real wage rate in Home is higher than that in Foreign.

Further, taking account of Eqs. (6.19), (6.20), and (6.23), we can show that the sign of the difference in the real wage rates in Home and Foreign is equivalent to the sign of $Z(\lambda, \phi)$ defined as follows:

$$Z(\lambda, \phi) \equiv [2\phi\lambda + B(1 - \lambda)] [\lambda + \phi(1 - \lambda)]^{\frac{\beta}{\sigma - 1}}$$

$$- [2\phi(1 - \lambda) + B\lambda] [\phi\lambda + (1 - \lambda)]^{\frac{\beta}{\sigma - 1}}.$$

That is, if $Z(\lambda, \phi) > 0$, skilled workers have an incentive to migrate into Home; in contrast, if $Z(\lambda, \phi) < 0$, they have an opposite incentive.

Symmetric dispersion equilibrium and the break point: If $\lambda = 1/2$, the situation becomes completely symmetric. Accordingly, we have $Z(1/2, \phi) = 0$ for any admissible ϕ (i.e., $0 < \phi \leq 1$). In this situation, no skilled worker has an incentive to move from the current country of residence to the other. That is, the completely symmetric situation always constitutes a spacial equilibrium — the *symmetric dispersion equilibrium*.

Although the completely symmetric situation always satisfies the condition for the spatial equilibrium, it may fail to be stable. Let us consider a small perturbation of the share parameter λ and suppose that λ happens to be slightly larger than 1/2 initially. If $Z(\lambda, \phi) > 0$, then the skilled workers in Foreign have an incentive to move toward Home. As some of skilled workers actually migrate from Foreign to Home, λ gets larger and the situation further deviates from the completely symmetric situation — the symmetric dispersion equilibrium cannot be stable. On the other hand, if $Z(\lambda, \phi) < 0$, then the skilled workers in Home want to move back to Foreign and, eventually, the symmetric dispersion equilibrium will be restored. In this case, we can say that the symmetric dispersion equilibrium is (locally) stable. The condition for the symmetric dispersion equilibrium to be stable is that $\partial Z(\lambda, \phi)/\partial \lambda$ evaluated at $\lambda = 1/2$ is negative, which is equivalent to

$$(\sigma - 1 + \beta)\{1 + (\beta/\sigma)\}\phi - (\sigma - 1 - \beta)\{1 - (\beta/\sigma)\} < 0. \tag{6.25}$$

If $(\sigma - 1 - \beta) \leqq 0$, the above inequality cannot be met for any admissible ϕ — the symmetric dispersion equilibrium will never be stable. Therefore, for the symmetric dispersion equilibrium to be stable for some ϕ, we must have $(\sigma - 1 - \beta) > 0$, which is known as the *no-black-hole condition*.

By solving Eq. (6.25) for ϕ, we obtain

$$\frac{\{1 - (\beta/\sigma)\}(\sigma - 1 - \beta)}{\{1 + (\beta/\sigma)\}(\sigma - 1 + \beta)} > \phi.$$

We write the left-hand side of the above expression as ϕ_B and call it the *break point*. By definition, we have

$$\phi_B \equiv \phi_R \times \frac{\sigma - 1 - \beta}{\sigma - 1 + \beta} < \phi_R.$$

If the freeness of trade ϕ is lower than ϕ_B or, equivalently, if the transportation cost is sufficiently high, the symmetric dispersion equilibrium is (locally) stable.

Agglomeration equilibria and the sustain point: Let us consider a situation where all the skilled workers concentrate in one of the countries, say, in Home (i.e., $\lambda = 1$). If $Z(1, \phi) > 0$, no skilled worker has an incentive to move back to Foreign. This situation becomes a spatial equilibrium — the agglomeration equilibrium in Home. Further, by the continuity of Z, we also have $Z(\lambda, \phi) > 0$ for λ slightly smaller than unity; therefore, the agglomeration equilibrium in Home is (locally) stable. Similarly, the situation in which all the workers concentrate in Foreign (i.e., $\lambda = 0$) is another stable agglomeration equilibrium if $Z(0, \phi) < 0$. An agglomeration equilibrium is always stable if it exists.

By simply calculating, we can confirm $Z(1, \phi) = -Z(0, \phi)$. Therefore, we have $Z(1, \phi) \geqq 0$ if and only if $Z(0, \phi) \leqq 0$; these conditions are equivalent to

$$2\phi^{(\sigma-1-\beta)/(\sigma-1)} \geqq 1 - (\beta/\sigma) + \{1 + (\beta/\sigma)\}\phi^2. \qquad (6.26)$$

Under the no-black-hole condition, the left-hand side of (6.26) is both increasing and concave in ϕ, while the right-hand side is both increasing and convex in ϕ. It is easy to verify that there are exactly two values of ϕ that solves (6.26) with equality. Obviously, $\phi = 1$ is one of such solutions. Let ϕ_S be the other solution, which is called the *sustain point*. Equation (6.26) holds if and only if $\phi_S \leqq \phi \leqq 1$.

Classification of equilibria: After conducting tedious calculation, we can verify that $\phi_S < \phi_B$. According to the levels of the freeness of trade ϕ, we can distinguish three cases: (i) $0 < \phi < \phi_S$; (ii) $\phi_S \leqq \phi \leqq \phi_B$; and (iii) $\phi_B < \phi \leqq 1$. Figure 6.2 measures λ horizontally and Z vertically and it illustrates the graphs of $Z(\lambda, \phi)$ for these three cases.

First, let us consider case-(i). In this case, the graph of $Z(\lambda, \phi)$ is represented by curve adb, which cuts the horizontal axis only once at point d (where $\lambda = 1/2$) from above. Since we have both $Z(0, \phi) > 0$ at point a and $Z(1, \phi) < 0$ at point b, none of the situations where all the skilled workers concentrate in one country can be a spatial equilibrium. The completely

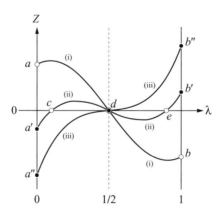

Fig. 6.2   Real Wage Differences and Spacial Equilibria

symmetric situation is the only spatial equilibrium, which is also stable. Each country accommodates a half of the skilled workers in the world.

Suppose $\lambda > 1/2$ in case-(i), which is *not* a spatial equilibrium. As shown above, the relative price index P/P^* is lower than in the symmetric dispersion equilibrium. This *cost-of-living effect* (or, price-index effect) tends to attract more skilled workers from Foreign to Home. That is, the cost-of-living effect works as an agglomeration force. At the same time, because the transportation cost is very high in case-(i), the relative skilled wage rate of Home is lower than in the symmetric dispersion equilibrium. This *relative-skilled-wage effect* gives the skilled workers in Home incentives to go back to Foreign and, therefore, works as a dispersion force. In case-(i), because the latter dominates the former, then the symmetric dispersion equilibrium results.

As the transportation cost becomes lower and international integration progresses, the economy goes into case-(ii). The graph of $Z(\lambda, \phi)$ rotates counterclockwise and becomes curve $a'cdeb'$. As shown in the figure, we have $Z(\lambda, \phi) = 0$ at points c, d, and e, which represent the dispersion equilibria; one of them (i.e., point d) is stable, while the other two (i.e., points c and e) are unstable.[15] In addition, we have both $Z(0, \phi) < 0$ at point a' and $Z(1, \phi) > 0$ at point b', which represent the agglomeration equilibria. The symmetric dispersion equilibrium still remains to be stable. There also emerge two agglomeration equilibria as stable outcomes. In this case, the relative-skilled-wage effect dominates the cost-of-living effect if λ is close to $1/2$, while the opposite is true if λ is close to either 1 or 0.

Lastly, if the transportation cost becomes very low, the economy goes into case-(iii). The graph of $Z(\lambda, \phi)$ in this case is represented by curve $a''db''$, which cuts the horizontal axis only once at point d from below. The symmetric dispersion equilibrium (i.e., point d) loses its stability, while the agglomeration equilibria remain stable. In this case, both the cost-of-living effect and the relative-skilled-wage effect work as agglomeration forces.

---

[15] Point e, for example, represents an *asymmetric* dispersion equilibrium (or, a *partial agglomeration equilibrium*), where not all but more skilled workers reside in Home than in Foreign. Note that the slope of curve $a'cdeb'$ at d is negative, but those at points c and e are positive; this implies the stability of point d and the instability of points c and e.

6.5 Remarks and Further Topics

In this section, we apply the monopolistically competitive trade model to Foreign Direct Investment (FDI) and the gravity equation.

6.5.1 *Firm Heterogeneity and FDI*

The Melitz model with firm heterogeneity can be extended to analyze various modes of operation such as domestic supply, exports, and FDI. Following Helpman *et al.* (2004), we show here how the basic model can be extended to accommodate FDI. By modifying Eq. (6.15), we can write the profit of a firm with productivity $\Theta \equiv \theta^{\sigma-1}$ obtained from a certain mode of operation as follows[16]:

$$\pi \equiv Rw^{1-\sigma}\Theta - f.$$

Here, R, w, and f are (re)interpreted as the market size, the variable cost (the wage rate), and the fixed cost, respectively, that correspond to the mode of operation concerned. It should be noted that π is both increasing and linear in Θ.

Modes of operation: If a Home firm with technology level Θ operates only in the Home market, it earns the profit $\pi_D(\Theta) \equiv Rw^{1-\sigma}\Theta - f_D$, where R is the market size of Home, w is the Home wage rate, and f_D is the fixed cost for domestic operation. In order to participate in international transactions, a Home firm can take one of two alternative modes of operation: export or (horizontal) FDI. If the firm chooses export, it produces goods in Home by employing Home labor and send the products to the Foreign market with incurring transportation costs. Then, the firm earns the additional profit $\pi_X(\Theta) \equiv R^*(\tau w)^{1-\sigma}\Theta - f_X$ from export, where R^* is the market size of Foreign, $\tau > 1$ represents the iceberg-type transportation cost, and f_X is the fixed cost for export. On the other hand, if the firm chooses FDI, it produces goods in Foreign by employing Foreign labor and serves the Foreign market *without* incurring transportation costs. Then, the firm earns

---

[16]In Eq. (6.15), the fixed cost was represented by the product of the wage rate and the fixed labor input. To ease the exposition, we assume that the fixed cost here is independent of the wage rate.

the additional profit $\pi_I(\Theta) \equiv R^*(w^*)^{1-\sigma}\Theta - f_I$ from FDI, where w^* and f_I denote the Foreign wage rate and the fixed cost for FDI, respectively.

It is plausible to assume $f_D < f_X < f_I$ because international transactions require larger overhead costs than the domestic operation and, also, because FDI requires some additional overhead costs that are not necessary for export, which may include the costs of constructing foreign factories, establishing new distribution channels in the host country, and finding local parts suppliers and so on.

Sorting pattern of firms: If two countries, Home and Foreign, are identical or similar in their characteristics, we have $R \approx R^*$ and $w \approx w^*$. Then we can show that the graphs of profits from various operations (i.e, π_D, π_X, and π_I) can be drawn as in Fig. 6.3. Let Θ_D, Θ_X, and Θ_I be the solutions to $\pi_D(\Theta) = 0$, $\pi_X(\Theta) = 0$, and $\pi_X(\Theta) = \pi_I(\Theta)$, respectively. Under our assumptions, it is easy to show that $0 < \Theta_D < \Theta_X < \Theta_I$; these cutoff points divide the range of productivity into four sub-intervals.

As shown in Fig. 6.3, we have (i) $\pi_I(\Theta) < \pi_X(\Theta) < \pi_D(\Theta) < 0$ if $\Theta < \Theta_D$; (ii) $\pi_I(\Theta) < \pi_X(\Theta) < 0 < \pi_D(\Theta)$ if $\Theta_D < \Theta < \Theta_X$; (iii) $0 < \pi_X(\Theta)$ and $\pi_I(\Theta) < \pi_X(\Theta) < \pi_D(\Theta)$ if $\Theta_X < \Theta < \Theta_I$; and (iv) $0 < \pi_X(\Theta) < \pi_I(\Theta) < \pi_D(\Theta)$ if $\Theta > \Theta_I$. From these observations, we can conclude that firms with heterogeneous productivities can be sorted out into four categories in the order of increasing productivities: (i) firms in the lowest productivity category (i.e., those with $\Theta < \Theta_D$) do not enter the market at

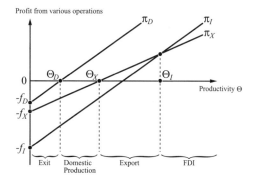

Fig. 6.3   Various Operations of Firms and the Cutoff Points

Source: Figure 3 in Helpman (2006, p. 598); see also Figure 1 in Helpman *et al.* (2004, p. 302).

the very outset; (ii) firms in the second lowest productivity category (i.e., those with $\Theta_D < \Theta < \Theta_X$) serve the domestic market, while stay away from the foreign market; (iii) firms in the second highest productivity category (i.e., those with $\Theta_X < \Theta < \Theta_I$) serve both the domestic and foreign markets and choose export as the mode of international transactions; (iv) lastly, firms in the highest productivity category (i.e., those with $\Theta > \Theta_I$) also serve both the domestic and foreign markets and engage in FDI.[17]

6.5.2   *The Gravity Equation Revisited*

In Chapter 2, we derived the gravity equation based on the Eaton–Kortum model, which is a many-good, many-country, stochastic-technology extension of the Ricardian model under perfect competition. Here, we show that a many-country extension of the basic monopolistically competitive model can serve as another theoretical basis for the gravity equation.

Many country extension: There is a finite number of countries, each of which is populated by identical households; that production technologies are the same for all varieties across all countries. For simplicity, we assume away the homogeneous (numéraire) good. Then, the preference of a household is represented by Eq. (6.1) with $\beta = 1$. Let N be the set of countries. For $i \in N$, let M^i, m^i, w^i, L^i, and Y^i be the set of varieties of the differentiated good produced in country i, the measure of M^i, the wage rate, the labor endowment (which is equal to the number of households), and the total income, respectively. The world total income is denoted by $Y^W \equiv \sum_{i \in N} Y^i$. For $i, j \in N$ and $k \in M^i$, $\tau^{ij} \geq 1$ denotes the amount of a variety that has to be shipped out from country i in order to deliver 1 unit of the variety to country j (i.e., the transportation cost from i to j); p_k^i is the producer (i.e., FOB) price of variety k produced in country i; and p_k^{ij} is the consumer (i.e., CIF) price of variety k produced in country i and consumed in country j. Obviously, we have $p_k^{ij} = \tau^{ij} p_k^i$ for all $i, j \in N$ and for all $k \in M^i$.

---

[17]Here we are considering only horizontal FDIs. By appropriately modifying the model to include a production chain consisting of several vertically related production processes or tasks, we can deal with vertical FDIs in which some combinations of processes/tasks (possibly, the production chain as a whole) can be transferred to the host country. See Helpman *et al.* (2004).

The demand of a household in country j for variety k produced in country i, denoted by x_k^{ij}, becomes as follows: for $i, j \in N$ and $k \in M^i$,

$$x_k^{ij} = \frac{(p_k^{ij})^{-\sigma} I^j}{(P^j)^{1-\sigma}},$$

where I^j denotes the income of a household in country j and

$$P^j \equiv \left[\sum_{i \in N} \int_{k \in M^i} (p_k^{ij})^{1-\sigma} dk \right]^{\frac{1}{1-\sigma}}$$

is the price index of the differentiated good consumed in country j. Similar to Eq. (6.6), the equilibrium producer prices are determined through profit maximization by firms: for $i \in N$ and $k \in M^i$,

$$p_k^i = \frac{w^i a \sigma}{\sigma - 1}.$$

The producer price of variety k produced in country i depends on the wage rate in country i, but not on the identity of the variety; we denote it by p^i.

Bilateral trade and the multilateral resistance terms: The amount of export from country i to country j is

$$
\begin{aligned}
X^{ij} &= \int_{k \in M^i} p_k^{ij} x_k^{ij} L^j dk = \int_{k \in M^i} \left(\frac{p_k^{ij}}{P^j} \right)^{1-\sigma} I^j L^j dk \\
&= m^i (p^i)^{1-\sigma} \left(\frac{\tau^{ij}}{P^j} \right)^{1-\sigma} Y^j,
\end{aligned}
\tag{6.27}
$$

where $Y^j \equiv I^j L^j$ represents the total income (i.e., GDP) of country j. In turn, the total income of country i, Y^i, is equal to its total sales:

$$Y^i = \sum_{\ell \in N} X^{i\ell} = m^i (p^i)^{1-\sigma} \sum_{\ell \in N} \left(\frac{\tau^{i\ell}}{P^\ell} \right)^{1-\sigma} Y^\ell.$$

Solving it for $m^i (p^i)^{1-\sigma}$ and substituting the result back into the definition of P^j, we obtain

$$P^j = \left[\sum_{\ell \in N} \left(\frac{\tau^{\ell j}}{Q^\ell} \right)^{1-\sigma} \mu^\ell \right]^{\frac{1}{1-\sigma}}, \quad j \in N, \tag{6.28}$$

where $\mu^{\ell} \equiv Y^{\ell}/Y^W$ denotes the income share of country ℓ and

$$Q^{\ell} \equiv \left[\sum_{k \in N} \left(\frac{\tau^{ik}}{P^k} \right)^{1-\sigma} \mu^k \right]^{\frac{1}{1-\sigma}} , \quad \ell \in N. \tag{6.29}$$

Similar to Eqs. (2.13) and (2.14) in Chapter 2, Eqs. (6.28) and (6.29) implicitly define the multilateral resistance terms (i.e., P^is and Q^is) as functions of the transportation costs of all pairs of countries, $\{\tau^{jk}\}_{j,k \in N}$, and the income shares, $\{\mu^j\}_{j \in N}$. If the transportation costs are symmetric, that is, if $\tau^{ij} = \tau^{ji}$ for all $i, j \in N$, we have $Q^i = P^i$ for all $i \in N$.

The gravity equation: With the definitions of the multilateral resistance terms, we can rewrite Eq. (6.27) as follows: for $i, j \in N$,

$$X^{ij} = \frac{Y^i Y^j}{Y^W} \left(\frac{\tau^{ij}}{Q^i Q^j} \right)^{1-\sigma}. \tag{6.30}$$

It is quite remarkable that the gravity equations, Eqs. (2.15) and (6.30), derived from two considerably different theoretical frameworks are almost identical. Apparently, the only difference between them appears in the powers to the *distance term* $\tau^{ij}/(Q^i Q^j)$. The distance term is raised up to "$-\theta$" in Eq. (2.15), while it is raised up to "$1 - \sigma$" in Eq. (6.30). Besides transportation costs, the gravity equation (2.15) and the multilateral resistance terms derived from the Eaton–Kortum model largely depend on the *technological* (supply side) parameter θ, which is an indicator of the comparative advantage, while the gravity equation (6.30) and the multilateral resistance terms derived from the monopolistically competitive model depend on the *preference* (demand side) parameter σ, which corresponds both to the elasticity of demand for each variety and to the elasticity of substitution between pairs of varieties.

Chapter 7

Trade Policy

In the competitive circumstance, *free trade* brings about a Pareto-efficient resource allocation in the world economy. Despite this remarkable theoretical result, the government of each individual country, in reality, often adopts interventional trade policies and somehow tries to affect the world resource allocations in favor of the country itself. Of course, the government of a country may have various "good" reasons for trade intervention. For example, the government may want to protect the domestic firms against harsher competition with foreign firms who can supply cheaper goods to the domestic market; to gain time to foster a new prospective industry that has just come into existence (i.e., an *infant industry*) until it becomes a mature well-established industry; to secure the health and safety of its nationals from those foreign food products that do not meet the appropriate sanitary/phytosanitary standards in the country, and so on. To see if those and other reasons for trade intervention can be theoretically justified or not, we have to get a good understanding of the effects of various trade policies and the way how they work. In this chapter, we first examine trade policies in the competitive circumstance. Our main focus will be on *tariffs*. The similarities and differences between tariffs and other policy measures will also be discussed. Then, we move on to the examination of trade policies in some imperfectly competitive circumstances. We discuss the so-called *strategic trade policy* arguments.

7.1   Tariffs and Subsidies

Trade taxes and subsidies are typical trade intervention measures, which affect trade flow by creating gaps between the domestic and world prices of traded goods. The tax imposed on imports of a country is *import tariff* and that on exports is *export tax*. Similarly, we can consider *import subsidy* and *export subsidy*, which correspond to *negative* import tariff and *negative* export tax, respectively. Unless necessary, we use simpler expressions such as "tariffs" or "tariff policy" to refer to trade tax/subsidy policy.

Methods of taxation: *Specific tax* (or *unit tax*) prescribes the amount of tax for a physical unit of a good. On the other hand, *ad valorem tax* specifies the amount of tax as a certain percentage of the value of a good. Suppose that a country imports good j and imposes import tariff on it. Let p_j and p_j^* denote the domestic and world prices of good j, respectively.[1] If a specific import tariff rate per unit of good j is given by t_j, the domestic price must be equal to the sum of the world price and the specific rate, that is, $p_j = p_j^* + t_j$. On the other hand, if an *ad valorem* rate is given by $\tau_j \times 100\%$, the domestic price must be equal to the world price multiplied by $1 + \tau_j$, that is, $p_j = (1 + \tau_j)p_j^*$.[2] For a given *ad valorem* tariff rate, we can find a corresponding specific rate and vice versa. That is, if $\tau_j p_j^* = t_j$, we have $p_j = (1 + \tau_j)p_j^* = p_j^* + \tau_j p_j^* = p_j^* + t_j$. In view of this, we can say that the *ad valorem* tariff and the specific tariff are equivalent as far as the world price remains unchanged.

7.1.1   *Small-Country Case*

Consider an economy of a *small country* with two traded goods (good 1 and good 2). Let $x \equiv (x_1, x_2)$, $y \equiv (y_1, y_2)$, and $z \equiv (z_1, z_2) \equiv x - y$ be the vectors of consumption, production, and net import of the country, respectively. Further, let $D_j(p, I)$ and $Y(p)$ be the ordinary demand function for good j

---

[1]The world price is the CIF price, where CIF stands for "Cost, Insurance, and Freight".

[2]If good j is an import of the country and if t_j and τ_j are negative, the expressions $p_j = p_j^* + t_j$ and $p_j = (1 + \tau_j)p_j^*$ correspond to import subsidies. In contrast, if good j is an export of the country and if t_j and τ_j are negative, these expressions correspond to export taxes.

and the GDP function, where $p \equiv p_1/p_2$ is the domestic relative price of good 1 in terms of good 2. The country imports good 1 under free trade. Let $p^* \equiv p_1^*/p_2^*$ and τ be the world relative price of good 1 and the *ad valorem* tariff rate on the import of good 1, respectively. Since $p_1 = (1 + \tau)p_1^*$ and $p_2 = p_2^*$, we have $p = (1 + \tau)p^*$. If the world price p^* is given and fixed, the introduction of import tariff or an increase in the tariff rate gives rise to an increase in the domestic price p.

Tariff revenue and the budget constraint: By imposing import tariff, the government receives tariff revenue: $\text{TR} \equiv \tau p^*(x_1 - y_1) \equiv \tau p^* z_1$. We assume that the collected tariff revenue is reimbursed (or transferred) to the household of the country in a lump-sum fashion. Let I be the real disposable income of the household. The disposable income consists of the factor income of the household, which equals to the GDP, and the transfer from the government. That is, $I \equiv Y(p) + \text{TR}$.

The budget constraint of the household can be expressed in three different ways: (i) $px_1 + x_2 = I$, (ii) $p^* x_1 + x_2 = p^* y_1 + y_2$, and (iii) $p^* z_1 = -z_2$. The first expression means that the actual expenditure by the household is equal to the disposable income; the second means that the value of the consumption evaluated at the world price is equal to the value of the production evaluated at the world price; and the third means that the value of imports evaluated at the world price is equal to that of exports, implying the balanced trade.

Production, import, and consumption: The first-order derivative of $Y(p)$ with respect to p yields the supply function $\tilde{y}_1(p)$ for good 1, which is increasing in p. Given the world price p^*, import tariff raises the domestic price p of the imported good and, thereby, increases the domestic production of good 1. That is, the import tariff promotes the expansion of the import-competing industry. This is the *protection effect* of import tariff. In contrast, an increase in the domestic relative price of good 1 induces a decrease in the domestic production of good 2. The import tariff is harmful to the exporting industry of the country. This is the *suppression effect*.

The import of good 1 (i.e., z_1) has to satisfy the following relation:

$$z_1 \equiv x_1 - y_1 = D_1\left([1 + \tau]p^*, Y([1 + \tau]p^*) + \tau p^* z_1\right) - \tilde{y}_1\left([1 + \tau]p^*\right), \quad (7.1)$$

which implicitly defines the net import function $\tilde{z}_1(p^*, \tau)$ for good 1. By totally differentiating Eq. (7.1), we can derive some properties of $\tilde{z}_1$:

$$\frac{\partial \tilde{z}_1}{\partial \tau} = \frac{p^*}{\Delta}\left[\frac{\partial \widetilde{D}_1}{\partial p} - \frac{\partial \tilde{y}_1}{\partial p}\right] < 0 \quad \text{and} \tag{7.2}$$

$$\frac{\partial \tilde{z}_1}{\partial p^*} = \frac{1}{\Delta}\left\{(1 + \tau)\left[\frac{\partial \widetilde{D}_1}{\partial p} - \frac{\partial \tilde{y}_1}{\partial p}\right] - z_1\frac{\partial D_1}{\partial I}\right\} \gtrless 0, \tag{7.3}$$

where $\widetilde{D}_1$ is the compensated demand function for good 1 and, therefore, $\partial \widetilde{D}_1/\partial p$ represents the (negative) *substitution term* in the Slutsky equation. In addition, we assume $\Delta \equiv 1 - \tau p^*\partial D_1/\partial I > 0$.[3] Equation (7.2) means that the introduction of import tariff or an increase in the tariff rate induces a decrease in the volume of imports. The trade balance condition implies that the reduction of imports entails a proportional reduction of exports. By the introduction of import tariff, the overall trade of the country shrinks. This is the *trade contraction effect*. In general, as shown in Eq. (7.3), the effect of an increase in the world relative price on the import of good 1 is ambiguous. However, if good 1 is a *normal good* (i.e., if $\partial D_1/\partial I > 0$), we have $\partial \tilde{z}_1/\partial p^* < 0$.

The effect of an increase in the tariff rate on the consumption of good 1 is represented by

$$\frac{dx_1}{d\tau} = p^*\frac{\partial \widetilde{D}_1}{\partial p} + \tau p^*\frac{\partial D_1}{\partial I} \cdot \frac{\partial \tilde{z}_1}{\partial \tau}.$$

If $\tau = 0$ initially, the second term in the right-hand side vanishes and we have $dx_1/d\tau < 0$. That is, a small increase in the tariff rate from zero brings about a decrease in the consumption of good 1. However, if good 1 is an *inferior good* and if $\tau > 0$ initially, it is possible to have $dx_1/d\tau > 0$. That is, the consumption of good 1 can increase against an increase in the tariff rate. Even if this is the case, the increase in the consumption of good 1 cannot exceed the increase in the production of good 1 against an increase in the tariff rate.

Welfare of the country: Let u and $V(p, I)$ be the utility level and indirect utility function of the country: $u = V(p, I)$. We normalize the marginal

---

[3]If $\tau = 0$, we have $\Delta = 1$. Furthermore, because we can show that $1 = (1 + \tau)p^*\partial D_1/\partial I + \partial D_2/\partial I$ from the budget constraint, we have $\Delta > 0$ if all goods are *normal* in consumption.

utility of income $\partial V/\partial I$ equal to unity.[4] Then, by making use of Roy's identity, we can derive the expression for the change in the utility level against an increase in the tariff rate as follows:

$$\frac{du}{d\tau} = \tau p^* \frac{\partial \tilde{z}_1}{\partial \tau} \leq 0.$$

The introduction of import tariff by a *small* country makes the country worse-off.

7.1.2 *Two-Country Case*

The import tariff of a country reduces the net import of the country and, thereby, disturbs the world market. Correspondingly, the world price will change, which gives rise to some secondary effects on the world economy. Now, taking full account of the endogenous determination of the world price, let us consider the effects of import tariff in a model with two goods and two countries (country A and country B), in which country A imports good 1 and imposes import tariff on one hand, country B imports good 2 but does not adopt any trade policy on the other.

The world market equilibrium: Let $\tilde{z}_1^A(p^*, \tau)$ and $\tilde{z}_1^B(p^*)$ be the net import functions of country A and country B, respectively. Due to the Walras law, it suffices to consider the world market clearing condition for good 1:

$$Z_1(p^*, \tau) \equiv \tilde{z}_1^A(p^*, \tau) + \tilde{z}_1^B(p^*) = 0, \tag{7.4}$$

which determines the equilibrium world price. Equation (7.4) does not guarantee the uniqueness of the equilibrium price; multiple equilibria are possible. Furthermore, each equilibrium may not be *stable* in the Walrasian sense. For an equilibrium to be locally stable in the Walrasian sense, it is necessary to have $\partial Z_1(p^*, \tau)/\partial p^* < 0$ at the corresponding equilibrium point.[5]

---

[4]This normalization is valid only for a local analysis.
[5]If $\partial Z_1(p^*, \tau)/\partial p^* < 0$ holds true for all possible p^*, the equilibrium price must be determined uniquely (if it exists at all) and the equilibrium is globally stable in the Walrasian sense.

By totally differentiating Eq. (7.4), we obtain the expression for the change in the equilibrium price against an increase in the tariff rate:

$$\frac{dp^*}{d\tau} = -\left[\frac{\partial Z_1}{\partial \tau}\right]\bigg/\left[\frac{\partial Z_1}{\partial p^*}\right] < 0, \tag{7.5}$$

where we make use of Eq. (7.2) and assume the Walrasian local stability of the equilibrium point. Note that, since country A imports good 1, the relative price of good 1 corresponds to the inverse of country A's terms of trade. Therefore, Eq. (7.5) means that, by imposing import tariff, the importing country can improve its terms of trade.

Figure 7.1 illustrates the effects of country A's import tariff on the world market equilibrium. Two solid curves OA and OB represent the non-tariff offer curves of countries A and B, respectively. The initial free trade equilibrium is point e^*, at which the offer curves OA and OB intersect. The equilibrium world price p^* is represented by the slope of line segment connecting O and e^*. The amount of trade in good 1 is $q_1^* \equiv \tilde{z}_1^A(p^*, 0) = -\tilde{z}_1^B(p^*)$ and that of good 2 is q_2^*. Given p^*, an import tariff by country A reduces the volume of trade of country A as indicated by Eq. (7.2). Then, country A's trade point moves from e^* to point a along the trade balance line Oe^* and, correspondingly, the tariff-ridden offer curve of country A shrinks to curve OA'. The equilibrium point moves to point e', at which OA' and OB intersect. The new equilibrium world price $p^{*\prime}$ is represented

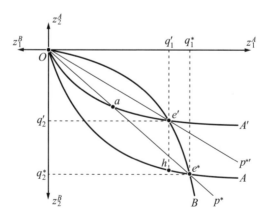

Fig. 7.1   Contraction of the Offer Curve and the Equilibrium World Price

by the slope of line segment connecting O and e'. Because the slope of segment Oe' is flatter than that of segment Oe^*, we have $p^{*\prime} < p^*$. The amount of trade in good 1 becomes $q_1' \equiv \tilde{z}_1^A(p^{*\prime}, \tau) = -\tilde{z}_1^B(p^{*\prime})$ and that of good 2 is q_2'. In the case of Fig. 7.1, the import tariff by country A reduces the overall volume of trade, that is, $q_1' < q_1^*$ and $q_2' < q_2^*$.[6]

Metzler paradox: Given the world price, an increase in the import tariff induces an increase in the domestic price. However, since an increase in the import tariff brings about a decrease in the world price as shown above, the domestic price of the imported good may decrease even when the tariff rate increases. The change in the domestic price against an increase in the tariff rate (evaluated at $\tau = 0$) becomes

$$
\begin{aligned}
\left.\frac{\mathrm{d}p}{\mathrm{d}\tau}\right|_{\tau=0} &= p^* + (1 + \tau)\frac{\mathrm{d}p^*}{\mathrm{d}\tau} \\
&= p^*\left[\frac{\partial Z_1}{\partial p^*}\right]^{-1}\left\{-z_1^A\frac{\partial D_1^A}{\partial I^A} + \frac{\partial \tilde{z}_1^B}{\partial p^*}\right\} \\
&= p^*\left[\frac{\partial Z_1}{\partial p^*}\right]^{-1}\left\{-z_1^A\frac{\partial D_1^A}{\partial I^A} + \left[\frac{\partial \widetilde{D}_1^B}{\partial p^*} - \frac{\partial \tilde{y}_1^B}{\partial p^*}\right] - z_1^B\frac{\partial D_1^B}{\partial I^B}\right\}.
\end{aligned}
$$

If we maintain the assumptions of the Walrasian stability and the normality in consumption, we have both $[\partial Z_1/\partial p^*]^{-1} < 0$ and $-z_1^A[\partial D_1^A/\partial I] < 0$ ($\because z_1^A > 0$). In this case, if the export by country B is increasing in p^* (i.e., $\partial \tilde{z}_1^B/\partial p^* < 0$), we obtain $\mathrm{d}p/\mathrm{d}\tau > 0$ as normally expected.[7] However, it is still possible to have $\mathrm{d}p/\mathrm{d}\tau < 0$. This, somewhat perverse, effect is known as the *Metzler paradox* (Metzler, 1949). A necessary condition for the paradox is $\partial \tilde{z}_1^B/\partial p^* > 0$, which corresponds to the case where the offer curve of country B is *inelastic*.[8] In the case of the Metzler paradox, the import tariff of a country fails to protect the import-competing industry of the country.

---

[6]Depending on the shape of country B's offer curve, the amount of country A's import under tariff can be greater than that under free trade.

[7]If both countries share the same homothetic preference, we have $\partial D_1^A/\partial I^A = \partial D_1^B/\partial I^B$. In this case, because the negative income effect in country A exactly offsets the positive income effect in country B, then we obtain $\mathrm{d}p/\mathrm{d}\tau > 0$.

[8]The offer curve of country B becomes inelastic if the positive income effect (i.e., $-z_1^B[\partial D_1^B/\partial I^B] > 0$) outweighs the negative substitution effect (i.e., $\partial \widetilde{D}_1^B/\partial p^* - \partial \tilde{y}_1^B/\partial p^* < 0$).

Welfare of the countries: Taking account of the change in the terms of trade against an increase in the tariff rate, we can derive the expression for the change in the utility level of the importing country (i.e., country A):

$$\frac{\mathrm{d}u^A}{\mathrm{d}\tau} = -z_1^A \frac{\mathrm{d}p^*}{\mathrm{d}\tau} + \tau p^* \frac{\mathrm{d}z_1^A}{\mathrm{d}\tau}, \tag{7.6}$$

where $\mathrm{d}z_1^A/\mathrm{d}\tau \equiv [\partial \tilde{z}_1^A/\partial p^*][\mathrm{d}p^*/\mathrm{d}\tau] + [\partial \tilde{z}_1^A/\partial \tau]$. The first term in the right-hand-side of Eq. (7.6) is called the *terms-of-trade effect*, which is positive. The second term is called the *volume-of-trade effect*. If $\mathrm{d}z_1^A/\mathrm{d}\tau < 0$ as normally expected, the volume-of-trade effect becomes non-positive. If $\tau = 0$ initially, the volume-of-trade effect vanishes and the terms-of-trade effect remains positive. Accordingly, the overall welfare effect becomes positive. This means that in the *large-country* case, the importing country can improve its welfare by introducing a small tariff. On the other hand, if τ is sufficiently large, the (negative) volume-of-trade effect may outweigh the (positive) terms-of-trade effect and, consequently, the overall welfare effect can be negative. That is, if the country has already adopted a sufficiently high tariff rate, a further increase in the tariff rate may worsen the welfare of the country.

When country A increases its tariff rate, the welfare of country B, who does not impose any tariffs, changes as follows:

$$\frac{\mathrm{d}u^B}{\mathrm{d}\tau} = -z_1^B \frac{\mathrm{d}p^*}{\mathrm{d}\tau} < 0.$$

Clearly, the import tariff by country A deteriorates the welfare of country B. The import tariff is a *beggar-thy-neighbor policy*. Moreover, after the introduction of an import tariff by country A, the agents in country A face $(1 + \tau)p^*$, while the agents in country B face p^*. Accordingly, some of the marginal conditions for Pareto-efficiency are violated; the new equilibrium under unilateral tariff fails to be Pareto-efficient.

7.1.3 *General Formula for Welfare Changes*

Let us consider the effects of tariffs/subsidies on the welfare of a country in a more general setting with n goods. We compare the utility levels in two different situations, which we call the comparison situation and the initial situation, respectively. Let x, y, z, t, p^*, p, and u denote the vectors of consumption, production, net import, specific tariff, world price, domestic price, and the utility level in the comparison situation, respectively. By definition, we have $z = x - y$, $p = p^* + t$, and $u = U(x)$, where U is the social utility function. The corresponding variables in the initial situation are denoted by attaching a bar ($^-$).

Derivation of the formula: By the definitions of the expenditure function and the GDP function, we have $E(p, u) \equiv px$, $E(p, \bar{u}) \leq p\bar{x}$, and $Y(p) \equiv py \geq p\bar{y}$. Combining these relations, we obtain

$$
\begin{aligned}
E(p, u) - E(p, \bar{u}) &\geq px - p\bar{x} = py + tz - p\bar{x} \\
&= py - p\bar{y} + p\bar{y} + tz - p\bar{x} + \bar{p}^*\bar{z} \\
&= \underbrace{p(y - \bar{y})}_{\text{production gain}} \underbrace{-(p^* - \bar{p}^*)\bar{z}}_{\text{TOT}} + \underbrace{t(z - \bar{z})}_{\text{VOT}}.
\end{aligned}
\tag{7.7}
$$

In the second line of the above derivation, we used the trade balance condition in the initial situation: $\bar{p}^*\bar{z} = 0$. The first term in the last line is the *production gain*, which is always non-negative. The second term represents the effect of changes in the world price weighted with the net export (i.e., $-\bar{z}$), which we call the *terms-of-trade effect* (TOT). The third term represents the effect of changes in the net import evaluated at the tariff rate in the comparison situation, which we call the *volume-of-trade effect* (VOT). Equation (7.7) provides us with a sufficient condition for welfare improvement: if the sum of TOT and VOT is positive, we have $E(p, u) - E(p, \bar{u}) \geq 0$, implying $u \geq \bar{u}$. Equation (7.7) is the counterpart of Eq. (7.6) when tariffs change discretely.[9]

Gains-from-trade proposition and more: By making use of Eq. (7.7), we can reconfirm the gains-from-trade proposition, which we proved in Chapter 4, and derive some new propositions.

---

[9] Equation (7.7) can be seen as a simplified version of more general formula for welfare improvement derived by Ohyama (1972, p. 47, Theorem 1), which is sometimes called *Ohyama's formula*. It should be noted that the welfare criterion used in Ohyama (1972) is based on the *Revealed Preference in the Aggregate*, while our welfare criterion in Eq. (7.7) is based on the *Social Utility Function*. For the relation among several welfare criteria, see Chapter 4.

Proposition 7.1 (Gains from Free Trade Revisited). *A country is better-off (not worse-off) under free trade than in autarky.*

Proof. Suppose that the initial situation corresponds to *autarky* and the comparison situation to *free trade*. Because $\bar{z} = 0$ from the autarkic equilibrium condition and $t = 0$, then both the terms-of-trade effect and the volume-of-trade effect vanish simultaneously and only the non-negative production gain remains. □

Next, suppose that the initial situation corresponds to autarky and the comparison situation to a tariff-ridden trade. For good j with $z_j > 0$, $t_j > 0$ means an import tariff. Similarly, for good j with $z_j < 0$, $t_j < 0$ means an export tax. If the tariff vector t includes only trade taxes (i.e., import tariffs and export taxes), we have $tz > 0$. Even if the tariff vector t includes some import/export subsidies, it is possible to have $tz \geq 0$. When the net tariff revenue tz is non-negative, the trade tax/subsidy policy represented by t is said to be *self-financing* (Ohyama, 1972, p. 49). With this terminology, we can show a more general proposition:

Proposition 7.2 (Autarky vs. Trade under Self-Financing Tariff). *Trade under a self-financing tariff is better than no trade.*

Proof. Because $\bar{z} = 0$, the terms-of-trade effect vanishes. Self-financing tariff means $tz \geq 0$. The right-hand side of Eq. (7.7) becomes $p(y - \bar{y}) + tz \geq 0$. □

Now suppose that the initial situation corresponds to a tariff-ridden trade, while the comparison situation corresponds to free trade. The following theorem shows that free trade is the optimal policy for a small country:

Proposition 7.3 (Free Trade vs. Tariff-Ridden Trade). *For a small country, free trade is better than trade under any tariffs and subsidies.*

Proof. By the small-country assumption, we have $p^* = \bar{p}^*$. Accordingly, the terms-of-trade effect vanishes. The volume-of-trade effect also vanishes because $t = 0$ under free trade. The right-hand side of Eq. (7.7) becomes $p(y - \bar{y}) \geq 0$. □

In a two-good model, an increase in the relative price of the export good is called an improvement of the terms of trade and, actually, it induces an improvement of the welfare of the country. In a many-good model, an improvement of the terms of trade can be defined as such a change in the world price vector that makes the net import vector in the initial situation less expensive. That is, if we have $(p^* - \bar{p}^*)\bar{z} < 0$, we call the change in the world price vector from $\bar{p}^*$ to p^* an "improvement" of the terms of trade.

Proposition 7.4 (Improvement of the Terms of Trade). *Under free trade, an improvement of the terms of trade induces a welfare improvement of the country.*

Proof. Free trade implies $t = 0$. Further, by the definition of terms-of-trade improvement, we have $-(p^* - \bar{p}^*)\bar{z} > 0$. The right-hand side of Eq. (7.7) becomes $p(y - \bar{y}) - (p^* - \bar{p}^*)\bar{z} > 0$. □

7.2 Other Policy Measures

Some policy measures or their combinations other than tariffs have effects that are similar or equivalent to tariffs. In this section, we examine some tariff-equivalent policy measures.

7.2.1 *Price Intervention Policies*

Import tariff and export tax: In a two-good model, import tariff and export tax of a country have exactly the same effects on the economy. This is known as *Lerner's symmetry theorem* (Lerner, 1936). To see this, it suffices to show that the relative price and the budget constraint under import tariff are identical to those under export tax. Suppose that the country imports good 1 and exports good 2. First, let us consider the case of import tariff and assume that the *ad valorem* tariff rate is given by τ. Because $p_1 = (1 + \tau)p_1^*$ and $p_2 = p_2^*$, the domestic relative price under import tariff becomes $p \equiv (1 + \tau)p_1^*/p_2^* = (1 + \tau)p^*$ and the budget constraint becomes $px_1 + x_2 = py_1 + y_2 + T$ with $T = \tau p^*(x_1 - y_1)$. In turn, let us consider the case of export tax and assume that the *ad valorem* tax rate is given by τ. Because $p_1 = p_1^*$ and $p_2^* = (1 + \tau)p_2$ in this case, the domestic relative price under export tax becomes $p = p_1^*/[p_2^*/(1 + \tau)] = (1 + \tau)p^*$ and the budget constraint under export tax becomes $px_1 + x_2 = py_1 + y_2 + T'$ with $T' = \tau(y_2 - x_2)$. The domestic relative price under import tariff is identical to that under export tax. Further, from the budget constraint under import tariff, we have $p^*(x_1 - y_1) = (y_2 - x_2)$. Accordingly, we obtain $T = T'$ as far as the import tariff rate and the export tax rate are the same, meaning that the budget constraints are identical in both cases.

Consumption tax and production subsidy: Import tariff can be identified with a combination of consumption tax and production subsidy. To see this, it suffices to show that the domestic price and the budget constraint under tariff vector t can be replicated by a certain combination of consumption tax and production subsidy. Let t^C and t^P be the consumption tax vector and the production subsidy vector, respectively. Further, let p^* be the world price vector. Then, the consumer price becomes $p^C \equiv p^* + t^C$ and the producer price becomes $p^P \equiv p^* + t^P$. The consumption tax revenue amounts to $t^C x$ and the subsidy payment to the producers amounts to $t^P y$, where x and y are the vectors of consumption and production, respectively. If the net government revenue (i.e., $T \equiv t^C x - t^P y$) is positive, it will be transferred to the household sector in a lump-sum fashion; if negative, it will be financed by a lump-sum tax on the household. The budget constraint under a combination of consumption tax and production subsidy becomes $p^C x = p^P y + T$. Now suppose that $t^C = t^P = t$. Then, because $p^C = p^P = p = p^* + t$ and $T = t(x - y)$, the budget constraint becomes identical to the one under import tariff t: $px = py + T$. Accordingly, the equilibrium under a tariff vector t can be replicated by the equilibrium under the combination of consumption tax and production subsidy such that $t^C = t^P = t$.

7.2.2   *Quantitative Restrictions*

Tariffs and other price intervention policies restrict trade flow of a country in an *indirect* manner. In contrast, quantitative restrictions such as import quota and export restraint *directly* control trade flow. In the competitive circumstance, the effects of quantitative restrictions are basically identical to those of price intervention policies. In this subsection, we show the similarities and differences between quantitative restrictions and price intervention policies.

Import quota: By imposing an upper bound of the amount of imports, import quota restricts the inflow of goods. The imported good in the domestic market will be in short supply and, therefore, the domestic price of the imported good tends to rise. On the other hand, because the effective import demand from the importing country in the world market decreases, the world price tends to fall. Consequently, as in the case of tariffs, there arises a gap between the domestic and world prices of the good, which yields *quota rent*.

In the case of tariffs, the amount of money corresponding to the gap between the domestic and world prices accrues to the government as tariff revenue. In contrast, in the case of import quota, who receive the quota rent depends upon the way how the import licenses are allocated to potential importers. If the licenses are rationed (based on, for example, the past records of imports by the applicants) without any payment, the licensed importers will receive the quota rent. If, on the other hand, the licenses are auctioned off competitively to many potential importers, the "price" of a license to import one unit of the good would rise up to the (expected) gap between the domestic and world prices. Consequently, the quota rent eventually accrues to the government as the sales of the import licenses. To avoid an analytical complexity, we assume here that the licenses are allocated among domestic importers through a competitive auction and that the sales of the import licenses will be transferred to the domestic household in a lump-sum fashion.

Figure 7.2 illustrates the effects of import quota. Suppose that country A imports good 1 and exports good 2 and that the economy is initially in the free trade equilibrium point e^*, where the non-distorted offer curves, OA and OB, intersect. The equilibrium world price of good 1 (in terms of good 2) is p^* and country A's import of good 1 is q_1^*. Let Q be the level of import quota by country A, which is assumed to be smaller than q_1^* (i.e., $Q < q_1^*$).[10] Under import quota, the offer curve of country A will

---

[10]If $Q \geq q_1^*$, the import quota fails to be binding and will have no effect on the economy.

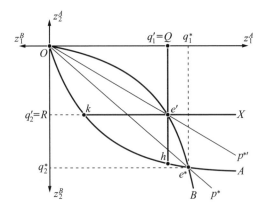

Fig. 7.2   Effects of Import Quota and Export Restraint

have a refraction point corresponding to Q. Actually, the effective offer curve of country A under import quota becomes a kinked curve OhQ as in Fig. 7.2. At the initial equilibrium world price p^*, the world market for good 1 is in excess supply. The world price declines and a new equilibrium will be established at point e', where the quota-distorted offer curve OhQ of country A and the non-distorted offer curve OB of country B intersect. The new equilibrium world price $p^{*\prime}$ is represented by the slope of the line Oe'. Obviously, $p^{*\prime}$ is lower than p^*. By comparing Figs. 7.1 and 7.2, we recognize that if the import quota Q is set equal to the import under tariff (i.e., $Q = q_1'$), the import quota replicates the equilibrium under tariff — in this sense, import quota can be said to be equivalent to import tariff.

Export restraint: By imposing an upper bound of the amount of exports, export restraint reduces the outflow of goods. The effective export supply from the exporting country in the world market decreases and, at the initial world price, the world market will be in excess demand. Then, the world price of the good tends to rise. On the other hand, the domestic market for the exported good will be in excess supply and the domestic price tends to decrease. There arises a gap between the world and domestic prices of the exported good. Similar to the case of import quota, this gap yields *quota rent*. The allocation of the export licenses generates a similar problem of income distribution. Once again, we assume that the export licenses are allocated among many potential exporters through a competitive auction and the sales of the export licenses are transferred from the government to the domestic household in a lump-sum fashion.

Figure 7.2 illustrates the effects of export restraint. Let R be the level of export restraint, which is assumed to be smaller than the free trade export q_2^*. Under export restraint, the offer curve of country A will have a refraction point corresponding to R. The effective offer curve under export restraint becomes a kinked curve OkX as in Fig. 7.2. A similar argument as the import quota case also applies well to the export restraint case. The new equilibrium becomes point e', at which the quota-distorted offer curve OkX of country A and the non-distorted offer curve OB of country B intersect. The equilibrium world price of good 2 (in terms of good 1) is $1/p^{*'}$, which is higher than $1/p^*$. By inspecting Fig. 7.2, we recognize that the export restraint can replicate the equilibrium under import quota. Similar to Lerner's symmetry between import tariff and export tax, we find the symmetry between import quota and export restraint. In a sense, we can say that import tariff, export tax, import quota, and export restraint are equivalent with each other.

Non-equivalence: The symmetry or equivalence among import tariff, export tax, import quota, and export restraint does not always hold true. Figure 7.3 illustrates a situation where import quota cannot replicate the equilibrium under tariff. It should be noted that the offer curve OB' of country B has a backward-bending portion and that the free trade equilibrium point e^* is on this portion.[11] If country A imposes a small import tariff, then the offer curve of country A shrinks toward the origin. The new equilibrium under tariff is established at point b', at which the tariff-ridden offer curve OA' of country A intersects with the non-distorted (but, inelastic) offer curve OB' of country B. As shown in the figure, the amount of imports of country A under tariff becomes greater than that under free trade in spite of the imposition of import tariff.

Now, let us examine whether an import quota can replicate the equilibrium point b' under import tariff. Let Q' be the level of import quota set

---

[11] At every point on the backward-bending portion of the offer curve, the *price elasticity of net import* becomes less than unity. In other words, at each point on the backward-bending portion, the offer curve is *inelastic*.

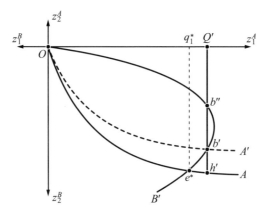

Fig. 7.3   Non-Equivalence of Import Quota and Tariff

equal to the import under tariff, which, of course, corresponds to point b'. By imposing the import quota Q', the (effective) offer curve of country A becomes a kinked curve $Oh'Q'$. Then, there arise three equilibria under import quota: points e^*, b', and b''. It should be noted that, under the Walrasian price adjustment, point b' under import quota is unstable, while points e^* and b'' are stable. There is no economic force that leads the economy toward point b'.[12] Therefore, under import quota, either one of points e^* and b'' will be realized and observed, but point b' will not. In particular, if the initial equilibrium is point e^*, the imposition of import quota Q' does not affect the economy at all; the world economy remains to be in point e^*. In view of the above observation, we can hardly say that point b' is replicated by the import quota.

7.2.3   *International Transfers and Tariffs*

Let us consider a two-good two-country model, where country A imports good 1. Suppose that country A imposes an import tariff with the unit tariff rate t and country B adopts an export subsidy with *the same* unit subsidy rate t. Then, the domestic prices of countries A and B become $p^A = p^* + t$ and $p^B = p^* + t$, respectively. Obviously, we have $p^A = p^B$. The budget constraints of the countries are $p^A x_1^A + x_2^A = p^A y_1^A + y_2^A + T^A$

---

[12]Point b' under import tariff is stable in the Walrasian sense.

and $p^B x_1^B + x_2^B = p^B y_1^B + y_2^B + T^B$, where $T^A \equiv t(x_1^A - y_1^A) > 0$ and $T^B \equiv -t(y_1^B - x_1^B) < 0$. Note that, due to the world market-clearing condition, we have $T^A + T^B = 0$. The household in country A receives a lump-sum transfer of the net tariff revenue from the government of country A, while the household in country B pays a lump-sum tax (used to finance the net subsidy payment) to the government of country B. In effect, this can be identified with an international lump-sum transfer (of the amount $T \equiv T^A = -T^B$) from country B's household to country A's household. Since all agents in both countries face a common relative price (i.e., $p^A = p^B = \hat{p}^* \equiv p^* + t$), the trade equilibrium under the combination of import tariff and export subsidy with the equilibrium world price being p^* is equivalent to the trade equilibrium under the international lump-sum transfer T from country B to country A with the equilibrium world price being $\hat{p}^*$ ($= p^* + t$). In a sense, tariffs and international transfers are equivalent.[13]

The above equivalence result can be extended to an n-good m-country model. To show this, we need to introduce some new concepts. Let M be the set of countries. An array of tariff vectors, $\gamma \equiv \{t^s\}_{s \in M}$, is called a *tariff structure*. Specifically, if there exists a common tariff vector t such that $t = t^s$ for all $s \in M$, the corresponding tariff structure is called an *equivalent tariff structure* with t and denoted by $\gamma_{eq}(t) \equiv \{t, t, \ldots, t\}$. A *feasible allocation* is an array of consumption and production vectors $\{x^s, y^s\}_{s \in M}$ such that $x^s \in \mathbb{R}_+^n$ and $y^s \in \mathcal{Y}^s$ for all $s \in M$. A feasible allocation $\{x^s, y^s\}_{s \in M}$ is called an *equilibrium allocation under* γ if there exists a world price vector p^* that satisfies the following conditions: for all $s \in M$, (i) $(p^* + t^s)y^s = Y^s(p^* + t^s)$; (ii) $(p^* + t^s)x^s \geq (p^* + t^s)x^{s\prime}$ implies $U^s(x^s) \geq U^s(x^{s\prime})$; (iii) $p^*(x^s - y^s) = 0$; and (iv) $\sum_{s \in M}(x^s - y^s) = 0$. Condition-(i) means that y^s maximizes the GDP evaluated at price $p^* + t^s$. Condition-(ii) reflects the household's utility maximization. Condition-(iii) is the trade balance condition evaluated at the equilibrium world price p^*. Condition-(iv) is nothing but the world market-clearing condition. The set of equilibrium allocations under γ is denoted by $\mathcal{E}(\gamma)$. Furthermore, an

---

[13]This equivalence between tariffs and international transfers has shown by Mundell (1968) in a two-good two-country framework.

array $\Gamma \equiv \{T^s\}_{s \in M}$ of net transfer receipts satisfying $\sum_{s \in M} T^s = 0$ is called a *transfer structure*. A feasible allocation $\{x^s, y^s\}_{s \in M}$ is called an *equilibrium allocation under* Γ if there exists a world price vector p^* that satisfies the following conditions: for all $s \in M$, (i′) $p^* y^s = Y^s(p^*)$; (ii′) $p^* x^s \geq p^* x^{s\prime}$ implies $U^s(x^s) \geq U^s(x^{s\prime})$; (iii′) $p^*(x^s - y^s) = T^s$; and (iv′) $\sum_{s \in M}(x^s - y^s) = 0$. Conditions-(i′), -(ii′), and -(iv′) are parallel to conditions-(i), -(ii), and -(iv), respectively. Condition-(iii′) is the *current account balance condition*, which means that the trade deficit is financed by the net transfer from abroad. The set of equilibrium allocations under Γ is denoted by $\mathscr{E}(\Gamma)$. The following theorem exhibits one side of the equivalence between tariffs and international transfers.

Proposition 7.5 (Existence of Equivalent Transfer Structure: Nakanishi, 1992). *Let* $\gamma_{eq}(t)$ *be an equivalent tariff structure with t. Then, for any equilibrium allocation* $\{x^s, y^s\}_{s \in M} \in \mathscr{E}(\gamma_{eq}(t))$, *there exists a transfer structure* $\hat{\Gamma} = \{\hat{T}^s\}_{s \in M}$ *such that* $\{x^s, y^s\}_{s \in M} \in \mathscr{E}(\hat{\Gamma})$.

Proof. Let p^* be the equilibrium world price under $\gamma_{eq}(t) = \{t, t, \ldots, t\}$. Define $\hat{p}^* \equiv p^* + t$ and $\hat{T}^s \equiv t(x^s - y^s)$. Note that, because $\sum_{s \in M} \hat{T}^s = t[\sum_{s \in M}(x^s - y^s)] = 0$ by the world market-clearing condition, the array $\{\hat{T}^s\}_{s \in M}$ is indeed a transfer structure, which is denoted by $\hat{\Gamma}$. Then, it suffices to show that $\hat{p}^*$ and $\{x^s, y^s\}_{s \in M}$ satisfy the conditions for $\mathscr{E}(\hat{\Gamma})$. Conditions-(i′), -(ii′), and -(iv′) are immediate from conditions-(i), -(ii), and -(iv). From condition-(iii), we have $0 = p^*(x^s - y^s) = p^*(x^s - y^s) + t(x^s - y^s) - t(x^s - y^s) = \hat{p}^*(x^s - y^s) - \hat{T}^s$, implying condition-(iii′). Hence, $\{x^s, y^s\}_{s \in M} \in \mathscr{E}(\hat{\Gamma})$.   □

To establish the "equivalence" of tariffs and international transfers, we have to show that the converse of the above theorem. The converse theorem, however, cannot be established without additional restrictions on the numbers of countries and goods and on the trade patterns.

Proposition 7.6 (Existence of Equivalent Tariff Structure: Nakanishi, 1992). *Let* $\Gamma \equiv \{T^s\}_{s \in M}$ *be a transfer structure. Suppose that the numbers of goods and countries are the same and that either one of the following conditions is satisfied in the equilibrium under* Γ*: (i) each country exports a single specific good and imports the others; or, (ii) each country imports* *a single specific good and exports the others. Then, for any equilibrium allocation $\{x^s, y^s\} \in \mathcal{E}(\Gamma)$, there exists an equivalent tariff structure $\gamma_{eq}(\hat{t}) = \{\hat{t}, \hat{t}, \ldots, \hat{t}\}$ such that $\{x^s, y^s\} \in \mathcal{E}(\gamma_{eq}(\hat{t}))$.*

We omit the proof; see Nakanishi (1992). In the context of piecemeal policy recommendation, both Nakanishi (1993) and Turunen-Red and Woodland (2001) have shown a similar result that the condition for the existence of Pareto-improving tariff changes *with* appropriate changes in international transfers is equivalent to that *without* changes in international transfers. Their results imply that some tariff changes are equivalent to transfer changes. In general, the existence of transfer-equivalent tariff structures heavily relies on the properties of an $n \times m$ matrix that consists of net import vectors of the countries: $Z \equiv [z^1, z^2, \ldots, z^m]$. To prove Proposition 7.6 by contradiction, Nakanishi (1992) has made use of the fact that the negation implies that Z be a matrix with dominant diagonals. Nakanishi (1993) and Turunen-Red and Woodland (2001) have shown that a sufficient condition for the equivalence is that the rank of Z is equal to the number of countries (i.e., m), which in turn implies that the number of traded goods should be no less than that of countries.[14]

7.3 Strategic Trade Policies

The term "strategic trade policy" refers to the governments' intervention by means of trade policy measures in the strategic interaction among firms in imperfectly competitive circumstances. The study on the strategic trade policy was originated from a series of articles by Brander and Spencer (1981, 1984, 1985). Since then, a vast number of contributions has appeared in the literature. The strategic trade policy argument sheds new light on the effects of trade policies and, also, on the governments' motivation for trade interventions. Since there is a wide variety of situations in imperfectly competitive circumstances according to various combinations of characterizing aspects, the effects of a particular trade policy

---

[14] Kemp and Wan (2005) have criticized the arguments of transfer-equivalent tariffs that they are based on the properties of endogenous variables (such as the matrix Z) and ignore the roles of fundamental variables (such as the endowments of goods/factors) of the model.

become dependent on subtle differences in the specifications of situations concerned. In this subsection, we examine the effects of several trade policies by making use of the basic model of differentiated duopoly introduced in Chapter 5.

7.3.1   *Import Tariff in the Cournot Case*

To begin with, let us consider the unilateral import tariff policy by country A imposed on firm B under the Cournot duopoly. We assume away transportation costs. Instead, we interpret the parameter t as the unit import tariff rate. Because the import tariff is imposed only on firm B, the behavior of both firms in the country-A market is identical to the case with positive transportation costs. In contrast, the behavior of both firms in the country-B market is identical to the case where the transportation cost is zero.

The Cournot–Nash equilibrium under import tariff: The equilibrium quantities in the country-A market are given by Eqs. (5.10) and (5.11): firm A's domestic supply is $x^*(t)$ and firm B's export supply (i.e., country A's import) is $y^*(t)$.[15] An increase in the tariff rate increases the *effective* marginal cost of firm B, inducing an inward-shift of the reaction curve of firm B. Then, the equilibrium point moves to the lower-right along the reaction curve of firm A. (The readers may refer to Fig. 5.1.) Consequently, $x^*(t)$ increases, while $y^*(t)$ decreases.

It is easy to verify that firm B's export supply reaches zero, $y^*(t) = 0$, if $t = \bar{t} \equiv (2\beta - \gamma)(\alpha - c)/(2\beta)$, which is the *prohibitive tariff rate* and equivalent to the *prohibitive transportation cost*. One important difference between the prohibitive tariff case and the prohibitive transportation cost case is that the prohibitive transportation cost affects both firms equally and replicates the autarkic situations in both countries, but the unilateral prohibitive tariff by country A affects the firms *unequally* and it only replicates the autarkic situation in country A but not in country B, because firm A is still able to enter the country-B market even under the prohibitive tariff by country A.

---

[15]The country-B market is not affected by the introduction of the import tariff by country A at all: firm A's export supply is $y^*(0)$ and firm B's domestic supply is $x^*(0)$.

Rent-shifting effect: Firm A obtains $\pi_D(t)$ and firm B obtains $\pi_{EX}(t)$ in the country-A market. Then, an increase in the tariff rate t induces both an increase in firm A's profit and a decrease in firm B's profit. In other words, by the import tariff, part of firm B's profit is taken away and moved from firm B to firm A. This is known as the *profit-shifting* or *rent-shifting* effect of import tariff.

Welfare of country A: The consumer in country A enjoys the surplus $\mathrm{CS}^*(t)$ in the domestic market, which is defined in Eq. (5.15). Firm A earns $\pi_D(t)$ in the domestic market and $\pi_{EX}(0)$ in the foreign market. The government of country A can collect the tariff revenue $\mathrm{TR}^A(t) \equiv ty^*(t)$. The welfare of country A is measured by the sum of the consumer surplus, the total profit of firm A, and the tariff revenue:

$$W^A(t) \equiv \mathrm{CS}^*(t) + \pi_D(t) + \pi_{EX}(0) + \mathrm{TR}^A(t).$$

Since the functions CS^*, π_D, and TR^A are quadratic in t, so is W^A, too. As shown in Chapter 5, $\mathrm{CS}^*(t)$ is decreasing, but $\pi_D(t)$ is increasing in t. The tariff revenue $\mathrm{TR}^A(t)$ is increasing in t at zero, while decreasing in t at the prohibitive tariff rate. Also, we have $\mathrm{TR}^A(0) = \mathrm{TR}^A(\bar{t}) = 0$. Changes in the welfare of country A is represented by

$$\frac{dW^A(t)}{dt} = [p_x^*(t) - c]\frac{dx^*(t)}{dt} + \left[1 - \frac{dp_y^*(t)}{dt}\right]y^*(t) + t\frac{dy^*(t)}{dt}.$$

By simple calculation, we can show that $1 - dp_y^*(t)/dt = 2\beta^2/\Delta^* > 0$, where $\Delta^* \equiv 4\beta^2 - \gamma^2 > 0$. This means that the consumer price of the imports increases less than the increase in the tariff rate, implying an incomplete *pass-through* of the tariff rate.[16] Further, we can show that

$$\frac{dW^A(0)}{dt} = [p_x^*(0) - c]\frac{dx^*(0)}{dt} + \left[1 - \frac{dp_y^*(0)}{dt}\right]y^*(0) > 0 \quad \text{and}$$

$$\frac{dW^A(\bar{t})}{dt} = [p_x^*(\bar{t}) - c]\frac{dx^*(\bar{t})}{dt} + \bar{t}\frac{dy^*(\bar{t})}{dt} = \frac{-(\alpha - c)(4\beta - 3\gamma)}{2\Delta^*} < 0.$$

That is, a small increase in the tariff rate from zero increases the total surplus of country A. In contrast, a small decrease in the tariff rate from

---

[16]This result heavily relies on the linearity of the demand function for the imports.

the prohibitive level increases the total surplus of country A. Let $\overline{W}$ be the autarkic welfare level of country A. Then, as shown in Chapter 5, we have $W^A(0) = W^*(0) > \overline{W}$. Further, because the prohibitive tariff rate does not replicate the autarkic situation for country A, we have $W^A(\bar{t}) > W^*(\bar{t}) = \overline{W}$. Because $W^A(t)$ is quadratic in t, the above results imply $W^A(t) > \overline{W}$ for all $t \in [0, \bar{t}]$.

Welfare of country B: Because the import tariff by country A does not affect the country-B market, the consumer in country B can enjoy the surplus $CS^*(0)$. Firm B earns $\pi_D(0)$ in the domestic market and $\pi_{EX}(t)$ in the foreign market. The welfare of country B is measured by the sum of the consumer surplus and the total profit of firm B:

$$W^B(t) \equiv CS^*(0) + \pi_D(0) + \pi_{EX}(t).$$

An increase in the tariff rate decreases $\pi_{EX}(t)$ and, thereby, deteriorates the welfare of country B. Introduction of a small import tariff by country A makes country A better-off, while country B worse-off. In this sense, the (small) import tariff can be said to be a *beggar-thy-neighbor policy*.

7.3.2   *Export Subsidy in the Cournot Case*

Next, let us consider the export subsidy policy. From the exporter's viewpoint, a positive export subsidy by the exporting country is equivalent to a negative import tariff by the importing country. Therefore, most of the effects of the export subsidy by country B are parallel to those of the import tariff by country A.

A negative t represents a positive export subsidy rate and its *decrease* corresponds to an increase in the export subsidy rate. Contrary to the import tariff case, an increase in the subsidy rate shifts the reaction curve of firm B outward and, thereby, brings about a decrease in firm A's domestic supply and an increase in firm B's export supply to the country-A market. The profit of firm A decreases, while the subsidy-inclusive profit of firm B increases.

Welfare of country A: The government of country A does nothing and, therefore, the welfare of country A is represented by the sum of the consumer surplus and the total profit of firm A:

$$W^A(t) \equiv CS^*(t) + \pi_D(t) + \pi_{EX}(0).$$

An increase in the export subsidy to firm B (i.e., a decrease in t) increases the consumer surplus of country A but decreases the profit of firm A. Simple calculation yields

$$\frac{dW^A(t)}{dt} = \frac{dCS^*(t)}{dt} + \frac{d\pi_D(t)}{dt} = [p_x^*(t) - c]\frac{dx^*(t)}{dt} - y^*(t)\frac{dp_y^*(t)}{dt}$$

$$= \frac{-(\beta - \gamma)(\alpha - c)}{\Delta^*} + \frac{\beta}{\Delta^*}t < 0. \quad (\because t \le 0)$$

That is, an increase in the export subsidy by country B is beneficial to county A as a whole.

Welfare of country B: The export subsidy by country B does not affect the country-B market. Then, the consumer of country B can enjoy $CS^*(0)$. Firm B earns $\pi_D(0)$ in the domestic market and $\pi_{EX}(t)$ in the foreign market. The government of country B bears the burden of subsidy payment $S(t) \equiv -ty^*(t)$. It is easy to check that $dS(t)/dt < 0$ for $t \le 0$; that is, an increase in the subsidy rate increases the burden of subsidy payment. The welfare of country B is represented by the sum of the consumer surplus and the total profit of firm B *minus* subsidy payment:

$$W^B(t) \equiv CS^*(0) + \pi_D(0) + \pi_{EX}(t) - S(t).$$

Simple calculation yields

$$\frac{dW^B(t)}{dt} = \frac{d\pi_{EX}(t)}{dt} - \frac{dS(t)}{dt} = [p_y^*(t) - c]\frac{dy^*(t)}{dt} + y^*(t)\frac{dp_y^*(t)}{dt}$$

$$= \frac{-\gamma(2\beta - \gamma)(\alpha - c)}{(\Delta^*)^2} - \frac{4\beta(2\beta^2 - \gamma^2)}{(\Delta^*)^2}t.$$

From this, we have $dW^B(0)/dt < 0$, which means that a small export subsidy improves the welfare of the exporting country.

Discussion: In the perfectly competitive circumstance, an export subsidy surely makes the exporting country worse-off, whether in the small-country case or in the large-country case. In contrast, in some oligopolistic circumstances, it is possible for the exporting country to improve its own welfare by introducing an export subsidy. This remarkable result has attracted a great deal of attention of the policy makers, because it seemed to provide them with a "good" rationale for trade intervention that aims to promote the exporting industry of the country. The strategic-trade-policy argument, however, should not be regarded as justification for such *mercantilistic policies*. The effects of a particular trade policy depend on subtle differences in the characterizing aspects of the imperfectly competitive situation under consideration. Therefore, by altering the characterizing aspects of the situation only slightly, they can be easily changed or even reversed. Since we do not (cannot) know exactly the characterizing aspects of the situation in reality, we may fail to achieve the desired/expected results or, even worse, we may suffer from undesired/unexpected results by implementing a particular strategic trade policy. After all, the strategic-trade-policy argument only indicates that the mercantilistic policies are not entirely groundless, but it cannot be a sound foundation for the mercantilistic policies.

7.3.3   *Export Tax in the Bertrand Case*

If we switch the situation from the quantity-setting duopoly to the price-setting duopoly, the effects of a trade policy can be changed or even reversed. To see this, let us consider the export tax policy in the Bertrand duopoly.

Suppose that the exporting country (i.e., country B) imposes a unit export tax t on firm B. The situation is similar to the case of the export subsidy by country B in the Cournot duopoly, except that t is now taken as a non-negative variable and that firms use prices as strategic variables. For simplicity, we assume positive trade equilibria, that is, the equilibrium quantities and prices are given by Eqs. (5.16)–(5.19). An increase in the export tax rate by country B (i.e., an increase in t) induces an increase in firm A's domestic supply $x^\circ(t)$, a decrease in firm B's export supply $y^\circ(t)$. Accordingly, the profit of firm A obtained from the country-A market, $\widetilde{\pi}_D(t)$, increases, while that of firm B, $\widetilde{\pi}_{EX}(t)$, decreases.

Welfare of country A: The consumer of country A enjoys $\mathrm{CS}^\circ(t)$ as defined in Eq. (5.21). Firm A can obtain $\widetilde{\pi}_D(t)$ in the domestic market and $\widetilde{\pi}_{EX}(0)$ in the foreign market. The welfare of country A is measured by the sum of the consumer surplus and the total profit:

$$W^A(t) \equiv \mathrm{CS}^\circ(t) + \widetilde{\pi}_D(t) + \widetilde{\pi}_{EX}(0).$$

Simple calculation yields

$$\frac{dW^A(t)}{dt} = [p_x^\circ(t) - c]\frac{dx^\circ(t)}{dt} - y^\circ(t)\frac{dp_y^\circ(t)}{dt}$$

$$= \frac{-\beta^2(\beta - \gamma)(\alpha - c)}{\Delta\Delta^*} + \frac{\beta^3}{\Delta\Delta^*}t.$$

Therefore, we have $dW^A(0)/dt < 0$, meaning that the introduction of a small export tax by the exporting country (i.e., country B) is harmful to the importing country (i.e., country A).

Welfare of country B: Because the consumer of country B is not affected by the export tax by country B, it enjoys $\mathrm{CS}^\circ(0)$. Firm B obtains $\widetilde{\pi}_D(0)$ in the domestic market and the net-of-tax profit $\widetilde{\pi}_{EX}(t)$ in the foreign market. The government of country B collect the tax revenue $\mathrm{TR}^B(t) \equiv ty^\circ(t)$. The welfare of country B is represented by the sum of the consumer surplus, the total profit, and the tax revenue:

$$W^B(t) \equiv \mathrm{CS}^\circ(0) + \widetilde{\pi}_D(0) + \widetilde{\pi}_{EX}(t) + \mathrm{TR}^B(t).$$

Changes in the welfare of country B with respect to t can be written as

$$\frac{dW^B(t)}{dt} \equiv \frac{d\widetilde{\pi}_{EX}(t)}{dt} + \frac{d\mathrm{TR}^B(t)}{dt} = \left[p_y^\circ(t) - c\right]\frac{dy^\circ(t)}{dt} + y^\circ(t)\frac{dp_y^\circ(t)}{dt}$$

$$= \frac{\gamma y^\circ(t)}{\Delta^*} - \frac{\beta(2\beta^2 - \gamma^2)}{\Delta\Delta^*}t.$$

On one hand, an increase in the export tax rate surely reduces the net-of-tax profit $\widetilde{\pi}_{EX}(t)$; on the other hand, it gives rise to an increase in the tax revenue if the tax rate is sufficiently small. From the above result, we can show that $dW^B(0)/dt > 0$.

7.4   Remarks and Further Topics

In this section, we deal with the issues concerning the regional trade agreements and the determination of tariffs under interdependent game-theoretic circumstances.

7.4.1 *Regional Trade Agreements*

Since the late 1980s, the world economy has witnessed a rapid increase in the number of *regional trade agreements* (RTAs), which are reciprocal preferential agreements between two or more countries. Typical forms of RTAs are *customs unions* (CUs) and *free trade agreements* (FTAs).[17] RTAs liberalize internal trade among the members, while maintain trade-intervention policies against the non-members: in the case of a CU, the members unify and coordinate their external trade policies; on the other hand, in the case of an FTA, each member country adopts its own external trade policies independently.[18] Although RTAs are apparently against the principle of *non-discrimination* in the World Trade Organization (WTO), they are authorized to form as far as they conform a certain set of rules.[19] RTAs' ambivalent nature of having both *liberalist* and *protectionist* sides makes it complicated to investigate the effects of RTAs. In this subsection, we briefly discuss the classical arguments of *trade creation* and *trade diversion* due to Viner (1950); show the Kemp–Wan theorem concerning the formation of a welfare-enhancing CU (Kemp and Wan, 1976); and also discuss other issues related to RTAs.

Trade creation: To see the effects of RTAs in a simple framework, let us consider a world economy with two goods and three countries A, B, and C. Suppose that country A is contemplating a formation of an RTA (either an FTA or a CU) with one of two candidate countries B and C. Country A is importing good 1 and both countries B and C are exporting good 1. Let p^B and p^C be the export prices of good 1 in countries B and C, respectively; for simplicity, we assume that they are fixed and $p^B < p^C$. Without RTA, country A applies the same tariff rate (say, $\tau^A > 0$) to all the imports of good 1 on the Most-Favored-Nation basis. Because $(1+\tau^A)p^B < (1+\tau^A)p^C$, country A comes to import good 1 only from country B and have no transaction with country C.

---

[17]Despite the adjective "regional" attached to its name, RTA does not require that the member countries should belong to the same region.

[18]The European Union is a notable example of CU. There is a great number of FTAs. According to the WTO website (as of 20 June 2017), the accumulated number of RTAs in force notified to the WTO have reached 445. In addition, more than 90% of them take the form of FTA.

[19]See the WTO website (https://www.wto.org/english/tratop_e/region_e/scope_rta_e.htm).

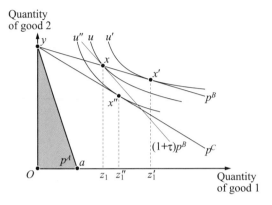

Fig. 7.4   Trade Creation and Trade Diversion

Figure 7.4 illustrates the situation. The shaded triangular area Oay represents country A's (Ricardian) production possibility set. Lines p^By and p^Cy represent the trade balance condition evaluated at p^B and that evaluated at p^C, respectively. Reflecting the comparative disadvantage of country A in good 1, country A completely specializes in good 2 (i.e., point y). Country A's consumption occurs at point x on the trade balance line with country B, where the slope of the indifference curve passing through point x is equal to the tariff-inclusive domestic price $(1 + \tau^A)p^B$ of the import from country B.

Now, suppose that country A decides to form an RTA with country B. Then, the tariff rate on the imports from country B reduces to zero, while that on the imports from country C is kept at $\tau^A > 0$. After the formation of the RTA, country B remains to be the most inexpensive source of good 1 for country A. Accordingly, country A keeps its trading partner unchanged. Due to the elimination of import tariff, country A's consumption point moves from x to x'; the import of good 1 increases from z_1 to z_1'; and the utility of country A increases from u to u' as illustrated in Fig. 7.4.

The formation of an RTA by countries A and B expands the volume of *internal* trade within the RTA, but does not affect *external* trade with country C at all.[20] The formation of the RTA expands the overall world

---

[20]Remember that country C has no transaction with country A in both pre-RTA and post-RTA situations.

trade — this is known as the *trade creation* effect. When the trade creation effect works well, as the volume of trade *within* the RTA increases, the welfare of the member countries tends to improve on one hand; the welfare of the outside country may not be affected on the other. In this sense, we can say that the trade creation effect tends to improve the welfare of the world as a whole.

Trade diversion: In turn, suppose that country A decides to form an RTA with country C. The tariff on the import from country C is eliminated, while that on the import from country B is kept at $\tau^A > 0$. Then, even if $p^B < p^C$ as assumed, we can have $p^C < (1 + \tau^A)p^B$. In this case, after the formation of the RTA, country A *switches* the trading partner from country B to country C, because country C is apparently the most inexpensive source of good 1. Country A's trade with country B is replaced by trade with country C — this is known as the *trade diversion* effect. The trade diversion effect creates country C's trade with country A, but destroys country B's trade with country A. In this sense, the trade diversion effect is beneficial to at least one of the member countries (i.e., country C), but harmful to the outside country (i.e., country B). The welfare of country A may or may not improve.

Figure 7.4 illustrates a case where the trade diversion effect worsens country A's welfare. Country A's pre-RTA consumption is point x and the post-RTA consumption is point x''. Country A's import increases from z_1 to z_1'', but the utility level decreases from u to u''. By changing trading partner from country B to C, the *terms of trade* of country A deteriorates: the tariff-exclusive import price of good 1 increases from p^B to p^C. This also causes the deterioration of country A's welfare. By carefully examining Fig. 7.4, we recognize that the welfare-deteriorating trade diversion is more likely if (i) the gap between the possible partners' export prices is bigger or if (ii) the initial MFN-tariff rate τ^A is lower.[21]

Trade circumvention and the rules of origin: Let us consider a case where countries A and B form an FTA, while country C stays outside. In the case of an FTA, each member country can adopt its trade policies

---

[21]Readers may draw by themselves a figure that illustrates a welfare-enhancing trade diversion.

against the outside countries independently of the other member countries. Suppose that the MFN tariff rate of country A (i.e., τ^A) is higher than that of country B (i.e., τ^B). If a firm in country C wants to export its product to country A in the absence of the FTA, it has to incur a high tariff rate of country A; the domestic price of country C's product in country A becomes $(1 + \tau^A)p^C$. In contrast, in the presence of the FTA, the firm in country C can avoid the high tariff rate by taking advantage of the difference in the tariff rates of countries A and B. If the firm in country C first exports its product to country B, only incurring a low tariff rate of country B, and redirects the product to country A, then the firm can supply the product to country A's market at a lower price of $(1 + \tau^B)p^C$. It is called *trade circumvention*.[22]

Trade circumvention undermines the intended effectiveness of an FTA to give favorable treatment to the goods produced in member countries and discriminate against the goods produced in non-member countries. Things become more complicated when a good is produced by using intermediate goods produced in different countries and/or when the production of a good is processed in several different countries. To prevent trade circumvention, *rules of origin* (ROOs) are usually introduced to an FTA. Based on certain criteria, ROOs determine whether a good is eligible — in the sense that the good is judged as a product of the member countries — for the preferential treatment of the FTA. There are three known criteria: for a country to be approved as the origin of a good, (i) the *value-added criterion* requires that the percentage of the value-added of the good generated/added in that country exceeds a specified level; (ii) the *tariff-headings criterion* requires that the tariff-heading of the good is obtained in that country; and (iii) the *technical criterion* requires that a specific process of the production of the good is carried out in that country.[23]

Formation of welfare-enhancing RTAs: Viner (1950)'s argument of trade creation and trade diversion has created an impression that the formation of an RTA intrinsically brings about ambiguous welfare effects.

---

[22] We are ignoring here the transportation costs and other impediments to trade among countries.

[23] Krishna and Krueger (1995) have examined the effects of ROOs based on the value-added criterion and discussed their relation to the *domestic content requirement*. Ishikawa *et al.* (2007) have focused on the roles of ROOs in the final good market. Takauchi (2014) has considered the cases where firms comply or do not comply with ROOs.

In the case of formation of CUs, however, Kemp and Wan (1976) have shown a much clearer positive result[24]:

Proposition 7.7 (Kemp and Wan, 1976). *Let any subset of the countries form a customs union. Then there exists a common tariff vector and a system of lump-sum compensatory payments, involving only members of the union, such that there is an associated tariff-ridden competitive equilibrium in which each individual country, whether a member of the union or not, is not worse off than before the formation of the union.*[25]

Grinols (1981) has extended the Kemp–Wan theorem to include a concrete compensation scheme based on the idea of the lump-sum transfer scheme developed by Grandmont and McFadden (1972),[26] and given a constructive proof of the theorem. Here, we show a sketch of the proof by Grinols (1981). Let M be the set of all countries in the world. A subset $K \subset M$ of countries is contemplating a formation of a CU. Let p^* and z^s be the world price vector and the net import vector of country $s \in M$, respectively; the corresponding *pre*-union variables are denoted by attaching a bar ($^-$). The GDP function of country s is denoted by $Y^s(\cdot)$.

Suppose that the world price vector (external to the union) in the post-union situation is kept the same as the pre-union world price vector, that is, $p^* = \bar{p}^*$. Then the behavior of the non-member countries remain unchanged. That is, $\bar{z}^s = z^s$ for all $s \in M/K$. Accordingly, the non-member countries in the post-union situation will be as well-off as in the post-union situation. Note that, under this condition, the world market clearing conditions in both the pre- and post-union situations imply $\sum_{s\in K} z^s = -\sum_{s\in M\backslash K} z^s = -\sum_{s\in M\backslash K} \bar{z}^s = \sum_{s\in K} \bar{z}^s$.

In turn, if each member country in the post-union situation can afford to buy the same consumption vector that the country actually consumed in the pre-union situation, then it can be made at least as well-off as in

---

[24] For the possibility of forming a welfare-enhancing FTA, see Panagariya and Krishna (2002) and also Krishna (2005).

[25] We are ignoring the problem of income (re)distribution among households within each single country by adopting the "single-household assumption" here. The original Kemp–Wan theorem has been proved based on the model without the single-household assumption.

[26] See Chapter 4, Section 4.2.

the pre-union situation. Let p be the common *internal* price vector that the union members face in the post-union situation. For country $s \in K$, the expenditure necessary to buy $\bar{x}^s$ evaluated at p is $p\bar{x}^s$ and the factor income is equal to $Y^s(p)$. Then, the following compensation payment $T^s(p)$ is sufficient for country s to buy $\bar{x}^s$ in the post-union situation: for $s \in K$,

$$T^s(p) \equiv p\bar{x}^s - Y^s(p). \tag{7.8}$$

To complete the proof, it suffices to show that the total amount of the compensation payments *within* the CU can be covered by the CU itself. By summing Eq. (7.8) over the member countries, we obtain

$$\sum_{s \in K} T^s(p) \equiv \sum_{s \in K} \{p\bar{x}^s - Y^s(p)\} \leqq \sum_{s \in K} \{p\bar{x}^s - p\bar{y}^s\} = p \sum_{s \in K} \bar{z}^s$$
$$= p \sum_{s \in K} z^s - p^* \sum_{s \in K} z^s = (p - p^*) \sum_{s \in K} z^s = t \sum_{s \in K} z^s. \tag{7.9}$$

The inequality in the first line follows from the definition of the GDP function; the second line follows from both the fact $\sum_{s \in K} \bar{z}^s = \sum_{s \in K} z^s$ and the trade balance condition $p^* \sum_{s \in K} z^s = 0$ in the post-union situation. As we set the *common tariff vector* of the CU equal to $t \equiv p - p^*$, then the last term can be seen as the union's tariff revenue in the post-union situation. Equation (7.9) means that, by redistributing the tariff revenue appropriately, the member countries can achieve the necessary compensation payments.[27]

Possibility of global free trade: Can the prevalence of RTAs lead the world economy eventually to *global free trade*? — this is known as the "dynamic time-path" question raised by Bhagwati (1991, 1993). There are two strands of theoretical investigation into the dynamic time-path question: the coalition formation game approach and the network formation game approach. Examples of the former coalition formation game approach include Yi (1996, 2000), Das and Ghosh (2006), and Saggi and Yildiz (2010). On the other hand, Furusawa and Konishi (2005, 2007) and Goyal and Joshi (2006) have followed the framework of network formation games as developed by Jackson and Wolinsky (1996). Other examples

---

[27]There may arise a strictly positive surplus $t \sum_{s \in K} z^s - \sum_{s \in K} T^s(p) > 0$. In order to deal with this case appropriately, it suffices to consider the following transfer payment to country s: $T^s(p) + \theta_s \{(p - \bar{p}^*) \sum_{k \in K} \bar{z}^s - \sum_{k \in K} T^k(p)\}$, where $\theta_s > 0$ for all $s \in K$ and $\sum_{s \in K} \theta_s = 1$.

include Aghion *et al.* (2007), Macho-Stadler and Xue (2007), Zhang *et al.* (2011), and Lake (2016). Further, in the framework of the network formation game, Zhang *et al.* (2013) and Nakanishi (2018) have considered situations in which the countries are fully farsighted enough to understand not only the immediate outcome of the formation of an RTA but also the ultimate outcome induced by a sequence of successive formation of RTAs.[28] In view of the above literature, we cannot make a definitive answer to the dynamic time-path question. The achievement of global free trade is one possibility, but not of necessity.[29]

7.4.2   *Tariff War and Trade Negotiation*

As shown in the previous sections, imposition of an import tariff by one country may improve its own welfare; at the same time, it worsens the welfare of trading partners. This policy externality provides the trading partners with a strong incentive to take some (possibly, retaliatory) policy measures. Taking account of these political interdependency, the governments have to make decisions on their trade policies. On one hand, each government can decide its trade policy independently of the others' policies; on the other hand, the governments can determine their policies somewhat cooperatively. In this subsection, we introduce a convenient analytical device called *tariff utility function*, which can be used to examine the determination of tariffs in some game-theoretic circumstances.

Tariff utility function: Consider a competitive world economy consisting of two countries (A and B) and two tradable goods (good 1 and good 2). Country A imports good 1, while country B imports good 2. For $s = A, B$, let τ^s be the *ad valorem* import tariff rate of country s. Further, let p^* be the world relative price of good 1 in terms of good 2. Then, similar to Eq. (7.1), the net import of country s can be written as a function of p^* and τ^s: $\tilde{z}^s(p^*, \tau^s) \equiv (\tilde{z}_1^s(p^*, \tau^s), \tilde{z}_2^s(p^*, \tau^s))$. Due to the Walras law, the

---

[28]To capture the farsightedness of the countries, Zhang *et al.* (2013) adopted the notion of *pairwise farsightedly stable set* developed by Herings *et al.* (2009) as the solution concept; on the other hand, Nakanishi (2018) adopted the *farsighted von Neumann–Morgenstern stable set.*

[29]Digging into the literature concerning the achievement of global free trade is beyond the scope of this book; for the first step, the readers may consult the articles listed here.

world market equilibrium obtains if

$$\tilde{z}_1^A(p^*, \tau^A) + \tilde{z}_1^B(p^*, \tau^B) = 0.$$

This determines the world equilibrium price as a function of the combination of the tariff rates of the countries: $\tilde{p}^*(\tau^A, \tau^B)$. Because the import tariff by one country improves its own terms of trade in the large-country case, $\tilde{p}^*$ becomes decreasing in τ^A, while increasing in τ^B.[30]

Substituting $\tilde{p}^*(\cdot)$ into $\tilde{z}^s(\cdot)$ and, further, substituting the result into the trade utility function $W^s(\cdot)$,[31] we can define a function $\mathcal{U}^s$ that associates each combination of tariff rates (τ^A, τ^B) with the equilibrium welfare level of country s: for $s = A, B$,

$$\mathcal{U}^s(\tau^A, \tau^B) \equiv W^s\left(\tilde{z}^s\left(\tilde{p}^*\left(\tau^A, \tau^B\right)\right)\right),$$

which is called the *tariff utility function*.[32] To see the properties of the tariff utility function, let us take $\mathcal{U}^A$ for example. Let $\bar{u}^A$ be the *autarkic utility level* of country A. Suppose $\tau^B = 0$, then there exists $\bar{\tau}^A > 0$ such that $\bar{u}^A = \mathcal{U}^A(\bar{\tau}^A, 0)$, which is the (unilateral) *prohibitive tariff rate*. Because a small increase in τ^A from zero improves country A's welfare, $\mathcal{U}^A$ is increasing in τ^A at $(0, \tau^B)$ as far as τ^B is not prohibitive. As an increase in country B's tariff rate aggravates the terms of trade of country A, $\mathcal{U}^A$ is decreasing in τ^B.

A *tariff indifference curve* is the graph of a set of tariff combinations that give rise to a certain utility level. In Fig. 7.5, bold curves u, u', and u'' are some examples of tariff indifference curves of country A on the τ^A–τ^B plane, where τ^A is measured horizontally and τ^B vertically. The lower a tariff indifference curve is located, the higher the corresponding utility level is. (With a slight abuse of notation, we have $u < u' < u''$.) Because $\mathcal{U}^A$ is increasing in τ^A at $(0, \tau^B)$ and decreasing in τ^B, each tariff indifference curve is upward-sloping at the intersection with the vertical axis.

---

[30] These properties of $\tilde{p}^*$ hold if (i) both $\tilde{z}_1^A$ and $\tilde{z}_1^B$ are decreasing in p^*, (ii) $\tilde{z}_1^A$ is decreasing in τ^A, and (iii) $\tilde{z}_1^B$ is increasing in τ^B. See, Eqs. (7.2)–(7.3).

[31] For the trade utility function, see Section 4.3.1.

[32] Mayer (1981) has introduced the notion of tariff utility function. Later, Dixit (1987) has examined the properties of the tariff utility function in some detail. For more detailed characterization of the tariff utility function, see Nakanishi (2010, Chapter 3).

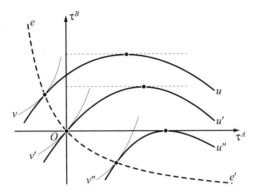

Fig. 7.5   Tariff Indifference Curves

Let p^s be the domestic relative price of good 1 in country s. By the assumption on the trade pattern, we have both $p^A = (1 + \tau^A)p^*$ and $p^B = p^*/(1 + \tau^B)$. If $p^A = p^B$, all the agents in the world face a common relative price and, consequently, all the marginal conditions for Pareto-efficiency are met. Therefore, a tariff combination (τ^A, τ^B) is Pareto-efficient if it satisfies

$$(1 + \tau^A)(1 + \tau^B) = 1. \tag{7.10}$$

Obviously, the origin $O \equiv (0,0)$, which corresponds to global free trade, satisfies Eq. (7.10). For a Pareto-efficient (τ^A, τ^B), we have $\tau^A \gtreqqless 0$ if and only if $\tau^B \lesseqqgtr 0$. This implies that, in order to achieve Pareto-efficiency, both countries cannot impose strictly positive import tariffs simultaneously: if one country levies import tariff, the other must adopt import subsidy. The graph of the Pareto-efficient tariff combinations is depicted by the dotted hyperbola ee' in Fig. 7.5. At each point on the hyperbola ee', a tariff indifference curve of country A is tangent to a tariff indifference curve of country B. Thin curves v, v', and v'' are country B's tariff indifference curves, which are tangent to country A's tariff indifference curves u, u', and u'', respectively, at some points on the hyperbola ee'.

The Nash tariff equilibrium: *Tariff war* is a situation where some countries adopt aggressive tariff policies against their trading partners and, in turn, the partner countries also take aggressive tariff policies in retaliation for the former countries' offensive policies. The situation of a tariff war can be modeled as a strategic-form tariff game $G = (\{A, B\}, \{X^s\}_{s \in \{A,B\}}, \{\mathcal{U}^s\}_{s \in \{A,B\}})$, where $X^s \equiv (-1, +\infty) \subset \mathbb{R}$ is the set of admissible tariff rates (i.e., strategies) of country s.[33] Then the consequence of a tariff war will be identified with the Nash equilibrium of G, which is the tariff combination (τ^{A*}, τ^{B*}) that satisfies the following conditions: for all $\tau^A \in X^A$ and for all $\tau^B \in X^B$,

$$\mathcal{U}^A(\tau^{A*}, \tau^{B*}) \geq \mathcal{U}^A(\tau^A, \tau^{B*}) \quad \text{and} \quad \mathcal{U}^B(\tau^{A*}, \tau^{B*}) \geq \mathcal{U}^B(\tau^{A*}, \tau^B).$$

The tariff reaction function ψ^A of country A is defined as follows: for $\tau^B \in X^B$,

$$\psi^A(\tau^B) \equiv \arg \max_{\tau^A \in X^A} \mathcal{U}^A(\tau^A, \tau^B).$$

The tariff reaction function ψ^B of country B can be defined in a similar way. The Nash equilibrium of G is a fixed point of a mapping ψ from $X^A \times X^B$ to itself such that $\psi : (\tau^A, \tau^B) \rightarrow (\psi^A(\tau^B), \psi^B(\tau^A))$.[34]

In Fig. 7.6, curves ψ^A and ψ^B depict the graphs of the tariff reaction functions (i.e., tariff reaction curves) of countries A and B, respectively. The Nash equilibrium of G is represented by the intersection of these curves, that is, point N. At point N, the tariff indifference curves of both countries intersect perpendicularly to each other. Obviously, the Nash equilibrium is not Pareto-efficient. Let $u^{A*} \equiv \mathcal{U}^A(\tau^{A*}, \tau^{B*})$ and $u^{B*} \equiv \mathcal{U}^B(\tau^{A*}, \tau^{B*})$ be the utility levels of country A and country B at the Nash equilibrium, respectively. Figure 7.6 illustrates a situation in which *both countries lose the tariff war* in the sense that both countries suffer from lower utility levels at the Nash equilibrium than under global free trade: $u^{A*} < \mathcal{U}^A(0,0)$ and $u^{B*} < \mathcal{U}^B(0,0)$. Falling together in the tariff war is not the only possibility; it might be the case that *one of the countries win the tariff war* in the sense

---

[33]The framework of strategic-form games and the Nash equilibrium may not capture the notion of "retaliation" appropriately. By adopting the framework of the *theory of social situations* (TOSS) developed by Greenberg (1990), Oladi (2005) has examined the tariff retaliation game; similarly, Nakanishi (1999) has examined the quota retaliation game. See also Nakanishi (2010, Chapters 2 and 3).

[34]It should be noted that the definitions of the strategic-form tariff game G and the tariff reaction functions here are not rigorous/precise enough to be used for analyzing *all the Nash equilibria* of this game. In the text, we concentrate on the Nash equilibrium with positive trade transactions. It is easy to verify that the combination of the prohibitive tariff rates, $(\bar{\tau}^A, \bar{\tau}^B)$, constitutes another Nash equilibrium of G (with no trade transaction).

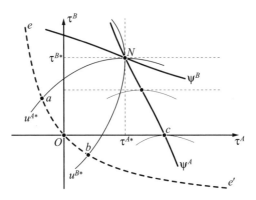

Fig. 7.6   The Nash Tariff Equilibrium and the Core

that the winning country achieves higher utility level at the Nash equilibrium than under global free trade. The possibility of winning the tariff war has been pointed out by Johnson (1953–1954) and, accordingly, it is called the "Johnson's case".

Cooperative tariff structures: On one hand, each country can determine its own tariff independently of the other countries; on the other hand, countries can coordinate their tariffs in order to facilitate mutual gains from cooperation. Here, we consider what kind of tariff structures will be established when the countries can negotiate over their tariffs and make binding agreements.

A country will not enter into a negotiation from the very outset if the utility level at the final outcome of the negotiation is expected to be lower than what the country can achieve by itself without negotiation. The outcome that will be realized when a negotiation breaks down or fails to start is called the *disagreement point* or the *threat point*. We regard the Nash equilibrium, (τ^{A*}, τ^{B*}), of the strategic-form tariff game G as the disagreement point of the tariff negotiation between countries A and B. Accordingly, if a tariff combination (τ^A, τ^B) were to be a candidate for one of the final outcomes of the negotiation, it must satisfy the following condition:

$$\mathcal{U}^A(\tau^A, \tau^B) \geq u^{A*} \quad \text{and} \quad \mathcal{U}^B(\tau^A, \tau^B) \geq u^{B*},$$

which are called the *participation constraint* or the requirement of *individual rationality*. Further, if a certain tariff combination reached through negotiation is *not* Pareto-efficient, the countries are still able to improve on it jointly; in this case, the very tariff combination cannot be the final outcome. Therefore, a candidate for the final outcome must be Pareto-efficient, that is, it must satisfy Eq. (7.10).

Mayer (1981) has proposed the *core* — the set of tariff combinations that satisfy both the individual rationality and the Pareto-efficiency — as the (set-valued) solution to the tariff negotiation.[35] Figure 7.6 illustrates an example of the core. Curves u^{A*} and u^{B*} represent the tariff indifference curves of countries A and B that correspond to the Nash equilibrium (i.e., the disagreement point). The spindle-shaped area $u^{A*}Nu^{B*}$ represents the set of individually rational tariff combinations. On the other hand, the hyperbola ee' represents the set of Pareto-efficient tariff combinations. Accordingly, the core is depicted by the segment ab on the hyperbola ee'. In this example, the origin O is included in the core, that is, global free trade can be a final outcome of the tariff negotiation. Unfortunately, in the Johnson's case, global free trade cannot be achieved through negotiations by the countries, because the origin O is excluded from the core.[36]

The core does not pinpoint a particular tariff combination as *the* final outcome of the negotiation. Rather, it only narrows down the range of possible candidates for the eventual consequence. Which particular outcome will be achieved through negotiation depends on the bargaining power of the countries. If country A is more powerful than country B, then the final outcome would be a tariff combination in the core close to point b; conversely, if country B is more powerful, then the final outcome would become closer to point a.[37]

---

[35]The notion of "core" has been introduced originally as the solution concept for characteristic function form games. See von Neumann and Morgenstern (1944) and Gillies (1959).

[36]By adopting the *Nash bargaining solution* as the solution concept, Riezman (1982) has examined a problem of tariff negotiation and obtained similar results.

[37]Bagwell and Staiger (1999, 2002) have extensively used the notions of trade utility function and trade indifference curves to examine the working of the reciprocity principle in the GATT/WTO system. See also Nakanishi (2010, 2017).

Bibliography

Aghion, P., P. Antràs, and E. Helpman, 2007, Negotiating free trade, *Journal of International Economics* 73: 1–30.

Anderson, J.E. and E. van Wincoop, 2003, Gravity with gravitas: A solution to the border puzzle, *American Economic Review* 93: 170–192.

Anderson, J.E. and E. van Wincoop, 2004, Trade costs, *Journal of Economic Literature* 42: 691–751.

Bagwell, K. and R.W. Staiger, 1999, An economic theory of GATT, *American Economic Review* 38(2): 291–319.

Bagwell, K. and R.W. Staiger, 2002, *The Economics of the World Trading Systems*, Cambridge, Mass.: MIT Press.

Bernard, A.B., J. Eaton, J.B. Jensen, and S.S. Kortum, 2003, Plants and productivity in international trade, *American Economic Review* 93: 1268–1290.

Bernard, A.B. and J.B. Jensen, 2004, Why some firms export, *Review of Economics and Statistics* 86: 561–569.

Bernard, A.B., J.B. Jensen, and P.K. Schott, 2006, Survival of the best fit: Exposure to low wage countries and the (uneven) growth of U.S. manufacturing plants, *Journal of International Economics* 68: 219–237.

Bhagwati, J.N., 1991, *The World Trading System at Risk*, Princeton University Press, Princeton, New Jersey, U.S.

Bhagwati, J.N., 1993, Regionalism and multilateralism: An overview, in: J. de Melo and A. Panagariya (eds.), *New Dimensions in Regional Integration*, Cambridge University Press, Cambridge, UK.

Boadway, R.W. and N. Bruce,1984, *Welfare Economics*, Basil Blackwell, UK.

Brander, J.A., 1981, Intra-industry trade in identical commodities, *Journal of International Economics* 11: 1–14.

Brander, J.A. and P.R. Krugman, 1983, A 'reciprocal dumping' model of international trade, *Journal of International Economics* 15: 313–321.

Brander, J.A. and B.J. Spencer, 1981, Tariffs and the extraction of foreign monopoly rents under potential entry, *Canadian Journal of Economics* 14(3): 371–389.

Brander, J.A. and B.J. Spencer, 1984, Trade warfare: Tariffs and cartels, *Journal of International Economics* 16: 227–242.

Brander, J.A. and B.J. Spencer, 1985, Export subsidies and international market share rivalry, *Journal of International Economics* 18: 83–100.

Brezis, E.S., P.R. Krugman, and D. Tsiddon, Leapfrogging in international competition: A theory of cycles in national technological leadership, *American Economic Review* 83(5): 1211–1219.

Brown, C. and G. Linden, 2009, *Chips and Change: How Crisis Reshapes the Semiconductor Industry*, Cambridge, MA: MIT Press.

Cairncross, F., 1997, *The Death of Distance*, Boston, Mass.: Harvard Business School Press.

Chipman, J.S., 1969, Factor price equalization and the Stolper–Samuelson theorem, *International Economic Review* 10: 399–406.

Chipman, J.S. and J.C. Moore, 1972, Social utility and the gains from trade, *Journal of International Economics* 2: 157–172.

Clarke, R. and D.R. Collie, 2003, Product differentiation and the gains from trade under Bertrand duopoly, *Canadian Journal of Economics* 36(3): 658–673.

Combes, P-P., T. Mayer, and J-F. Thisse, 2008, *Economic Geography:The Integration of Regions and Nations*, Princeton University Press: Princeton.

Das, S.P. and S. Ghosh, 2006, Endogenous trading bloc formation in a North-South global economy, *Canadian Journal of Economics* 39: 809–830.

Davis, D.R., 1998, The home market, trade, and industrial structure, *American Economic Review* 88: 1264–1276.

Demiroglu, U. and K.K. Yun, 1999, The lens condition for factor price equalization, *Journal of International Economics* 47: 449–456.

Dettmer, B., 2011, International service transactions: Is time a trade barrier in a connected world? Jena Economic Research Papers #2011-003.

Deardorff, A.V., 1994, The possibility of factor price equalization, revisited, *Journal of International Economics* 36: 167–175.

Deardorff, A.V., 1994, in: A.V. Deardorff and R.M. Stern (eds.), *The Stolper–Samuelson Theorem: A Golden Jubilee*, Amsterdam: The University of Michigan Press.

Debreu, G., 1959, *Theory of Value: An Axiomatic Analysis of Economic Equilibrium*, Cowles Foundation for Research in Economics, Yale University.

Diewert, W.E., 1980, Symmetry conditions for market demand functions, *Review of Economic Studies* 47: 595–601.

Dixit, A., 1987, Strategic aspects of trade policy, in: T. Bewley (ed.), *Advances in Economic Theory: Fifth World Congress*, New York: Cambridge University Press.

Dixit, A. and V. Norman, 1986, Gains from trade without lump-sum compensation, *Journal of International Economics* 21: 111–122.

Dixit, A. and V. Norman, 1980, *Theory of International Trade: A Dual, General Equilibrium Approach*, Cambridge: Cambridge University Press.

Dixit, A.K. and J.E. Stiglitz, 1977, Monopolistic competition and optimum product diversity, *American Economic Review* 67: 297–308.

Dornbusch, R., S. Fischer, and P.A. Samuelson, 1977, Comparative advantage, trade, and payments in Ricardian model with a continuum of goods, *American Economic Review* 67: 823–839.

Dornbusch, R., S. Fischer, and P.A. Samuelson, 1980, Heckscher–Ohlin trade theory with a continuum of goods, *The Quarterly Journal of Economics* 95(2): 203–224.

Eaton, J. and S. Kortum, 2002, Technology, geography, and trade, *Econometrica* 70(5): 1741–1779.

Flam, H. and M.J. Flanders, 1991, *Heckscher–Ohlin Trade Theory*, Cambridge, Mass.: The MIT Press.

Forslid, R. and I.P. Ottaviano, 2003, An analytically solvable core-periphery model, *Journal of Economic Geography* 3: 229–240.

Fujita, M., P.R. Krugman, and A.J. Venables, 1999, *The Spatial Economy: Cities, Regions, and International Trade*, Cambridge, Mass.: The MIT Press.

Fujita, M. and J-F. Thisse, 2013, *Economics of Agglomeration: Cities, Industrial Location, and Globalization*, 2nd edn., New York: Cambridge University Press.

Furusawa, T. and H. Konishi, 2005, Free trade networks with transfers, *Japanese Economic Review* 56: 144–164.

Furusawa, T. and H. Konishi, 2007, Free trade networks, *Journal of International Economics* 72: 310–335.

Gillies, D.B., 1959, Solutions to general non-zero-sum games, *Annals of Mathematics Studies* 40: 47–85.

Gorman, W.M., 1953, Community preference fields, *Econometrica* 21: 63–80.

Gorman, W.M., 1955, The intransitivity of certain criteria used in welfare economics, *Oxford Economic Papers* 7: 25–35.

Goyal, S. and S. Joshi, 2006, Bilateralism and free trade, *International Economic Review* 47: 749–778.

Grandmont, J.M. and D. McFadden, A technical note on classical gains from trade, *Journal of International Economics* 2: 109–125.

Greenberg, J., 1990, *The Theory of Social Situations: An Alternative Game-Theoretic Approach*, New York: Cambridge University Press.

Grinols, E., 1981, An extension of the Kemp–Wan theorem on the formation of customs unions, *Journal of International Economics* 11: 259–266.

Grossman, G.M. and E. Helpman, 1995, Technology and trade, in: G. Grossman and K. Rogoff (eds.), *Handbook of International Economics* III (Chapter 25), Amsterdam, the Netherlands: Elsevier Science B.V.

Grubel, H.G. and P.J. Lloyd, 1975, *Inta-Industry Trade*, London: Macmillan.

Gupta, A. and S. Seshasai, 2007, 24-hour knowledge factory: Using internet technology to leverage spatial and temporal separations, *ACM Transactions on Internet Technology* 7(3), Article 14.

Head, K., and J. Ries, 1999, Rationalization effects and tariff reductions, *Journal of International Economics* 47: 295–320.

Head, K., T. Mayer, and J. Ries, 2009, How remote is the offshoring threat? *European Economic Review* 53: 429–444.

Heckscher, E.F. and B. Ohlin, 1991, *Heckscher–Ohlin Trade Theory*, translated, edited, and introduced by H. Flam and M.J. Flanders, Cambridge, Mass.: The MIT Press.

Helpman, E., 1981, International trade in the presence of product differentiation, economies of scale and monopolistic competition: A Chamberlin–Heckscher–Ohlin approach, *Journal of International Economics* 11: 305–340.

Helpman, E. and P.R. Krugman, 1985, *Market Structure and Foreign Trade: Increasing Returns, Imperfet Competitiion, and the International Economy*, Cambridge: The MIT Press.

Helpman, E., M.J. Melitz, and S.R. Yeaple, Export versus FDI with heterogeneous firms, *American Economic Review* 94: 300–316.

Helpman, E., 2006, Trade, FDI, and the organization and firms, *Journal of Economic Literature* 44: 589–630.

Herings, P.J-J, A. Mauleon, and V. Vannetelbosch, 2009, Farsightedly stable networks, *Games and Economic Behavior* 67: 526–541.

Hicks, J.R., 1940, The valuation of the social income, *Economica* 7: 105–124.

Hotelling, H., 1932, Edgeworth's taxation paradox and the nature of demand and supply functions, *Journal of Political Economy* 40(5): 577–616.

Hurwicz, L. and H. Uzawa, 1971, On the integrability of demand functions, in: J. Chipman *et al.* (eds.), *Preferences, Utility, and Demand*, New York: Harcourt, Brace, Jovanovich.

Ikemoto, K., 1969, Specific factors of production and the comparative costs theory, *Kobe University Economic Review* 13: 23–32.

Ishikawa, J., H. Mukunoki, and Y. Mizoguchi, 2007, Economic integration and rules of origin under international oligopoly, *International Economic Review* 48(1): 185–210.

Jackson, M. and A. Wolinsky, 1996, A strategic model of social and economic networks, *Journal of Economic Theory* 71: 44–74.

Johnson, H.G., 1953–1954, Optimum tariffs and retaliation, *Review of Economic Studies* 55: 142–153.

Jones, R.W., 1961, Comparative advantage and the theory of tariffs: A multi-country, multi-commodity model, *Review of Economic Studies* 28: 161–175.

Jones, R.W., 1965, The structure of simple general equilibrium models, *Journal of Political Economy* 73: 557–572.

Jones, R.W., 1971, A three-factor model in theory, trade, and history, in: J.N. Bhagwati, R.W. Jones, R.A. Mundell and J. Vanek (eds), *Trade, Balance of Payments and Growth*, Amsterdam: North-Holland.

Jones, R.W. and J.A. Scheinkman, 1977, The relevance of the two-sector production model in trade theory, *Journal of Political Economy* 85(5): 909–935.

Jones, R.W., S. Marjit, and T. Mitra, 1993, The Stolper–Samuelson theorems: Links to dominant diagonals, in: R. Becker, M. Boldrin, R.W. Jones, and W. Thomson (eds.), *General Equilibrium, Growth, and Trade II: The Legacy of Lionel McKenzie*, New York: Academic Press.

Kaldor, N., 1939, Welfare propositions of economics and interpersonal comparisons of utility, *Economic Journal* 49: 549–552.

Kawamata, K., 1991, *Market Mechanisms and Economic Welfare* (in Japanese: *Shijo-Kikou-To-Keizai-Kousei*), Tokyo, Japan: Sobunsha Publishing Co.

Kemp, M.C., 1962, The gain from international trade, *Economic Journal* 72: 803–819.

Kemp, M.C., 1969, *The Pure Theory of International Trade and Investment*, Englewood Cliffs, N.J.: Prentice-Hall.

Kemp, M.C., 1995, *The Gains from Trade and the Gains from Aid: Essays in International Trade Theory*, New York: Routledge.

Kemp, M.C., 2006, Factor price equalization in a world of many trading countries, *Review of International Economics* 14(4): 675–677.

Kemp, M.C. and K. Shimomura, 2001, Gains from trade in a Cournot–Nash general equilibrium, *Japanese Economic Review* 52: 284–302.

Kemp, M.C. and H. Wan Jr., 1976, An elementary proposition concerning the formation of customs unions, *Journal of International Economics* 6: 95–97.

Kemp, M.C. and H. Wan Jr., 1986, Gains from trade with and without lump-sum compensation, *Journal of International Economics* 21: 99–110.

Kemp, M.C. and H. Wan Jr., 2005, On the existence of equivalent tariff vectors — When the status quo matters, *Singapore Economic Review* 50: 345–359.

Kemp, M.C. and L.L. Wegge, 1969, On the relation between commodity prices and factor rewards, *International Economic Review* 10: 407–413.

Kemp, M.C. and K-y. Wong, 1995, Gains from trade when markets are possibly incomplete, in: M.C. Kemp (ed.), *The Gains from Trade and the Gains from Aid*, London: Routledge.

Kikuchi, T., 2006, Time zones, outsourcing and patterns of international trade, *Economics Bulletin* 6(15): 1–10.

Kikuchi, T., 2009, Time zones as a source of comparative advantage, *Review of International Economics* 17(5): 961–968.

Kikuchi, T. and N.V. Long, 2011, Shift working and trade in labour services with time zone differences, *Pacific Economics Review* 16(5): 553–564.

Kikuchi, T. and S. Marjit, 2011, Growth with time zone differences, *Economic Modeling* 28: 637–640.

Krishna, K. and A.O. Krueger, 1995, Implementing free trade agreements: rules of origin and hidden protection, in: A.V. Deardorff, J. Levinson, and R.M. Stern (eds.), *New Directions in Trade Theory*, Ann Arbor: University of Michigan Press, pp. 149–187.

Krishna, P., 2005, *Trade Blocs — Economics and Politics*, Cambridge University Press, New York.

Krugman, P.R., 1979, Increasing returns, monopolistic competition, and international trade, *Journal of International Economics* 9: 469–479.

Krugman, P.R., 1980, Scale economies, product differentiation, and the pattern of trade, *American Economic Review* 70: 950–959.

Krugman, P.R., 1981, Intraindustry specialization and the gains from trade, *Journal of Political Economy* 89: 959–973.

Krugman, P.R., 1991, *Geography and Trade*, Cambridge, Mass.: MIT Press.

Lake, J., 2016, Free trade agreements as dynamic farsighted networks, *Economic Inquiry*, Online version, DOI:10.1111/ecin.12360.

Lancaster, K., 1966, A new approach to consumer theory, *Journal of Political Economy* 74: 130–157.

Leahy, D. and J.P. Neary, 2011, Oligopoly and Trade, in: D. Bernhofen, R. Falvey, D. Greenaway, and U. Kreickemeier (eds.), *Palgrave Handbook of International Trade*, New York: Palgrave Macmillan.

Lerner, A.P., 1936, The symmetry between import and export taxes, *Economica* 3: 306–313.

Macho-Stadler, I. and L. Xue, 2007, Winners and losers from the gradual formation of trading blocs, *Economica* 74: 664–681.

Mandal, B., S. Marjit, and N. Nakanishi, 2017, Outsourcing, factor prices and skill formation in countries with non-overlapping time zones, *Eurasian Economic Review*, available on line (https://doi.org/10.1007/s40822-017-0086-9).

Mangasarian, O.L., 1969, *Nonlinear Programming*, New York: McGraw-Hill.

Marjit, S., 2007, Trade theory and the role of time zones, *International Review of Economic and Finance* 16: 153–160.

Marjit, S. and B. Mandal, 2017, Virtual trade between separated time zones and growth, *International Journal of Economic Theory* 13: 171–183.

Matsuoka, Y. and M. Fukushima, 2010, Time zones, shift working and international outsourcing, *International Review of Economic and Finance* 19: 769–778.

Mayer, W., 1974, Short-run and long-run equilibrium for a small open economy, *Journal of Political Economy* 82: 955–967.

Mayer, W., 1981, Theoretical considerations on negotiated tariff adjustments, *Oxford Economic Papers* 33: 135–153.

McKenzie, L.W., 1953, Specialization and efficiency in world production, *Review of Economic Studies* 21: 165–180.

Melitz, M.J., 2003, The impact of trade on intra-industry reallocations and aggregate industry productivity, *Econometrica* 71: 1695–1725.

Metzler, L., 1949, Tariffs, the terms of trade and the distributions of national income, *Journal of Political Economy* 57(1): 1–29.

Mitra, T. and R.W. Jones, 1999, Factor shares and the Chipman condition, in: J.R. Melvin, J.C. Moore, and R. Riezman (eds.), *Trade, Theory and Econometrics: Essay in honor of John S. Chipman*, New York: Routledge.

Motta, M., J-F. Thisse, and A. Cabrales, On the persisitence of leadership or leapfrogging in international trade, *International Economic Review* 38(4): 809–824.

Mundell, R., 1968, *International Economics*, New York: McMillan.

Mussa, M., 1974, Tariffs and distribution of income: The importance of factor specificity, substitutability, and intensity in the short and long run, *Journal of Political Economy* 82: 1191–1203.

Mussa, M., 1979, The two sector model in terms of its dual: A geometric exposition, *Journal of International Economics* 9: 513–526.

Nakanishi, N., 1992, On the equivalence of tariffs and international transfer, *Kobe University Economic Review* 37: 85–96.

Nakanishi, N., 1993, Welfare analysis of tariff change with and without international transfers, *Journal of International Economics* 35: 377–387.

Nakanishi, N., 1999, Reexamination of the international export quota game through the theory of social situations, *Games and Economic Behavior* 27: 132–152.

Nakanishi, N., 2010, *Game-Theoretic Analysis of Trade Policies under Interdependent Circumstances: Applications of the Theory of Social Situations and the Stable Set Approach*, Kyoto, Japan: Minerva Shobo Publishing Co. (in Japanese).

Nakanishi, N., 2017, Implication of the "status quo" in theoretical trade policy analyses — piecemeal policy and the stable set approach, *The International Economy* 19: 23–37.

Nakanishi, N., 2018, Farsightedly stable FTA structures — the roles of pre-existing tariff rates, in: S. Marjit and S. Kar (eds.), *International Trade, Welfare, and the Theory of General Equilibrium*, Cambridge, UK: Cambridge University Press.

Nakanishi, N. and N.V. Long, 2015, The distributional and allocative impacts of virtual labor mobility across time zones through communication networks, *Review of International Economics* 23(3): 638–662.

Nakanishi, N. and N.V. Long, 2018, A new impetus for endogenous growth: R&D offshoring via virtual labor mobility, unpublished manuscript.

Neary, J.P., 1978, Short-run capital specificity and the pure theory of international trade, *Economic Journal* 88: 488–510.

Neary, J.P., 2003, Presidential Address: Globalization and market structure, *Journal of the European Economic Association* 1(2/3): 245–271.

Negishi, T., 1963, On social welfare function, *Quarterly Journal of Economics* 77: 156–158.

Newbery, D.M.G. and J.E. Stiglitz, 1984, Pareto inferior trade, *Review of Economic Studies* 51: 1–12.

Nikaido, H., *Convex Structures and Economic Theory*, New York: Academic Press.

Ohlin, B., 1933, *Interregional and International Trade*, Cambridge: Harvard University Press.

Ohyama, M., 1972, Trade and welfare in general equilibrium, *Keio Economic Studies* 2: 37–73.

Oladi, G., 2005, Stable tariffs and retaliations, *Review of International Economics* 13(2): 205–215.

Ottaviano, G., T. Tabuchi, and J.F. Thisse, 2002, Agglomeration and trade revisited, *International Economic Review* 43: 409–435.

Ottaviano, G. and J.F. Thisse, 2004, Agglomeration and economic geography, in: J.V. Henderson and J.F. Thisse (eds.), *Handbook of Regional and Urban Economics* 4, Elsevier, Amsterdam.

Panagariya, A. and P. Krishna, 2002, On necessarily welfare-enhancing free trade areas, *Journal of International Economics* 57: 353–367.

Pavcnik, N., 2002, Trade liberalization, exit, and productivity improvements: Evidence from Chilean plants, *Review of Economic Studies* 69: 245–257.

Qi, L., 2003, Conditions for factor price equalization in the integrated world economy model, *Review of International Economics* 11(5): 899–908.

Qi, L., 2010, Why the lens condition cannot imply factor price equalization, *Review of International Economics* 18(4): 772–779.

Ricardo, D., *On the Principles of Political Economy and Taxation*, London: John Murray.

Riezman, R., 1982, Tariff retaliation from a strategic viewpoint, *Southern International Economics* 30: 267–283.

Roy, R., 1947, La distribution du revenu entre les divers biens, *Econometrica* 15: 205–225.

Rybczynski, T., 1955, Factor endowment and relative commodity prices, *Economica* 22(84): 336–41.

Scitovszky, T. de, 1941, A note on welfare propositions in economics, *Review of Economic Studies* 9: 77–88.

Saggi, K. and H.M. Yildiz, 2010, Bilateralism, multilateralism, and the quest for global free trade, *Journal of International Economics* 81: 26–37.

Samuelson, P.A., 1938, Welfare economics and international trade, *American Economic Review* 28: 261–266.

Samuelson, P.A., 1939, The gains from international trade, *Canadian Journal of Economics and Political Science* 5: 195–205.

Samuelson, P.A., 1950, Evaluation of real national income, *Oxford Economic Papers* 2: 1–29.

Samuelson, P.A., 1953–1954, Prices of factors and goods in general equilibrium, *Review of Economic Studies* 21: 1–20.

Samuelson, P.A., 1956, Social indifference curves, *Quarterly Journal of Economics* LXX, No. 1.

Samuelson, P.A., 1971, Ohlin was right, *Swedish Journal of Economics* 73: 365–384.

Shephard, R.W., 1953, *Cost and Production Functions*, Princeton: Princeton University Press.

Shy, O., 1988, A general equilibrium model of Pareto inferior trade, *Journal of International Economics* 25: 143–154.

Stolper, W.F. and P.A. Samuelson, 1941, Protection and real wages, *Review of Economic Studies* 9: 58–73.

Takauchi, K., 2014, Rules of origin and strategic choice of compliance, *Journal of Industry, Competition and Trade* 14: 287–302.

Takayama, A., 1970, *International Trade: An Approach to the Theory*, New York: Holt, Rinehart and Winston.

Takayama, A., 1985, *Mathematical Economics 2nd edition*, Cambridge University Press.

Tinbergen, J., 1962, *Shaping the World Economy: Suggestions for an International Economic Policy*, New York: Twentieth Century Fund.

Turunen-Red, A. and A.D. Woodland, 2001, The anatomy of multilateral trade policy reform, in: S. Lahiri (ed.), *Regionalism and Globalization: Theory and Practice*, London: Routledge.

Viner, J., 1950, *The Customs Union Issue*, New York: Carnegie Endowment for International Peace.

von Neumann, J. and O. Morgenstern, 1944, *Theory of Games and Economic Behavior* (2nd edn., 1947; 3rd edn., 1953), Princeton, N.J.: Princeton University Press.

Wachter, R.M., 2006, The dislocation of US medicine — The implications of medical outsourcing, *New England Journal of Medicine* 354(7): 661–665.

Weymark, J.A., 1979, A reconciliation for recent results in optimal taxation theory, *Journal of Public Economics* 12: 171–189.

Woodland, A.D., 1982, *International Trade and Resource Allocation*, Amsterdam: North-Holland.

Wong, K.-y., 1995, *International Trade in Goods and Factor Mobility*, Cambridge: The MIT Press.

Yeaple, S.R., A simple model of firm heterogeneity, international trade, and wage, *Journal of International Economics* 65: 1–20.

Yi, S.-S, 1996, Endogenous formation of customs unions under imperfect competition: Open regionalism is good, *Journal of International Economics* 41: 153–177.

Yi, S.-S, 2000, Free-trade areas and welfare: An equilibrium analysis, *Review of International Economics* 8: 336–347.

Zhang, J., L. Xue, and X. Yin, 2011, Forming efficient free-trade networks: A sequential mechanism, *Review of International Economics* 19(2): 402–417.

Zhang, J., L. Xue, and L. Zu, 2013, Farsighted free trade networks, *International Journal of Game Theory* 42: 375–398.

Index